RICHARD BRINSLEY SHERIDAN
by Sir Joshua Reynolds

UNCORKING OLD SHERRY
The Life and Times of Richard Brinsley Sheridan

Uncorking Old Sherry

The Life and Times of

RICHARD BRINSLEY SHERIDAN

~~~~~~

"Thou art a friend indeed and my only request shall be that you continue to love me and look on my imperfections with more affection than judgment."

SHERIDAN'S *Pizarro*

~~~~~~

by

OSCAR SHERWIN

TWAYNE PUBLISHERS, INC. • NEW YORK

© 1960 by Oscar Sherwin

Library of Congress Catalog Card Number: 60–12916

Manufactured in the United States of America

To
My Children

CONTENTS

ILLUSTRATIONS

Illustrations follow pages 96 and 128.

BOOK ONE

THE AGE

THE AGE

IT IS AN AGE of orators and actors. The House of Commons is the theatre of the country. Indeed, its lobbies are a green room where men sit up till five in the morning on chance of hearing one of the protagonists. Members as well as reporters take notes of the speeches, and great ladies anxiously await the result of the performance. Lady Chatham, Lady Temple, and the Duchess of Rutland, and two or three others, wait in an adjoining room and ask every Commons man they see, "Well, sir, how do you think it will go? Who's up now?"

It is a demonstrative time in England, one of capitals, italics, and notes of exclamation. Tears do not go out of fashion till 1808 when the surtout comes in and the eighteenth century dies. For some forty years they are cultivated in both houses and are as common as Latin quotations. Burke weeps when Fox praises him in 1790, and Fox weeps at Burke's irrevocable farewell from his friend and pupil in the following year. Fox is the inveterate weeper on political emergencies. Tears trickle down the fat cheeks of this spoiled child of fifty in 1799 when he hurries up for two days from his Arcadian self exile in the vain hopes of at length defeating Pitt. Fox and Burke are emotional, but Pitt, the unruffled, weeps also, "pressing his hat upon his brow," when the vote impeaching his beloved Dundas, Lord Melville, is recorded. The stiff Elliot (afterwards Lord Minto) sometimes "feels the bone in his throat" at another's eloquence—and once even at his own (that dull speech on the Impey charge against Warren Hastings) which, he declares "had the honour of squeezing tears from several." Jenkinson (Lord Liverpool), the power behind the throne, frequently sheds them too, airing his handkerchief for the purpose. Even dry Barré weeps to hear Burke's

[11]

denunciation of Red Indian levies in the American War. In 1789 the browbeating and beetle browed Thurlow ("None can be so wise as Thurlow looks," says Fox) does the same, protesting sham loyalty from the woolsack. And in the preceding autumn the solemn Chancellor goes into hysterics at the sight of his master's madness.

Great and stormy speeches always draw the downpour. Sheridan's wife and Mrs. Siddons both swoon at Burke's invectives against Warren Hastings. On the same occasion the whole assembly cries aloud on hearing him and Fox. Sheridan himself bursts into tears in full sight of an audience when he sees his father (to whom he is as yet unreconciled) present with his sisters at a performance of *The Duenna*. The heir apparent during his colloquies with Fox about Mrs. Fitzherbert literally breaks down, for he rolls on the carpet. In his shifts to win her he gnashes himself with knives (like a priest of Baal) and threatens to commit suicide (like Mr. Mantalini). And when at last he weds the luckless Caroline, he is actually seen tearing his hair in the gardens of Carlton House. To crown it all, his august father weeps on the neck of the impassive Duke of Portland over the tyranny of the coalition.

In the theatre tears are not so surprising, but they fall there in waterfalls. Garrick when he bids farewell to Drury Lane pauses till a gush of them relieves him, while when Mrs. Siddons makes her second appearance on its boards, Sheridan's father and the whole house sob and cry aloud. Fox, once more, sitting in the orchestra to be nearer the same tragedienne, on one occasion bedews the instruments.

As for gesticulation, it has never been more in evidence. Burke's dagger scene in 1792, when he throws down a Birmingham weapon on the floor of the House to point his hatred of the Jacobins, is famous. But Burke also keeps pressing Elliot's hand at a dinner party to mark his rapture over a speech, and he also airs a knack of catching speakers in his arms, for not only Sheridan experiences the compliment, but Elliot also, a fact which lessens Sheridan's pleasure. Burke again has literally to be dragged down to his seat by Fox and Sheridan when infuriated by criticisms on his conduct in reinstating corrupt officials. No one has less command of his passions or overdoes his violence more than Burke. In 1778 he flings a book of estimates at the Treasury bench, knocks down a candle, and injures Welbore Ellis's shins. And two years later, aiding Fox at the Westminster election and indignant at the insinuations that he is a Papist, he responds to cries of "Tip him the long oath" by kissing the book and then hurling it at the populace.

Nor is attitudinizing restricted to scenes like these. The notorious Duchess of Kingston (Foote's Lady Kitty Crocodile), parading her pomp and grievances all along the Bath road, is carried at night to her inn kicking and screaming. While great ladies, aided by the tight lacing, go into continual swoons. Even as late as at Nelson's obsequies a Miss Bayne actually dies of hysterics.

Macaronies in 1773, the year of their birth, run gorgeous races in Kensington Gardens on Sunday evenings, belles pose as dairymaids, give Cossack dances in uniforms, and sometimes masquerade as men to hear the great debates in the House of Commons. The beaux follow suit, and Jack Willett-Payne, the Prince's secretary, attends a fancy ball dressed as a young lady and chaperoned by Mrs. Fitzherbert.

Frivolity is not confined to the youthful, the foolish, or even the idle. The Duke of Grafton flaunts at Ascot races with a mistress whom he has picked up in the street, and parades her at the Opera when the royal party is in their box. But George III is willing that the Duke of Grafton should bring whom he pleases under the same roof as the Queen—so long as he keeps such people as Rockingham and Burke and Richmond out of the cabinet.

It is a moist age. "They tell me, Sir John," says George III to one of his favorites, "that you love a glass of wine." "Those who have so informed your Majesty," is the reply, "have done me a great injustice; they should have said a bottle."

Men of all ages drink abominably, and the higher one

mounts in rank the more one drinks. Almost every member
of the Royal Family except the King drinks heavily. It is
considered bad form not to leave a feast half drunk at
least. The wise drink heavily in order to sparkle on subjects
of importance. The foolish drink to escape solitude. Fox
drinks a great deal, though he is not reckoned to do so by
his superiors, Sheridan excessively, and Grey more than
any of them. The Prince is portrayed in the shops of Bond
Street as a "Voluptuary in the agonies of Indigestion," his
waistcoat unbuttoned, his respiration impeded by repletion,
and the board before him covered with bottles of mara-
schino or cedrato. Few escape the penalties of self-indul-
gence. More gout is manufactured in this century than in
any other, and from its outset, to quote Congreve, its
heroes are fellows "whom the flood cannot wash away."

Sheridan calls wine "a vile habit, never to be excused,"
and twice nearly subdues it, yet it gains on him by leaps
and bounds, and at length becomes as necessary for his
displays as it was for Hudibras. Doctor Bain, his physician
for the last twenty-five years of his life, being summoned
one morning, finds him in a high fever, but is assured by
the butler that his master on the preceding night drank
"nothing particular, only two bottles of port." Much earlier,
when Sheridan sprains his foot, Tickell guesses it is gout
and recommends him "patience and claret." Yet that same
drinking habit to which Sheridan yields seems a badge of
manhood in an age when Wellington drinks hard in his
youth, when "Diddy," the Protestant Duke of Norfolk, lies
down in his bouts on logs of wood in the street till he is
taken for dead, when Speaker Cornwall in the House of
Commons sits barricaded by pints of porter—a president
in keeping with his rubicund subjects. This hard drinking
does not die out nearly so soon as the tears which mix
with the port stains on the paper. Long afterwards, when a
pious lady offers Theodore Hook a tract headed, "Three
Words to a Drunkard," "Oh, yes, of course," is the rejoinder,
"Pass the bottle."

Sheridan is thrown early with Fox who can vie with

the imperturbable Dundas in his potations—and then read Homer, or gamble at Brooks's, or rattle the dice box at Crockford's with a fresh set of more seasoned roysterers. But the highly strung Sheridan copes ill with such competitors and succumbs sooner than topers like Dundas or soakers like Pitt, who have more claret than blood in their veins. Pitt, usually a solitary drinker, once driving home with that friend from Hollwood, settles a score for seven bottles at an inn on the old Kent road. He is observed, says the *Morning Chronicle*, "in walking to his carriage after a Canterbury Corporation banquet during September, 1792, to oscillate like his own bills." With Dundas again he joins in the roystering dinners of the time, where, no doubt, the conversation takes a convivial and improving turn. The pair once stagger arm in arm into the House in no condition to do business—

> "I can't see the Speaker.
> Pray, Hal, do you?"
> "Not see the Speaker, Bill?
> Why I see two."

And Pitt on another occasion is obliged to retire behind the Speaker's chair where he is violently sick.

The business of Great Britain is transacted over oceans of liquor and continents of food. Erskine never pleads a cause without a small flask of madeira in his pocket. Rigby, paymaster of the forces, says that the only merit he possesses or cares to claim is that he drinks fair. This virtue stands him in good stead when he becomes secretary to the Duke of Bedford in Ireland, for he washes away disaffection in floods of vice-regal claret. Rigby, however, does not observe what Burke calls "the morality of geography." As he drinks at Dublin, so he drinks in London, and as he drinks in London, so he drinks in the country.

Dundas and Thurlow drink port; Fox champagne and burgundy; Sheridan, first claret, then port, latterly rackpunch, hot negus, brandy, and eventually back to port again. Wilkes alone drinks bock (as Boswell, given to drink and repentance, does later), and Burke, who begins with a modicum of claret, ends by copious draughts of hot water, though in earlier days he once assures the Speaker, "I am not well. I eat too much, I drink too much, and I sleep very little." Pitt's last phase is port and water, and most of these drink less as they grow older, but Sheridan (alas! alas!) more and more. Now and then the good King indulges in "a pear and water," but the Prince of Wales drinks everything till everything palls and his cloyed palate has to decline on curacoa and cedrato.

Lord Weymouth boozes till daylight and dozes into the afternoon. The Earl of Carlyle accounts for a headache which he suffers at Lord Clermont's dinner on the ground that he drank all the wine within his reach. Kemble, who waxes majestic as he grows mellower, drinks claret by the pailful. Once he flings a decanter at Sheridan and then immediately shakes hands. Sir Philip Francis cannot always get through an after dinner sitting without losing his head, although he sips thumbfuls while his companions are draining bumpers. And Porson, the greatest scholar of the age, is so dependent on stimulants that he once consumes a bottle of methylated spirits under the impression that it is gin.

Nor is the cloth exempt. The Duchess of Devonshire records that a clergyman invited to Chatsworth arrived intoxicated and had to be expelled for his gross behavior to Lady Elizabeth Foster and a friend.

The English are amorous only when intoxicated. Major General Pillet is carried home one day after dinner by a very respectable widow who maintains a distinguished rank in the world. According to custom the company has drunk copiously. The widow has her daughter in the carriage, a young girl of about eighteen whose sweetheart sits beside the General on the forward seat. Never in any place would a collection of hussars or grenadiers conduct themselves in such a scandalous manner as does this sweetheart. Pillet cannot repress some expressions of indignation or hide his uneasiness at seeing the mother calmly occupied in refitting the disordered garments of her daughter. She is satisfied with observing to him, and repeating it with a sort of confusion, "The poor man is in liquor."

We read of a party at Mrs. Crewe's where three young men become so drunk "and begin at last to talk so plain" that Lady Frances and Lady Palmerston flee from the table while Mrs. Sheridan who tries to follow them does not make her escape till her arms are black and blue and her apron torn off.

Mrs. Fitzherbert never retires till her royal spouse comes home. Often when she hears the Prince and his drunken companions on the staircase, she seeks refuge from their presence under a sofa. The Prince finding the drawing room deserted, draws his sword in joke, and searching about the room, at last draws forth the trembling victim from her place of concealment.

Wives are not ashamed to chronicle that their spouses return to them in the small hours "pretty drunk, pretty cold, and pretty cross," or to relate how they are kept awake all night by the sound "of every cruel pop of that odious five shilling claret in the pantry."

However, women of all classes follow the men—at a distance. In drawing rooms, when the tea is brought forward, ladies are in that state which is called "half seas over."

Though they drink port and even porter with their lobsters, they vary their cups with a cheering and colorful selection: Oil of Venus, Spirit of Saffron, Spirit of Cinnamon, Spirit of Adonis, Orange Flower, Mint, Tansey, Usquebaugh Green, Yellow, White, Coffee Water, chocolate water, Belle de Nuit, Parfait Amour, Turkey Visney, Lilly-cum-Valley, Marasquino, Flora Granata, Eau Cordiale de Genève, Eau Divine, Eau de Millefleurs, Eau d'Or, Orangasse, Linette des Indes, Cedra, Rouge and Blanc, Eau de Bergamotte, red and brown Jacomonoodi, Quinces red and white, Chamberry, Neuilly, Fine Cholic Water, Surfeit, plague, and peppermint waters.

The superiority of port, however, over all other wines becomes part and parcel of the creed of every true born and true hearted English gentleman. "To which university," says a lady to the sagacious Dr. Warren, "shall I send my son?" "Madam," replies he, "they drink, I believe, near the same quality of port in each of them."

But beer remains the national drink, morning, noon, and night. The breweries in 1760 turn out 35,107,812 gallons of beer, 70 gallons a head for Londoners excepting infants, boys, and girls, and 47 gallons including them. The popular drinks are beer, "bub," Christian bub, excellent bub, mighty bub, "humming bub," (affectionate for ale). And for cordials: sweet apple, punch, gin, egg flip, gill ale, stout, brandy, rum of Barbadoes, stocky, half and half, cider, cherry, amber beer, mild beer, purl, old Pharaoh, knock me down, humtie-dumtie, stipple, shouldree, rum shrub, possets and cups of many kinds. There are also Dr. Butler's ale, Dr. Quincey's ale, and Scurvy Grass Ale—all extremely popular as medicines, no doubt with the additional recommendation that while you are being cured, you are also getting drunk.

There are 17,000 gin shops in London, and painted boards are suspended from the door of almost every seventh house inviting the poor and Bohemian to get drunk for a penny, dead drunk for two pence, and have straw whereon to lie and recover free.

As for the Bohemians, they are always waiting for something or somebody to turn up, and employing the intervals in wrangling or being reconciled to their countless clubs and taverns, the weirdest of which is the terrible "Two in the Morning"—a ghastly conclave of wizened hell-rakers who resemble a Dance of Death. Their bond of union is the alcohol of human kindness. The bumper heals quarrels nearly as often as it provokes them—

> A bumper of good liquor
> Will end a contest quicker
> Than Justice, Judge, or Vicar;
> So fill the cheerful glass
> And let the good humour pass. . . .

(Oh! to have been present when "all was hiccough and happiness.")

Gambling vies with drinking. One is ruinous to the purse as the other to health. All fashionable England gambles and not to know the game in vogue is to argue oneself lowered. People of quality, lawyers, physicians, army and navy men, actors, politicians, even clergymen gamble prodigiously and systematically. From court to scullery everyone gambles. Society is one vast casino.

On whatever pretext, and under whatever circumstances, when half a dozen people of fashion find themselves together—whether for music or dancing or politics or drinking the waters or each other's wine—the box is sure to be rattling and the cards are being cut and shuffled.

The passion for gambling is not weakened by the rival attractions of female society, for the surest road into the graces of a fine lady is to be known as one who bets freely and loses handsomely. Horace Walpole in town at Lady Hertford's loses fifty guineas before he can say an *Ave Maria*. On a summer night at Bedford House, with windows open on the garden, and French horns and clarionets on the grand walks, the guests have no ears for anything beyond the cant phrases of the card table. Nor is the craze limited to the harsher sex. Coteries of ladies, young and old, single and married, have their regular nights of meeting. Doubtless, when jewels and trinkets have been successively staked and lost, the pearl of greatest value—the most brilliant ornament of the sex—is in danger. There is limited loo for the Princess Amelia, and unlimited loo for the Duchess of Grafton, and it is noticed that when a piper and tabor are introduced and the furniture shifted for a minuet, her royal highness takes advantage of the confusion to desert her own for the Duchess's party.

During a long and fierce debate on Wilkes and a close division—so close that two votes are purchased with two peerages and invalids are brought down in flannels and blankets, till the floor of the House is compared to the pavement of Bathseda—eight or nine Whig ladies who cannot find room in the gallery, after a cosy dinner, are found contentedly sitting round a pool in one of the Speaker's chambers.

Georgiana, Duchess of Devonshire, plays for stakes and is made miserable by her debts, and once Sheridan hands the Duchess into her carriage when she is literally sobbing at her losses.

Mrs. Lumm loses two or three hundred on a night, but Mrs. Fitzroy is very angry she does not win it. And the lady who has been so unlucky in Ireland takes practical measures to balk the spite of fortune—and carries pams in her pocket to the loo table. But ladies who cheat in the long run are less dangerous associates than ladies who cannot pay. No man of honor expects his fair debtor to face an angry husband with the equanimity with which he himself encounters the surliness of his banker or the remonstrances of his steward. And to the end of his gambling days, it is not in Charles James Fox to be stern with a pretty defaulter, crying as she has never cried before at the prospect of having on her return home to confess that she has lost her pin money three times over in the course of a single evening.

Whist spreads its universal opium over the whole nation. It makes courtiers and patriots sit down to the same pack of cards. Edmund Hoyle writes a treatise on the subject which passes through no fewer than seven editions in the space of twelve months. There never is so excellent a book printed. People are in raptures with it. They eat with it, sleep with it, go to Parliament with it, go to Church with it. They pronounce it the gospel of whist players. They want words to express their favor of the author, and so can look on him in no other light than a second Newton. It is the subject of all conversation and has the honor to be introduced in the cabinet. After 1783 faro becomes the rage, and then "EO."

Still the play goes on. Morning, noon, and evening, the sport of chance is to be witnessed in White's, in Brooks's, in Boodle's, reducing the multitudes to beggary and many hundreds to starvation. Even the green rooms of theatres are scenes of great doings. Thousands are frequently lost there in a night—rings, brooches, watches, salaries in advance, wardrobes, stays. Gambling in all its forms is rather a profession than a pastime to the leaders of the London world. The fierce delights of the political arena seem insipid and its prizes paltry to these depraved palates, while sums exceeding the yearly income of a secretary of state are continually depending upon the health of a horse or the sequence of a couple of cards. Sir James Lowther wins about £7000, Meynell wins £4000, and Pigot £5000 in one evening. At a gala ball Lord Clermont wins a much larger sum. But at another the Duke of Northumberland loses no less than £20,000 over the quinze before the Queens of hearts at the other end of the room finish their cotillons. Pitt gambles and George Selwyn, and Sheridan, and Fox, who, of course, is possessed by the demon and is very unlucky. Fox loses £20,000 in a night. Once he plays for twenty-four hours and loses £500 an hour. He sits down to cards after dinner, plays all night and next morning, and in that time loses £12,000; by five that afternoon he loses £12,000 and then £11,000 more.

> At Almack's of pigeons I'm told there are flocks,
> But it's thought the completest is one Mr. Fox;
> If he touches a card, if he rattles a box,
> Away fly the guineas of this Mr. Fox.

(Up to a point he carries his gambling habits into public life. For years he plays pitch and toss with his own and his party's prospects.)

The gaming at Almack's, which takes the place of White's, is worthy the decline of an Empire or Commonwealth, which you please. They play for stakes of £50 each rouleau, and generally there is as much as £10,000 in specie on the table at one time. Nor are the manners of the gamesters or even their dress for play undeserving of notice. They begin by pulling off their embroidered clothes, and put on great frieze coats or turn their coats inside out for luck. They then put on pieces of leather (such as are worn by footmen when they clean the knives) to save their laced ruffles, and to guard their eyes from the light and to prevent the tumbling of their hair, wear high crowned straw hats with broad brims, adorned with flowers and ribbons—and masks to conceal their emotion when they play at quinze. They have small neat stands by them with large rims to hold their tea or wooden bowls with edges of ormulu to hold their rouleaus. They borrow great sums of Jewish moneylenders at exorbitant premiums. Charles Fox calls his outward room where those moneylenders wait till he rises, his Jerusalem chamber. It is he who says that the greatest pleasure in life, after winning, is losing. His bad luck is notorious, and Walpole wonders what he will do when he has sold the estates of his friends.

> But hark! the voice of battle shouts from far,
> The Jews and Macaronies are at war.
> The Jews prevail, and thundering from the stocks,
> They seize, they bind, they circumcise Charles Fox.

But this happens long before he retires to roses and prosody at St. Anne's where Fitzpatrick finds him sitting on a haycock reading novels and watching the jays steal his cherries.

With that same kinsman he plays cards at Brooks's from ten at night till six the next afternoon, a waiter standing by all the time to warn them whose deal it is when they grow drowsy.

Here at Brooks's the play is often taken seriously, and conversation is resented. Sir Philip Francis comes to Brooks's wearing for the first time the ribbon of the Order of the Bath for which Fox recommended him. "So this is the way they reward you at last," remarks Roger Wilbraham coming up to the whist table. "They have given you a little bit of red ribbon to hang about your neck, and that satisfies you, does it? Now I wonder what I shall have. What do you think they will give me, Sir Philip?" "A halter and be damned to you," roars the infuriated player.

Many a man commits suicide through his reverses at the gaming tables. In 1755 Lord Mountford makes his quietus with a pistol owing to that cause. Having lost tremendous sums of money at play and being in mortal dread of beggary, his lordship makes application to the Duke of Newcastle for the governorship of Virginia or the Foxhounds, inwardly resolving to stake his existence on the result. Receiving an unfavorable reply, he takes counsel with his friends as to the earliest method of committing suicide. On New Year's Eve, Mountford sups at White's Chocolate House and afterwards plays whist till the small hours of the following morning. Later in the day he sends for a lawyer and three witnesses, in whose presence he executes a will which he orders to be read over thrice, clause by clause. As soon as they have done so, he inquires whether such a will will hold good in the event of his taking his life. On receiving the assurance that it will, he politely requests them to excuse his absence, and stepping into the adjoining room, deliberately makes away with himself—so quietly that no report of the pistol is heard.

But there are heartier losers in those days. It is a very necessary quality to possess since all play and most lose. Lord Carlisle (who complains of *cette lassitude de tout et de moi même qu'on s'appelle ennui*), General Fitzpatrick, Lord Hertford, Lord Sefton, the Duke of York, and many other squander vast sums in this amusement. There are not a great many winners. The Duke of Portland is one and his father-in-law, General Scott, another. The latter wins £200,000, but it is said (with scorn) that his success is due to his notorious sobriety. A fortunate man too is Colonel Aubrey who has the reputation of being the best whist and piquet player of the day. He makes two fortunes in India and loses them both and makes a third at play from a five pound note which he borrows.

The celebrated faro bank at Brooks's is kept by Lord Cholmondeley, Mr. Thompson of Grosvenor Square, Tom Stepney, and another. It ruins half the town and a Mr. Paul, who has come home with a fortune from India, punting against the bank, loses £90,000 in one night and at once goes Eastward ho! to make another.

Foreigners are made honorary members of the Clubs. During a visit of the allied sovereigns, Blücher, an inveterate gambler, loses £20,000. Count Montrond, on the other hand, is a winner. "Who the deuce is this Montrond?" the Duke of York asks Upton. "They say, sir, that he is the most agreeable scoundrel and the greatest reprobate in France." "Is he, by Jove?" cries the Duke. "Then let us ask him to dinner immediately."

Montrond is a witty fellow. The Bailli de Ferretti is always dressed in knee breeches, with a cocked hat, and a court sword, the slender proportions of which resemble those of his legs. "Do tell me, my dear Bailli," says Montrond one day, "have you got three legs or three swords?"

The Duke D'Orleans wins vast sums. No one has a good word for this Prince. "Vile Egalité," Lady Bunbury writes him down. *"Paresseux sur mer, poltron sur terre, polisson partout,"* another phrase maker sums him up. The Prince of Wales meets him at Cumberland House and is frequently seen with him in public. He wishes to pay him a visit at Paris, but the King wisely withholds the necessary permission, suggesting instead a visit to Hanover. The Prince declines. It is not the same thing.

The greed of gain has no pity for the ignorance and weakness of youth and spares neither relative nor benefactor, nor host, nor guest. A lad fresh from his public school, if he is known to have parents who love him well enough to stand between him and dishonor, walks into a London club like a calf eyed by the butcher. The young men lose five, ten, fifteen thousand pounds in an evening. Lord Stavordale, not yet one and twenty, loses £11,000 this Tuesday but recovers it by playing one great hand at hazard. He swears a great oath—"Now, if I had been playing deep, I might have won millions."

The Duke of Queensberry is a dangerous man at a card table. The turf has no mysteries for him. He is ever ready to bet and he prefers to bet on something that is very close to a certainty. He is full of resource, and his success is due at least as much to his cleverness as to his luck. His is the day of wagers, and at White's a betting book is laid upon the table for all bets made in the building to be inserted. His name frequently occurs therein. "The Duke of Queensberry bets Sir John Lade a £1000 as to which can produce a man to eat the most at one sitting." The Duke cannot be present at the contest, but he receives the result from a representative. "I have not the time to state particulars but merely to acquaint your Grace that your man beat his antagonist by a pig and an apple pie."

(Old Q.—his profligacy is a byword, and he pursues pleasure to the end of his days. He builds a palace at Richmond where many orgies take place, but he tires of that residence as he wearies of most everything else—people and things. "What is there to make so much of in the Thames? I am quite tired of it. There it goes, flow, flow, always the same." At the end of his days, he often sits on the balcony of a ground floor room of his Piccadilly mansion and ogles the passersby, while a footman holds a parasol over his head and another is ready to follow and find out the residence of any pretty girl that passes. Yet "Old Q." has wit in plenty, loves music, and is not without appreciation of letters and art. One of his greatest friends is George Selwyn, and while both accredit themselves with the paternity, neither knows which was the father of Maria Fagniani.)

Boswell is rescued from "a rage of gaming" by Thomas Sheridan, who lends him money to pay his debts on condition that he give up gambling. But the rage returns and proves irresistible. Night after night Boswell sits at cards.

There is a mania for betting:

Fifty guineas that Lord Ilchester gives his first vote in opposition and hits six of his first ten pheasants.

Five guineas down to receive a hundred if the Duke of Queensberry dies before half an hour after five in the afternoon of June 27, 1773.

March 11, 1775. Lord Bolingbroke gives a guinea to Mr. Charles Fox and is to receive a thousand from him whenever the debt of this country amounts to one hundred and seventy-one millions. Mr. Fox is not to pay the thousand pounds till he is one of his Majesty's cabinet.

29th January, 1793. Mr. Sheridan bets Mr. Boothby Clopton five hundred guineas that there is a Reform in the Representation of the people of England within three years from the date thereof.

29 January, 1793. Mr. Sheridan bets General Fitzpatrick fifty guineas that a corps of British troops are sent to Holland within two months of the date hereof.

Mr. Sheridan bets General Tarleton one hundred guineas to fifty guineas that Mr. Pitt is first Lord of the Treasury on the 28th of May, 1795. Mr. S. bets Mr. St. A. St. John fifteen guineas to five guineas ditto. Mr. S. bets Lord Sefton one hundred and forty guineas to forty guineas ditto.

Lord Maidstone bets Lord Kelbourne six bets of £50 each that he has six horses now in his own stable which he will ride over and shall clear a five foot wall in the Leath Country in Lincolnshire.

Lord Adolphus Fitzclarence bets Mr. George Bentinck £10 that during the year there is not a shot fired in anger in London.

Mr. F. Cavendish bets Mr. H. Brownrigg 2/1 that he does not kill the bluebottle fly before he goes to bed.

No subject is thought unfit for a bet. One morning in 1750 a man is suddenly observed to fall down just outside White's Coffee House. Instantly odds are laid and taken by bystanders and spectators on the chances of his being alive. Somebody, however, proposes to bleed the poor fellow, whereupon loud protestations arise from a section of the betting men on the ground that the use of a lancet will affect the fairness of the betting.

Mr. —— bets £1500 that a man can live twelve hours under water, hires a desperate fellow, sinks him down in a ship, by way of experiment, and both ship and man have not appeared since.

And of course, wagers are made as to which of two unmarried ladies will first give birth to a live child, as to which of two men will marry first; and men bet with equal heartiness on the duration of a ministry or the life of a minister, on a horse or dog, on a prizefight, billiard match, or cock fight. Everyone bets high, drinks deep, and has his affairs.

And then there is the lottery craze. It affects all classes of people from the nobleman who can afford to purchase a whole ticket to the servant who raises the sum (often by pilfering) necessary to purchase a sixteenth. Legislators themselves fall victim to the craze. The people, they argue, patronize the lottery, and why shouldn't they? Was it not by lot that the land of Canaan was divided among the tribes? Was it not by lot that Saul was selected King? . . .

The eventful day which is to decide the fortunes of thousands approaches. The sanguine holder of a lottery ticket, already the confident possessor of a prize of £20,000, disdains to walk to the scene of his anticipated triumph, and hires a hackney coach from the nearest stand, or perhaps a brass nailed leather chair to carry him to Guildhall. What! walk? He, the holder of a ticket which will soon be drawn for a prize! Psha! "Coach! Coach! To Guildhall—as fast as you like!" No quibbling about the fare. There is no occasion for economy now; the only consideration is speed, for the speculator is impatient to grasp his coming fortune. How crowded is the old hall with anxious faces! Some express hope, others betray a mixed sensation, half hope, half fear; others again look seriously on the ground, their owners wondering evidently when the drawing will commence— when their respective numbers will be drawn—what they will be, prizes or blanks—if prizes, of what amount; if blanks—. See! the sleeves of the Bluecoat boy who is to draw the numbers are turned up at the wrist. Why is this? To prevent his concealing, as he was once suspected of doing, a prize beneath his cuff. And now the wheel revolves. A prize is drawn! What? No? Yes. Hush! Silence there! Ha! is it possible? Yes. Yonder buxom servant, whose countenance is alternately changing from white to red, is the happy possessor of £12,000, a sixteenth of the prize. A buzz at

[27]

the upper end of the hall. Everything is hushed. Once more the wheel of fortune flies around—there is a straining and stretching of necks—and this time there is drawn—a blank.

It is an era of debt—of debt this era is the millenium. Nor is it viewed as a drawback to character. "Long corks and long credit" is a toast. Burke in criticising the debt laws, complains bitterly that every man is presumed to be solvent, an assumption, he adds, by no means in accordance with the facts. In low and high Bohemia debt is a matter of course. Murphy and Cumberland, both wits and scholars as well as playwrights, owe everywhere, and the former (with no desire to deceive) pays in dishonored bills and by the assignment of a copyright already sold. Even poor Tickell is "teazed to death," as his wife assures us, "for money which God knows we can very ill spare." In society fine ladies will borrow five pounds from their footmen whose eternal nose-gays and silk stockings cost a small fortune. Rodney is so embarrassed that he owes his extrication to the generosity of a French Field Marshall. Fox in 1773 owes £100,000 and suffers nine executions in his house. Fox's ally, General Burgoyne, is forced to take hiding from his creditors in France before he takes the field in America. Even Pitt is not free from bailiffs; and in 1786 a sheriff's officer is actually in occupation of the Prince's Carlton House for two days and in respect of a sum not exceeding £600. The insolvent draw on the insolvent, and the most amazing instance is where Fox, on the eve of starting for Newmarket, has recourse for a loan to Sheridan.

Fox's huge liabilities are defrayed not only by a rich father but also by the subscriptions of friends who ensure him a competence. Years earlier he is collected for at Brooks's, and this is the occasion when a member, discussing the proposal, delicately asks Selwyn how Charles will "take it" and is answered with "immediately, of course." Moreover in 1802 the Duke of Bedford bequeathes him no less than £10,000.

Pitt in his turn is subscribed for, nor is a voluntary loan of £12,000 ever repaid, though the nation votes £40,000 to defray his debts after his death. Sheridan has no rich father. His wealthy friends never subscribe for him, and the sole private offer ever made to him is declined. He gets no legacies, and no minister ever procures him a penny. Yet his debts—not half of Burke's or a sixth of Pitt's or a thirtieth of Fox's—are amply discharged by his survivors.

It is a mammon worshiping age. Pleasure, ambition, and politics exact their golden tribute. Everything is farmed— even America—and "Farmer George" himself has to furnish £12,000 for each election. Members' votes are bartered for pensions, and Sheridan urges that the ordinary waste in this direction is "so great as to be sufficient to maintain all the laboring poor." Lord North's son expresses his indignation at not having received any sinecure for the last three weeks. Lord Chatham himself has recourse to pensions as a means of shaking off inconvenient aspirants to office, and Wilkes when he returns from his French exile makes no scruple of demanding £5,000 and an annuity as "compensation." When it is objected in 1811 that "our Cato," Lord Grenville (Grenville whose virtue nothing can satiate) can scarcely come in, so difficult will he find his distribution of offices, a wit (and a woman) answers that there need be no difficulty, for Lord Grenville will be quite willing to take them all himself. Grenville and his brother Buckingham are exemplary harpies.

Dundas is an arch pluralist, holding three places. Pitt, indeed, invents a third secretaryship for his especial benefit, and this causes Sheridan to remark in a speech of 1795— "We certainly had a most gentlemanlike administration, and Mr. Secretary Dundas was three times as much a gentleman as any of them, for he had three places."

Pitt himself, however, like Fox, Grey, and Sheridan, is wholly unbribeable. He despises lucre as proudly as his father did. He rejects a city offer of £10,000 a year and a continental present of £100,000, while the pictures despatched by foreign potentates are left to be claimed by dishonest servants or to moulder in the cellars of the custom house. On declining to take the helm in March, 1783, his purity and steadiness are declared by Jenkinson, Lord Liverpool, to be "absolutely incompatible with the morals, manners, and grounds of attachment of those by whose means alone the government of this country can be carried on." But though he abolishes many sinecures he is forced to cement his party by a system of oblique bribery.

The commerce in honors is worse. Traffic in titles started with James I, but now it is an unblushing business on a colossal scale. During Pitt's first thirteen years of power, he makes no less than eighty-three new peers. He manages to confer no less than one hundred and forty coronets before he dies, and even when he relinquishes the reins of power, almost half the House of Lords are his offspring. He creates a plebeian aristocracy. He makes peers of second rate squires and fat graziers. He catches them in the alleys of Lombard Street and clutches them from the counting house of Cornhill. One of these fat graziers, recommended as worth a baronetcy, is sent up on approval and rejected because Pitt shudders at his atrocious dialect.

A minister's antechamber is a court of requests. "My dear Madam," says Goldsmith's place-monger Lofty, "all this is but a mere exchange. We do greater things for one another every day. . . . Let me suppose you the first Lord of the Treasury; you have an employment in you that I want; I have a place in me that you want; do me here; do you there; interest on both sides, few words, flat, done and done, and it's over."

Not without reason forty years earlier did Swift scratch on the window of Lord Carteret's vestibule—

> My very good lord, 'tis a very hard task
> For a man to wait here who has nothing to ask.

As for decorations, the bitter and renegade Philip Francis receives his Order of the Bath, yet Sheridan goes undecorated, lacking what he himself terms, "an ornament which favored peers wear all the year round, chimney sweepers only on the first of May."

It is an age of insolent hauteur heightened by the exclusiveness which limits society to less than three hundred and the cabinet till 1801 to seven. Old Lady Albemarle once says to a gentleman beneath her notice—"You have heard that I have abused you, but it is not true, for I would not take the trouble of talking about you, but if I *had* said anything of you, it would have been that you look like a blackguard on weekdays and on Sundays like an apothecary." Even Georgiana of Devonshire, when she first meets and is fascinated by the Sheridans, doubts whether she ought to invite a singer and the son of a player.

There is a story that a lady sees a man fall into the water and earnestly entreats the dandy who accompanies her and who is a notoriously good swimmer to save his life. Her friend raises his lorgnette with the phlegm indispensable to a man of fashion, looks earnestly at the drowning man, whose head rises for the last time, and calmly replies, "It's impossible, madam. I never was introduced to that gentleman."

It is an age of conversation—like all ages influenced by women and in touch with France. Wit and eloquence unlock the gates of the great houses, though the golden key is cast in a political mold. The Guelphs and the Ghibellines were not more at daggers drawn than are the followers of Fox, almost always in opposition, and the followers of Pitt, continually in power. Devonshire House and the salons of Mrs. Crewe and Mrs. Bouverie draw the former; the latter repair to the Duchesses of Gordon and Rutland or to Lady Salisbury—the first a bel esprit, the two others mature beauties. While later Lady Hester Stanhope, always a despot, becomes her Uncle Pitt's generalissima. Most of the wits, however, are on the Whig side. (There is no way of approaching an English lady so good as politics; in fact, ofttimes nothing but politics is heard at dinner or at the opera; nay, Lord E—— complains that his wife disturbs him with politics at night. She frightens him by suddenly calling out in her sleep, "Will the Premier stand or fall?")

The Blues, on the other hand—Mrs. Thrale who civilizes

Dr. Johnson, Mrs. Cholmondeley. Mrs. Montagu, and their sisterhood—are less partisan and more catholic in their assemblies. There are wits like Sheridan, Fox, Luttrell, George Selwyn, and "the Hare of many friends"; there are, of course, full cartloads of bores. There is even a club of these— "The Botherers." Authors pester their friends with manuscripts as much as in the Augustan days, and vote every success a plagiarism. One of these unhappy men—George Dyer—despairing of an audience elsewhere, betakes himself to Dr. Graham's mud patients who, immersed in earth up to their perukes, are powerless to escape from listening.

It is beyond all an age of scandal. The newspapers form a whispering gallery of libels and innuendos that spare neither age nor sex. Pasquin—as Williams calls himself—reduces slander to a fine, or rather, a gross art; the coarsest caricatures are hung in every print shop. Privacy is the privilege of the poor. When Mrs. Thrale dares Dr. Johnson and marries Piozzi, the mass of malevolent gossip forms a "bloterature" of its own. And scandal does not only stir abroad; like charity it begins at home. The wild Lady Wallace (the Duchess of Gordon's sister), seated one evening at a whist party, overhears herself traduced, and when her partner inquires whether she has "honors," she replies in broad Scotch—"I was waiting to see if those ladies would leave me any honor at all."

Rough personalities disfigure parliamentary debates. Pitt is often rallied on his cold distance from the fair sex. And Pitt only two years before he dies, singles out Sheridan's fiery countenance for a rude onslaught. Burke, who constantly passes the bounds, calls Lord Shelburne, "a Borgia and a Catiline." The Crown itself is not spared. In the Lower House he shouts that God has hurled the King from his throne when madness overtakes George in 1788 and 1789. When Thurlow, meaning to rat from the King's sinking ship to the cockle shell of Fox and the heir apparent, asseverates before the peers, "When I forsake my King, may my God forsake me," Wilkes who is in hearing exclaims, "He'll see you damned first." And Burke standing by him adds, "The sooner the better." When one member enters Parliament with the qualification of one volume on grammar and another on virtue, Townsend only observes that the House of Commons is the wrong market for such wares.

It is a literary age. Literature since the days of Defoe has walked in the markets and highways of life and mixed with the people. Through its very freedom it is turning democratic and Sheridan differs from the Restoration dramatists by never introducing noblemen in his plays. His characters are citizens—citizens of some quality, it is true, but citizens all the same, with scant reverence for old things or old age.

And yet it is an age of color and costume—when Lord Villiers, who "fashions away" his fortune, can come to court in a pale purple velvet turned up with lemon color and embroidered all over with SS of pearls big as peas, and in all the spaces little medallions in beaten gold in various figures of Cupid and the like; when Warren Hastings himself appears at his trial in puce satin and with a diamond hilted sword; when Lord Egmont's postillions wear white jackets trimmed with muslin and new ones every day; when up to the eighties youths of fashion carry white satin muffs (such as Fox loves in his days of dandyism and Sheridan sends for after his elopement); when, too, the ladies' headdresses are so high that a pantomime in Drury Lane exhibits Harlequin scaling a ladder to reach them; and when beauties are entitled "cloud-capped belles." The perfection of figure according to the ton is the smallest circumference into which an unfortunate waist can be compressed. Many poor girls hurt their health materially by trying to rival the Duchess of Rutland who squeezes herself to the size of an orange and a half. Small hoops are worn in the morning and larger ones for a dress, some going outwards as they go downwards, something in the form of a bell. Sacques are very common and gauze handkerchiefs trimmed with blonde are worn on the neck. As for the other sex, powdered hair, sword, folding hat, embroidered coat, pink heels, lace ruffles and rattan cane proclaim the man of breeding, who to be in fashion must dance well, fence well, and air his repartees with his snuff.

Queen Charlotte makes snuff taking fashionable, but the habit begins to die out. George carries a box, but he has no liking for it. Conveying it with a grand air between his right thumb and forefinger, he is careful to drop it before it reaches his nose. He gives up the custom of offering a pinch to his neighbors, and it becomes recognised as a breach of good manners to dip uninvited into a man's box. But then when Lord Petersham dies, his snuff is sold by auction. It takes three men three days to weigh it and realizes £3,000.

Private theatricals reflect public ostentation. Lord Barry-more pays £60,000 for a building to house his audience, performs buffoon dances, and acts Scaramouche. Lord Villiers acts "Pygmalion and the Statue" in a barn near Henley. To the people peers are still demigods, and the luckless Lord Ferrers (condemned by his peers for the murder of an old family steward, Johnson) drives in state to the gallows and is hanged with a silken rope in his silver embroidered wedding suit. If Sheridan loves pageants, pageants flash all around him. It is an age at once precious and brutal, of taste and turbulence. Mrs. Montagu presides over the Cupidon saloon which costs thousands, discoursing all night of Shakespeare and the musical glasses to a circle that comprises Dresden china, like the Duchess of Devonshire, and cast iron, like Dr. Johnson. While her poor mathematical husband has retired to kindly rest and oblivion. His colleries defray her expenses. Her dressing room is frescoed with roses and jessamine. "Of what good are the cupids to a middle aged woman," rails Mrs. Delany, "unless she looks upon herself as the wife of old Vulcan and the mother to all these little loves."

Our ladies titter at the most distressing scenes in *Romeo and Juliet,* grin over the anguish of a Monimia or Belvidera, and fairly laugh King Lear off the stage.

Duelling is one of the sincerities of life. No gentleman

is ever looked upon the worse for killing a man in his own defence, and if business cannot be carried on without it, what would you have a gentleman do? There are few men of any eminence who have not been called out. The passion, like gambling, is not confined to any one class or rank. It pervades all without exception.

Outside brawl chairman and linkboys; cityward lurk footpads and ruffians—all the scum which the Gordon riots upheave. Or, on a hot May night, young members vote against their opinions for fear that the heat may melt their rouge and wither their nosegays. While in the galleries above them the sturdier winebibbers snor lustily.

Burke rises to speak in volumes and is coughed down by the curt sons of Belial. Lord Ellenborough, years later, on seeing a Whig member yawn at a speech of a Whig bore, observes that while the yawn shows the yawner's taste, it is hardly fair thus to encroach on the province of the other side.

Four hours sleep is compatible with good health, good looks, and good spirits. The vices of men are coupled to the spirits of children, and parliamentary athletes romp like boys. Great geniuses sit up till midnight playing at cross purposes, crooked answers and what's my thought like. You have never heard a set of wits utter half so much nonsense. We can listen to Fox sportive over the stubbles, or watch him bear fighting in the corridors of St. Anne. We can see Pitt playing at blindman's buff at Wimbledon, or trying to recover his dignity when his secretaries surprise him with a face half blacked by burnt corks. Hellgate Lord Barrymore—whose amiable kindred (one of them a clergyman) are nicknamed respectively Cripplegate, Newgate, and Billingsgate—plays beau in St. James' or Mohawk in St. Giles' and rides into the hunting field more like a King of France and Navarre than an English gentleman, while his Negro trumpeter plays fantasias in the forest. Finical dilettanti buy spurious Titians and collect curios that image their surroundings. One of these cognoscenti brandishes aloft a tooth of Scipio Africanus, swearing to fix it in his own gums, while George Selwyn wonders that "such a thing could come into anybody's head."

Fashion dines early, goes to the opera or the playhouse, and returns to a late supper, where the wits and statesmen, fresh from the House of Commons debates on the doctrines of liberty, sit with the most beautiful women of the day, until the candles gutter and bend in the gilded candelabra and the sedan chairs with their weary chairmen and footmen in the courtyard show tawdry in the light of dawn.

Life is pretty much a "dolce far niente." The great world is not alive before two o'clock in the afternoon. A curious foreigner who wishes to see all the gradations of social life can hardly hold out a London season. More than forty invitations will be on his table—five or six for each day. (All these fête-givers, of course, must be called upon in a morning, and to be courteous one must go in person. "C'est la mer à boire.")

Sensation hobnobs with sensibility. There is the craze for balloons which enables Lunardi to play gallant to a duchess and the craze for animal magnetism when all the world flocks to Dr. Maineduc. There is the craze for Ambigu suppers (half dinners). There is the silly craze for vying in dressed dolls which the fashionable of both sexes dandle in the Park. There is the grim craze for making a gazing stock of the scaffold, and grandees turn waiters for a morning to secure the best view. Next night finds the same fribbles figuring with equal nonchalance at Ranelagh, or masquerading in domino at the Pantheon. Newgate or Tyburn, Ranelagh or Vauxhall, Foley or Marylebone Gardens, it is all the same—a maze of mumming.

Countless are the specimens. We can wonder at Soubise, the adopted black page (when black pages are the mode) of Gay's and Prior's Duchess of Queensberry. A dashing Negro, this young Othello, who pens verses, kills hearts, goes the pace, and dies training Arab horses in India. Nor are we less astounded by that great enigma, the Chevalier D'Éon himself, the friend of Sheridan, Wilkes, and General Paoli—

once a dragoon, still proud to wear his red uniform with pea green lapels and silver lace, a wit and a scholar, a paragon at feats of arms and horsemanship, the pensioner and agent of the French government and probably a pensioner of the British minister too—D'Éon who keeps his counsel as to his politics and his sex, D'Éon who lives as a soldier and expires in petticoats. Quite as eccentric is Lady Hester Stanhope's father, Lord Stanhope, a patrician Jacobite with the face of an Italian cardinal, who shocks his friends by sleeping with open windows under twelve blankets and studying science in a home that the King calls Democracy Hall.

It is certainly not a squeamish age, though frivolity is born of appetite, not of languor. Elopements, duels, and intrigues follow fast on one another. There is much low life above stairs and Mayfair imports everything from France but the finesse of her manners, combining the morals of Richelieu with the elegance of Dutch Sam. The Duke of York turns the Duchess of Gordon out of the Pantheon supper room for rudeness to his Lady Tyrconnel; the Whig and Tory duchesses hiss each other as they enter a drawing room; and Fox is considered much improved in the early nineties from the days when he spat on Lord Shelburne's carpet. (Dull decorum enters in the next century, after the Regency. Of all the offences against English manners which a man can commit, the three following are the greatest: to put a knife in his mouth instead of a fork; to take up sugar or asparagus with his fingers, or, above all, to spit anywhere in a room. The last named crime is so pedantically proscribed in England that you may seek through all London in vain to find such a piece of furniture as a spitting box.)

Rousseau is in the air and laxity is extreme. Beauty and talent kick over the traces at a time when, as Chesterfield says, "Everybody's son married nobody's daughter." Mysterious children appear suddenly, exchanged by their mothers, returned to their fathers, or screened in convenient dower houses. Lovers are rife, but love dwindles, and any gust of real passion soon dashes all the porcelain swains and shepherdesses to fragments. The sense of home is far fainter than it was fifty years earlier, but the Duchess of Devonshire, though she moves distracted between literature and license, does set the example of nursing her babies, which is followed later by Mrs. Siddons, to the derision of the Drury Lane green room.

And women take a prominent part not only in art and literature, but in philanthropy and politics. The French Revolution ushers in the woman's age and the woman's standpoint, so that Thomas Paine's *Rights of Man* is matched by Mary Wollstonecraft Godwin's *Rights of Woman*. Yet the century that began with Bolingbroke somehow ends in giving birth to Shelley. . . .

But the Georgian era is a carnival of the animal man in which leading roles are played by Sheridan and his circle.

BOOK TWO

THE MAN: LITERATURE

CHAPTER 1

PORTRAIT GALLERY

FIRST IN OUR GALLERY is the Reverend Thomas Sheridan, Doctor of Divinity and friend of Jonathan Swift. A punster, a quibbler, a fiddler, and a wit, hopelessly improvident and hopelessly devoid of tact, a sportsman, a linguist and practical jester, a classical translator, saturated with books, yet ignorant of men, he initiates the Sheridan tradition.

The dominie of Drumlane is a true Rabelaisian, though at the same time he is par excellence a great student and "doubtless," writes Swift, "the best instructor of youth in these kingdoms or perhaps in Europe, and as great a master of the Greek and Latin languages." He is a man of "good sense, modesty and virtue," Swift again records. "His greatest fault is a wife and four children"—for which there is no excuse but that a wife is thought necessary to a schoolmaster.

The veteran owes much to the man who brushes up his scholarship, soothes his saturnine moods (till he is designated the David of the clerical Saul) and rashly agrees to remind him of his parsimony—which provokes the taunt that he plays Gil Blas to the Archbishop of Granada. A nomad like Gil Blas he remains, loving his ease and his bottle, and never owning a real home.

He roams from school to school, from living to living, the prey of his own caprices and of "quondam" friends— "quon—damn them all," he says—who steal his pupils (some of whom he teaches gratis) and batten on his hospitality. He is appointed one of the chaplains to the Lord Lieutenant of Ireland but is promptly struck off the list for a good reason. It falls to his lot to preach at Cork on the first of August anniversary of the Brunswick accession and he chooses for his sermon, "Sufficient unto the day is the evil thereof," shooting his fortune dead by a single text. Swift mildly rebukes him. "Too much advertency is not your talent, else you had fled from that text as from a rock." For as Don Quixote says to Sancho, "What business had you to speak of a halter in a family where one of it was hanged?"

He loses his chaplaincy, and all the ways of promotion are closed to him forever. But his spirit is not broken by his evil luck. Still he remains a punster, a quibbler, a fiddler, and a wit. Not a day passes without a rebus, an anagram, or a madrigal. His pen and his fiddle are constantly in motion. At the outset he is earning £1200 a year; at the close he leaves more children than banknotes.

His foes indeed are of his own household. The termagant wife, Elizabeth Macfadden of Ulster, whom he calls "Ponsy" but Swift "Xantippe, the greatest beast in Europe," "a most filthy slut, lazy, slothful luxurious, ill-natured, envious, and suspicious" quarters a whole tribe of her poor relations on him, including her mother; nor is it long before their rapacity has twice spent her dowry of £500 a year. She stints his scholars and wastes his substance. Remote kinsmen of his own complete the ruin till he confesses to Swift that he is entirely "be-Sheridaned." But he still laughs away care with a madrigal, or, what is more likely, drowns it in a social jorum.

"He will invite," says Swift of his friend, "six or more people of condition to dine with him. On the day appointed he will be absent and know nothing of the matter. When he is told of this, he is pleased because it shows him to be a genius and a man of learning."

Yet Swift and Stella trust their "second Solomon" beyond all others. At Sheridan's country retreat, Quilca, Swift, despite the scolding wife, spends many months writing *Gulliver's Travels*. To Sheridan in 1726 he opens his heart in that poignant sentence when he thinks Stella is dying, "I conclude the fairest soul in the world hath left its body."

And when next year, a few months before she breathes her last, it is to him that he addresses the words, "The last act of life is always a tragedy at best." To him Stella on her deathbed entrusts Swift's private correspondence, the publication of which he prevents. She prefers him to all Swift's friends and appoints him one of her executors. Despite his crippled circumstances, he refuses her offer of a legacy, just as years earlier he rejected Swift's intended preferment of him to the Armagh headmastership. "You cannot make him a greater compliment," Swift avows, "than by telling before his face how careless he was in any affair that related to his interest and fortune."

But Sheridan dares to tell Swift the truth which is the less palatable as Swift's infirmities of mind and body increase, and the friends are temporarily estranged. The last words of Dr. Sheridan deserve record. It is remarked that the wind is in the East. "Let it blow east, west, south, or north," whispers the doctor, "the immortal soul will take its flight to the destined point."

Dr. Sheridan's son is a different man. From start to finish he appears a pedant among Bohemians and a Bohemian among pedants. Warned perhaps by his father's example, he declines to become a pedagogue and decides to reform the stage. It sorely needs reformation. Political brawlers and fashionable rakehells disturb its peace, taste is neglected, and the actors are jealous of each other. Sheridan is ambitious. He thinks himself eminently qualified to regulate the chaos and transform the theatre from a cockpit into an academy. An excellent scholar, he aspires to classicise the stage; a just actor, he is also a dull one. His deep voice and measured gestures make him out as an ideal impersonator of Addison's Cato.

In January of 1743 the part of Richard the Third is performed at the Smock Alley Theatre in Dublin by "a young gentleman." So great is his success that soon afterwards the name of Thomas Sheridan appears in the playbills, and in a short time, when Quin comes over to triumph, the veteran quits the city in disgust at the reigning favorite. By 1745, when Swift breathes his last, young Sheridan finds himself undisputed master of the Royal Theatre.

He next visits London, acts at Covent Garden and at Drury Lane. He piques Garrick's jealousy and offends his pride; he invites the famous actor-manager to Dublin on the understanding that profit sharing shall be the basis of their contract. However, Garrick does come over, and Chesterfield, then Lord Lieutenant, patronizes the performance and popularizes himself by flattering Sheridan.

But Sheridan's rise has been too rapid. Already a war of pamphlets has raged over his claim to a gorgeous robe for the part of Cato. And within the space of eight years he meets with two organised reverses, the first of which establishes his reputation while the second practically ruins his fortunes.

On an evening in January, 1746, when a bevy of distinguished beauties are gathered to see Sheridan as Horatio in *The Fair Penitent*, one Mr. Kelly, an inflammable and inebriated young gentleman from Galway, clambers on the stage, uses grossly improper language, and rushes after that sentimental adventuress, Miss Bellamy, who takes refuge in her dressing room and bolts the door. Sheridan appears, and instead of winking at this playful freak as is customary, orders the attendants to conduct the disturber back to his place in the pit. Kelly takes a basket of oranges from a girl and pelts Sheridan with them, calling out that he is a rascal and a scoundrel. Sheridan retorts with perfect truth, "I am as good a gentleman as you are." This arouses Kelly's wrath. He goes to the manager's room, repeats his offensive epithets, and receives a public thrashing. An uproar follows, the curtain is rung down, the audience disperses in factions, and the Kellyites and Sheridanites are the Montagus and Capulets of the hour. For some time Sheridan's life is in danger. Kelly goes off vowing vengeance against the player who has dared to be a gentleman. When he prosecutes Sheridan for assault, he declares that he has seen a gentleman soldier and a gentleman tailor but never before a gentleman player. Whereupon Sheridan bows and says, "Sir, I hope you see one now." Acquitted amid loud applause, he takes a gentleman's revenge. When the rioter is prosecuted and condemned to a heavy fine, he beseeches the government for its remission and emerges the most popular man in Dublin.

Among the audience that evening sits a dark haired and dark eyed young lady of twenty-one, Miss Frances Chamberlaine, already an authoress and already enshrined as one of the "three literary graces." (Mrs. Cowley and Mrs. Griffiths are the other two.) Dr. Parr, who first meets her before he is a master at Harrow, calls her "truly celestial."

Thomas Sheridan's conduct under this ordeal makes him Miss Chamberlaine's hero. She at once publishes a pamphlet, which helps turn the tide in his favor, and a poem, "The Owls," in which the birds of night are rebuked and abashed by Apollo. In a word she falls in love with the persecuted actor. It is not long before they meet at the house of his sister and are betrothed.

In the spring of 1747 they are married and take up their abode at 12 Dorset Street, Dublin. They move in the best society—the Lanesboroughs, Charlemonts, Orrerys, and Cunninghams are their friends. Sheridan founds the Dublin Beefsteak Club as a meeting ground for the Castle and the Green Room and dares public opinion by installing saucy Peg Woffington in the presidential chair. Yet he is a martinet and a man of regular religious observance, who never misses family prayers. These, however, are often lightened by a well shaken mixture of brandy, sugar, and water, less potent than the Prince Regent's "Diabolino," but strong enough in after years to make him drop from his chair while he lectures his two sons on the perils of intoxication.

Sheridan finds no other fault with his wife than that she dresses too plainly. She attires herself in brown silk and most usually puts on a cap of a grave and matronly form. Yet the fairness and beauty of her bust, neck, and arms are allowed to have been seldom rivalled. She is as little covetous of admiration as she is averse to display. In common

[45]

with many other ladies of her day from the Queen downwards, she is addicted to taking snuff. Having seen her draw off her glove to indulge in a pinch, a fellow traveler in the public coach which runs between London and Windsor remarks, "There are few ladies, madam, who would have concealed such a hand and an arm so long."

The Sheridans raise a family and live happily in Dublin until the second outburst at the Royal Theatre drives the father away from home and kingdom.

His Beefsteak Club has been viewed askance as the political support of an unpopular government, and when a version of Voltaire's *Mahomet* is revived in February, 1754, some lines in it reflecting upon the rulers of the land are frantically applauded. Mr. Digges, a gentleman actor who speaks the lines, is called upon to repeat them. Sheridan disapproves of the actor's response to the summons and delivers a dreary lecture on the subject to the members of his company, in which he dwells on the disgrace of stealing popularity by party strokes or by any unusual emphasis, gesture, or significant look. Digges asks what he shall do if a fresh encore is demanded, and is curtly told to use his own discretion. He resents being lectured and watches for an opportunity to revenge himself. This occurs on the second of March, 1754, when the same play is again performed.

When a call is made for a repetition of the unpoetical but partisan lines—

If ye powers divine!
Ye mark the movements of this nether world,
And bring them to account, crush, crush those vipers,
Who, singled out by the community
To guard their rights shall, for a grasp of ore
Or paltry office, sell them to the foe,

Digges has the impudence to tell the public that Sheridan has forbidden it. Violent cries of "Manager, manager" rend the air. Sheridan, convinced that personal mischief is intended, slips away home and for a whole hour the malignants await his return. The call is renewed. Still no manager. A loyal cry of "God bless His Majesty King George" sets the Nationalists in motion and at the end of the third huzza the work of destruction begins. The benches are torn up, the chandeliers shattered, a legion jumps on the stage and slashes the valuable curtain with their swords, a grate of burning coals deluges the box room, and the property is wrecked.

Nor do Sheridan's misfortunes end here. His wife brings forth her fourth born only to see him die in convulsions three months afterwards, and though the Duke of Dorset offers his protegé a pension of £300 a year, the proud Stoic declines it. The whole work of nine years is undone. There is nothing left for this mismanaging manager but to let his theatre and make his exit to London.

There he begins to act Hamlet with Rich at Covent Garden, but the venture is not a success, and Drury Lane battens on its failure. Indefatigable, though in broken health, he now thinks he sees the hand of heaven pointing out another way of life, the way which from the beginning he has had in view. He at once girds to his mission as educationalist and in three weeks composes an essay proving that immorality, ignorance, and false taste are due to a defective system which a "Revival of the Art of Speaking and the Study of our own Language" may contribute to cure. He will mend mankind by rhetoric.

He sends for Mrs. Sheridan and the children, and they settle at Bedford Street, Covent Garden, in a house at the corner of Henrietta Street, which till 1768 remains their London abode. Here they stand evenings at the open window expecting the great lexicographer still busy with his Dictionary. "Take out your opera glass," says Sheridan, "Johnson is coming; you may know him by his gait."

The summer of 1756 recalls Sheridan and his wife to Dublin. He makes peace with his audience, he invites Foote, his future satirist, and the Italian dancers, but all in vain. New enemies undermine his fame. Sherry grows out of date—and again he recurs to his schemes for "perfecting human nature." In December, 1757, with the Duke of Bedford for patron, he gives a fashionable breakfast at the music hall in Fishamble Street, succeeded by an oration—the same dull oration—on the instruction of youth, which preludes the foundation of a new Hibernian Society. Subscribers pour in. Professors are appointed at fabulous salaries to regenerate the young, and Sheridan is made president of the school. Elated with success, he crosses the channel to further the project. But no sooner is his back turned than foes, political and theatrical, blight his hopes. An actor, it is said, has no right to direct an academy. (And why should an Irishman teach Englishmen English?) Kelly's old taunt is revived, and once more the mob of Dublin does not permit a player to be a gentleman. For a year the Hibernian Society flourishes without him, and then it dies the death of the impecunious. Sheridan leaves Dublin and transfers his debts and his harangues to London. (Alas! poor Yorick!)

In London halcyon days begin with his lectures. Oratory, he insists, offers a specific for every ill on earth. Declamation, pronunciation, emphasis, but be it also said, advanced education occupy his days and nights. He speaks with great success in the Pewterers' Hall, Spring Garden, and afterwards at Oxford and Cambridge. Boswell hears him and thinks he reads very well though he complains he is ill. These lectures gradually become the rage. For one of his courses in 1762 no less than sixteen hundred subscribe at a guinea a piece, and they buy his publications at "half a guinea in boards."

He receives private pupils, including Lord Percy, and mends the action of Boswell. Nor is his fame confined to London, for in 1758 he receives honorary degrees at both the universities. Two years later he reappears on the boards and with such success that critics are split into his faction and Garrick's. By the beginning of 1761 Mrs. Sheridan can write that he stands "in high reputation with a prospect of being every day more and more esteemed."

At the same time her own fame enhances her husband's. The manuscript of her novel *Sidney Biddulph* receives the approbation of Samuel Richardson who arranges for its publication. When he writes to her, expressing admiration of it, she replies in these terms: "I think vanity under a show of modesty is of all lights it can appear in, the most contemptible! How ridiculous then would it be for me to say, I don't think the novel worth printing, after it has had your approbation. Before it was honored with that, I looked upon it as a thing written in a manner so different from the present taste that I did not suppose anybody would read it."

But everybody does. It takes London by storm. Richardson, of course, is in raptures, and Dr. Johnson remarks, "I know not, madam, that you have a right upon moral principles to make your reader suffer so much." The Abbé Prévost translates it into French; a dramatised version is put on the Paris stage; it pleases as a play as well as a book, and thus the success of *Sidney Biddulph* is twofold in France. In after years Charles James Fox pronounces it to be the best novel in the English language, while Georgiana, Duchess of Devonshire, at the age of fifty-one gravely consults her mother as to whether she may be allowed to read it.

The moral of the book is that virtue is not always rewarded, the unfortunate heroine having alone the consciousness of acting uprightly to sustain her under innumerable woes. Love is reduced to a subordinate place and made subservient to the triumph of wedded constancy and the exercise of the domestic duties and affections.

The welcome Mrs. Sheridan receives as a novelist makes her ambitious of shining as a playwright, and accordingly she composes two comedies, one a success and the other a failure. For the latter she receives a token of sympathy alike rare and welcome. It comes from Millar the bookseller who pays her handsomely for the rights to publish the comedy. He writes to say that its rapid sale is "an undeniable proof of its merits" and encloses a further payment of £100. Sympathy in this form is very precious. Mrs. Sheridan composes an Ode to Patience to show how philosophically she can bear misfortune. The first three out of the sixty lines run thus—

UNCORKING OLD SHERRY:

Unawed by threats, unmoved by force,
My steady soul pursues her course,
Collected, calm, resigned.

Her resignation and calm are rendered the easier owing to Millar's liberality.

A crowd of celebrities visit the Sheridans in the years following. There are Garrick, Beauclerk, Dr. Robertson, Mrs. Cholmondeley and Mrs. Macaulay, the great Johnson and Johnson's shadow, Boswell, a thin, eager looking young man dressed in black who talks much of General Paoli. "I suppose," Sheridan remarks, "you are in mourning for Corsica," and Boswell answers in the affirmative. Another guest is the novelist Samuel Richardson, who is dull as a drowning fly when vainly struggling with the melancholy that oppresses him.

The lexicographer is a frequent visitor. One day, observing that her eldest daughter is attentively employed in reading the *Rambler,* the mother hastens to assure Dr. Johnson it is only works of that unexceptionable description which she suffers to meet the eyes of her little girl. "In general," adds Mrs. Sheridan, "I am very careful to keep from her all books as are not calculated, by their moral tendency, expressly for the perusal of youth."

"Then you are a fool, madam!" vociferates the Doctor. "Turn your daughter loose into your library. If she is well inclined, she will choose only nutritious food; if otherwise, all your precautions will avail nothing to prevent her following the natural bent of her inclinations."

Though Dr. Johnson is fond of Mrs. Sheridan, he is already prejudiced against her husband, half through his hereditary association with Swift and half because Garrick never conceals his jealousy. Bozzy fans the flame which a pension and Dictionary soon turn into a conflagration. "Why, sir, Sherry is dull, naturally dull," he once says in pique, "but it must have taken him a great deal of pains to become what he is. Such an excess of stupidity is not in nature. Besides, sir, what influence can Mr. Sheridan have upon the language of this great country through his narrow exertions? It is burning a farthing candle at Dover to show light at Calais." And when a pension of £200 is given to Sheridan shortly after he has received his own, "What!" he roars, "have they given him a pension? Then it is time for me to give up mine." (It happens, as Boswell discovers from Loughborough that Sheridan has "rung the bell' for Johnson's pension.)

Johnson's joke has a "splenetic explosion." Sheridan says Johnson is a bully, that he has never feared him, and that Johnson never said an ill-bred thing to him but once, which was, "Sir, you have said this three times already. I do not see why you should say it again."

Such bludgeoning is not in Sheridan's manner. Instead of returning the cudgels, he quietly avoids the man who has so often knocked him down. Johnson afterwards repents, and confides to Boswell in his big bow-wow way, "Sir, Sheridan is not a bad man. No, sir. Were mankind to be divided into good and bad, he would stand considerably within the ranks of the good." Johnson is ready to be reconciled, but Sheridan is not and they never meet again. This rupture with Sheridan deprives the Doctor of one of his most agreeable resources for amusement in his lonely evenings, for Sheridan's bustling mind never suffers conversation to stagnate, and Mrs. Sheridan is a most agreeable companion—sensible, ingenious, unassuming—yet communicative.

In 1754 Sheridan with his family goes to live in France, partly for Mrs. Sheridan's health, partly to study the system of education, but mostly to escape his debts. There they live happily on a fifth of what would command comfort in England. The father, sighing that he is forgotten, toils at his grammars and dictionaries, the mother at her literary ventures, the children at French and music. Suddenly good tidings reach them. An English Act for insolvent debtors has been passed, and in 1766 influential friends press Sheridan to profit by it. He wavers, but they work zealously on his behalf in Dublin. It is hoped that his petition, favored by great names in the Irish Parliament, may prevail without personal attendance. But an opposition is raised, and Sheridan is on the verge of setting out for Ireland when his wife is seized with her last illness. She is buried at the end of the month in an enclosure of a Protestant family. Not only is this exceptional privilege accorded, but her funeral, at night and by torchlight, is followed by the Catholics who love her, and by a military escort. Her husband is desolate indeed. "I have lost," he writes, "what the world cannot repair—a bosom friend, another self. My children have lost— oh, their loss is neither to be expressed nor repaired. But the will of God be done."

The widower returns to London and gathers all his family around him in Frith Street, Soho Square. The household becomes a merry one, but Mr. Sheridan keeps a tight hand over his children. He is a strict disciplinarian, and he manages them as sternly as he does a theatre. He exacts unquestioning obedience from those dependent upon him, though he takes great offence if his superiors require submission from him. He "pours lava," as he says, upon those who offend him. He is very methodical and precise in all his ways. He has morning prayers regularly, and on Sunday evenings he either comments on the sermon of the day or expounds to the children a passage in the Bible. He is still fond of Dr. Johnson's *Ramblers,* and his daughters are often wearied and disheartened with the task of reading them aloud, because he is exacting with regard to enunciation and cadence, and careful in correcting what he deems their faults in speech.

The impression made on Richard Brinsley by life in his father's household is more agreeable than may be supposed, and it is fondly cherished during many years. In later days he calls to see his father but does not find him at home. His sister receives him in the dining room where the cloth is laid, and he exclaims, "Ah! I could fancy myself back among old times, seated with Charles and my sisters at this table and my father looking round us and giving his favorite toast—'Healths, hearts, and homes.'"

CHAPTER 2

CHILDHOOD

RICHARD BRINSLEY SHERIDAN is born at 12 Dorset Street, Dublin, towards the close of September, 1751. The precise day and month of his birth are unknown. Allthough he is baptized Thomas Brinsley, his parents soon afterwards change their minds and call him Richard after one of his uncles.

He is the third child. Thomas, the eldest, is born in 1747 but dies in 1750. Charles Francis is born in June, 1750. Then follow in January, 1753, Alicia, afterwards Mrs. Joseph Le Fanu, Sackville, born and buried during the theatre riots in 1754, and Anne Elizabeth Hume Crawfurd, born in 1758, a Londoner, and afterwards the wife of Henry Le Fanu, her brother-in-law's brother.

Dick and Lissy begin their education under the charge of schoolmaster Sam Whyte to whom they are committed by parents who are perpetually shifting their quarters. Whyte, an illegitimate son of Mrs. Sheridan's uncle, opens a school in Grafton Street, Dublin, under the sounding title of "Seminary for the Instruction of Youth," and thither the two children repair, first as day pupils and then as boarders. The schoolmaster is long the father's most zealous champion. When the elder Sheridan embarks on grammar, Whyte must needs follow his lead. Like his patron too, he starts literary assemblies, lectures on eloquence, and composes several works for which his pupils pay.

Dick fails to distinguish himself at the Seminary and spends his time dashing off repartees and lampoons. The boy, however, is no dullard, for he makes some progress in French, though he continues to pronounce "malheureux"

[53]

as "malheroo." In the fall of 1759 he joins his family in London where for three years he fully enjoys himself. He is a dare-devil and resents his father's open favoritism of Charles whose "domestic and sedentary disposition" qualifies him for a life at home and who has already been paraded on the lecturer's platform. Charles reads Eve's speech to Adam from Milton, beginning "O thou from whom and for whom I was formed," and Dick and Lissy occupy front places in their Sunday best.

Through Charles Sumner, headmaster of Harrow School, who shares Sheridan's fastidiousness in pronunciation, Dick is sent to Harrow-on-the-Hill. In 1762 it presents the appearance of a village grammar school with a small cluster of adjacent boarding houses. At first the little fellow is low spirited, taunted as a player's son, frequently in tears, and even downright unhappy. He sees next to nothing of his parents, is not taken home at the regular holidays, and is left without pocket money. But he soon warms up to his schoolmates and enters with zest into their sports and amusements. Among his friends he counts Jones and Halhed, and also Glanville, Horne, and Cummings, of whom nothing is known but their names. He is indolent, winning, brilliant without book, mischievous, and Irish—which qualities not only serve to attract his fellows but in his worst scrapes disarm the wrath of his masters. He keeps an apple loft for the supply of which all the gardens in the neighborhood are taxed.

Parr enters into his life, Parr who in due course is to be regarded as the Whig Dr. Johnson, to write learned treatises, look "Pomposo" to the life, and be responsible for Lady Byron's Latin. Parr is one of the last of the great classical pedants in whose eyes an exact knowledge of the Greek and Latin grammar and a minute acquaintance with the Greek and Latin classics constitute a title to universal respect and everlasting fame.

The master attempts to wean the varlet from his idle ways, but still Sheridan's Greek and his diligence remain woefully out of gear. He is often called up to construe and made to stand near the headmaster's desk where the voice of no prompter can reach him. Strange to say, he distinguishes himself by the delivery of a Greek oration. The speech—from Demosthenes—has to be delivered in the character of a military commander, for Demosthenes fought and fled at Chaeroneia. Master Dick calmly orders the scarlet and gold regimentals of an English general officer and thus resplendent does honor, doubtless, to his colors. (When his uncle, Dr. Richard Chamberlaine, who is supporting him, receives the tailor's bill, he remonstrates with him upon this unexpected piece of extravagance.)

Yet he dabbles in Virgil, Lucian, Lucan; his steps are noiseless and his taste silently improved.

One of his sisters now and then visits Harrow, and in the house where he is lodged she triumphantly repeats Dryden's "Ode in Honor of St. Cecilia's Day," according to the instruction given her by her father. Take a sample—

> *None* but the brave,
> None but the *brave*,
> None *but* the brave deserves the fair.

Whatever the zeal or proficiency of the sister, Richard cares nought for these things.

He takes the world lightly and gaily, and no laborious mental exertion tempts him. And when he returns to Frith Street at seventeen with his Irish charm and Harrow breeding, he is a young hero in the eyes of his sister. "I admired him," says Alicia. "I almost adored him."

His school chum, Nathaniel Brassey Halhed, enters into a correspondence with him, deferring with humility to his judgment and owning a want of "common sense, taste, nicety, and invention." All these qualities Halhed finds to perfection in his friend whose slips in spelling and punctuation, however, he does not fail to reprove.

They form a literary partnership, compose an operatic burlesque, *Jupiter* (the germ of The *Critic*), and translate in verse the love epistles of an obscure and dubious Greek author, Aristaenetus, which see light in August, 1771. The epistles are favorably reviewed but not remunerative.

Meanwhile, without the aid of his ally, he dashes off several pieces in verse and prose—a dramatic sketch of the *Vicar of Wakefield*, a weekly periodical entitled *Hernan's Miscellany*, in the style of the *Spectator*, a series of epigrams, and two rhymed satires, *Clio's Protest* and the *Ridotto of Bath*. A collection of occasional poems and a volume of *Crazy Tales* perish in embryo. He comes fresh from Horace, Theocritus, and Anacreon, has dabbled in Lucian's sardonic prose, loves Dryden, and above all is steeped in the lyrics of the sixteenth century. He strikes a miniature lyre. His love songs are fanciful and tuneful.

Parr steps forward and presses for an Oxford education, but paternal finances cannot bear the strain. It does not follow that old Sheridan is careless of his son's future. He is at this time maturing his educational scheme, and in 1769 it is published with a letter to the King in which the author offers to devote his life to its cause on the receipt of a sufficient pension to enable him to abandon the theatre. Visions of an academy in which he is to be the guiding spirit and his sons executives float before the gaze of this sanguine Irishman, and with that view he instructs them daily in elocution. At the same time they receive lessons in Latin and mathematics from a Mr. Lewis Ker, a portentous bore. The remainder of a polite education is acquired at old Angelo's fencing and riding schools close by. Dick teaches young Angelo rhetoric in return for his father's fencing lessons.

The royal ear is invoked in vain. And old Sheridan retires in 1771 to Bath where he works away at his Dictionary which ultimately appears in 1780.

"Why, sir," says Dr. Johnson to Boswell who has defended Sheridan's method of marking the pronunciation of vowels, "Consider how much easier it is to learn a language by the ear than by any marks. Sheridan's Dictionary may do very well, but you cannot always carry it about with you, and when you want the word, you have not the Dictionary.

It is like the man who has a sword that will not draw. It is an admirable sword, to be sure, but while your enemy is cutting your throat, you are unable to use it. Besides, sir, what entitles Sheridan to fix the pronunciation of English?"

CHAPTER 3

THE SCHOOL FOR SCANDAL

ON THE MORNING of Saturday, January 19, 1771, about half an hour before noon, a nonchalant youth may be seen strolling towards Simpson's, one of the lower Assembly rooms, which are then the twin attractions of the city of Bath. Cocked hat and scarlet waistcoat, dark piercing eyes, glowing cheeks, and full lips. About the whole countenance, however, there lurks an air of watchfulness in ambush, contrasting somewhat with its freshness. The youth glances around, then quickens his footsteps, for he is about to hear the voice of one whom already he admires in secret beyond every living and every singing creature.

He is bound for a concert room where his father has advertised recitations and a discourse on rhetoric "with a view to the improvement of human nature." Poor old Sherry, such are his "Attic entertainments." His art is of the old school, sonorous and formal, while his voice is that of one crying in a wilderness of pleasure seekers. He needs youth and radiance and beauty to commend it, and he finds them all in the genius of Elizabeth Ann Linley, eldest daughter of Thomas Linley, director of provincial oratorios and now of the Bath concerts.

She has barely turned sixteen. And though for over four years already an enchantress of the public and exposed to the rude gaze of mankind, she remains "the most modest, pleasing, and delicate flower" in Nature's garden—as voluptuary Wilkes styles her when he dines with the family in the following year. She has trodden a thorny path without contamination. Purity and beauty embodied, she consecrates her art to that Handel whom her sister Maria dies singing, whom their father reveres and resuscitates, and after whom he christens his eldest son. She is one who speaks in song, who moves in light. In after years a bishop terms her the connecting link between mortals and angels. A statesman who says the same sits up half the night to hear her. The King himself hangs on her every tone. And her voice is an emblem of herself.

Contemporaries unite in hyperbole. The musician Jackson of Exeter owns that "her countenance while singing is like nothing earthly." Calibans stand abashed at this Miranda. The evil-minded Pasquin is awed into respect by her presence. When she helps Fox in the Westminster election of 1784, obscure pamphleteers not only spare her, but are hushed into admiration. Leonora's charms turn vice into virtue, treason into truth. Whatever points at her is pointed right.

She irradiates the whole atmosphere. Twice or thrice during 1770 she sings at Oxford and takes it by storm. Her very name sheds perfume. When it is bruited that she has eloped to Scotland with a man of £3,000, general consternation ensues. To the young and chivalrous she shines, a being ensphered and ethereal, "a bright particular star" amid the mists of her profession. Her pathetic voice holds all hearers spellbound—

> Oh, soul of harmony that knows
> No touch of discord to disclose;
> So well her mind and voice agree,
> That every thought is ravishment.

And the singer Dibdin quotes the words of Comus as best expressing the quality of her voice.

> Can any mortal mixture of earth's mould
> Breathe such divine enchanting ravishment?
> Surely something holy lodges in that breast
> And with these raptures moves the vocal air
> To testify his hidden residence.

In a family of artists she is artistic to her finger tips. Like her sister Mary she sketches as well as sings, like her brother William she composes delightful verses, like her father and her brother Thomas she is a skilled instrumentalist, like her future husband an excellent mimic and impersonator. Gainsborough constantly draws and paints her—he twice models her face in clay. Ozias Humphry, the west-country painter, is another of her devotees, and Sir Joshua Reynolds (who cannot be charged with ecstasies) records his intense admiration. Not only does he twice depict her as St. Cecilia, but she is the model for the Charity in the window of New College, Oxford, and the Virgin in his picture of the Nativity.

She is as much tormented by suitors as Penelope. The list of men known to be in love with her before her marriage runs well into two figures. It includes Sheridan's brother Charles as well as his old Harrow schoolfellow Nathaniel Halhed. Directly Halhed hears her rehearse, "I am petrified," he sighs. "My very faculties are annihilated with wonder." And her image haunts him.

Sheridan, still uncertain of his own feelings, cautions a friend so susceptible against being over-enchanted. Eventually Halhed retires to India, and when at last he is off to the land of pagoda trees, he urges his friend to follow his footsteps—!

Charles, prudent and cautious even at twenty-two, after taking counsel with himself and deciding that his attachment to Miss Linley will certainly bring him more trouble than happiness, sends her a formal letter of farewell and goes to lodge at a farmhouse some miles away. But Halhed and Charles are among those who entertain honorable designs.

The previous year finds Miss Linley the unenviable center of a sensation which still agitates Bath. Mr. Walter Long, an old Wiltshire squire of vast estates and ancient lineage, but mean, ill bred, and avaricious, is added to the list of suitors. Mrs. Linley thrusts the match on the reluctant girl, who at this time is engaged in a dangerous friendship with a ci-devant Captain Mathews, a married rake who has known her ever since she stood as a mere child with her basket of concert programs. To the stern father whom she always loves she has been bound apprentice till she comes of age. And her talent is already worth an income of a £1000 a year to the family whose improving fortunes have just removed them from their small house in Pierpoint Street to one of the large mansions in the new Crescent. If she must cease to sing then, she must marry a wealthy husband. And thus love-diamonds are presented, wedding clothes prepared, and settlements drawn up.

Captain Mathews questions the little flame—*la petite Rossignol*—and is told she is going to be buried alive to be married to that "old, fusty, shabby, shuffling, money-loving, water-drinking, mirth-marring, amorous old hunks." Mrs. Linley hastens to reassure her daughter. She is convinced there is some little, low, paltry passion that lurks in her breast. "Ten thousand a year. There's not a lady in town would refuse him."

"Not his fortune," says Miss Linnet.

"Well," answers her mother, "who nowadays marries anything else? Would you refuse an estate because it happens to be a little encumbered? You must consider the man in this case a kind of mortgage." Then her mother reminds her that she has only a baby face and can bawl a few ballads—and she is bound, moreover, to support her family.

But suddenly, whether by the girl's own tears and entreaties, or by the remonstrances of Long's relations, or, as is reported, by her refusal to pass a night at his lodgings before the marriage, this match of sixteen and sixty is broken off, and the enraged parents threaten the lecherous lover with a lawsuit. Elizabeth, shrinking from publicity, now fears the exposure of her correspondence with Mathews whom she cannot help regarding with a pure but passionate attachment. That odious person, Samuel Foote, the comedian, to whom nothing is sacred, chances to be on the spot and at once scents an opportunity. Within a year he utilizes the whole story for a play, *The Maid of Bath*, which exhibits the girl's innocence, her mother's management, the captain's philanderings, and the lover's avarice, to the curiosity of a London audience. David Garrick writes the prologue, comparing Foote to Jack the Giant Killer and Long to a monster who seeks to devour a young and tender virgin—

> "Tally-ho!—a rank old fox we now pursue,
> So strong the scent, you'll run him full in view;
> If we can't kill *such brutes* in human shape,
> Let's fright 'em that your *chickens* may escape."

Mr. Long is frightened into payment of a handsome sum. He allows Elizabeth to retain his gifts and presents her with £3,000 to be settled on her till her majority—half of which she at once surrenders to her father. All Bath, all London, exclaim against him, and he remains pilloried as Squire Solomon Flint. While Miss Linley, famed hitherto as the linnet, the nightingale, the siren, is now known everywhere by the title of the comedy—Hapless Maid of scandal-mongering Bath! Tears are shed for and by her in plenty, and she often pours out her heart to her new friends, the Sheridan sisters, Lissy, a year older than herself, and Bessy, who is only twelve.

Still she lends her aid to the "Roman Father" in his Attic entertainments on Thursdays and Saturdays. The elocutionist as usual undertakes the reading part and Miss Linley the singing. On this occasion he recites verses from Milton and Goldsmith and Pope. She sings "Rosy Bowers" from Purcell, "Black-eyed Susan," and a Scotch ballad.

But while Miss Linley warbles and her lover listens, a short ramble must be made through Bath past and present though it is hard to be torn away from St. Cecilia and her minstrel.

A loud ringing of the Abbey bells announces to all and sundry the arrival of Horace Walpole and her ladyship, the Marchioness of Salisbury. Invalids are fond of news. Upon the first round of the bells they send out to inquire for whom they ring. But all visitors are received in the same way—even Mr. Bullock, an eminent cowkeeper of Tottenham who comes to drink the waters for indigestion.

Bath is the hotel of the eighteenth century. All sorts and conditions of men and women flock here: notables and notorieties, chaplains and members of Parliament, noblemen with ribbons and stars, quacks, duchesses, dove-colored Quakers, fortune hunters, lackeys, lank-haired Methodists, clerks and captains, usurers, brokers, bishops and boarding school misses, Ferdinand, Count Fathom, as well as my Lord Ogleby, Lady Bellaston, Geoffrey Wildgoose, Commodore Trunnion and Tugwell the cobbler, Lismahago and Tabitha Bramble. Be certain too you will encounter Mrs. Candour and Lady Sneerwell, Sir Benjamin Backbite and his uncle Mr. Crabtree—for Bath is their fitting environment. In fact they were born in Bath.

Persons go to Bath for gout, for the vapours, for all sorts of real or fake diseases, or, as my Lady does, because it is the thing to do if one wishes to remain in fashion. Some go by stage coach, some on horseback, some in their own carriages. They arrive well and return home cured. "Go to Bath" means "You are mad." The people of Bath never need to light their fires except as a luxury, for the waters spring out of the earth ready boiled for use. They drink nothing else there and seem to enjoy it, seeing how they swallow it down.

It is the queen of watering places—a heaven to impressionable and uncritical young ladies—a new world, all gaiety, good humor, and diversion. The merry bells ring round from morn to night. There is music in the Pump Room every morning, cotillons every forenoon, balls twice a week, and concerts every other night, besides private assemblies and parties without number. As soon as the guests are settled in their lodgings, they are visited by the Master of Ceremonies, a pretty little gentleman, so sweet, so fine, so civil and polite that in any other country he would pass for a Prince of Wales.

At eight in the morning my lady goes in dishabille to the Pump Room which is crowded like a Welsh fair. There you see the highest quality and the lowest tradesfolk jostle each other without ceremony—hail fellow well met. The noise of the music playing in the gallery, the heat and flavor of such a crowd, and the hum and buzz of their conversation give my Lady the headache and vertigo the first day, but afterwards all these things become familiar and even agreeable. Right under the Pump Room windows is the King's Bath, a hugh cistern where you see the patients up to their necks in hot water. As the music plays my Lady into the Bath, the women who tend her present her with a little floating wooden dish, like a basin, into which she puts a pocket handkerchief, a snuffbox, and a nosegay, and of late some patches, though the bath, occasioning a little perspiration, the patches do not stick as kindly as they should.

The Bath is small, not over clean, but it is a gay crowd that fills it. The ladies' costumes are hideous and unbecoming. They wear jackets and petticoats of brown linen, with ordinary chip hats in which they often fix their handkerchiefs to wipe the sweat from their faces. But truly whether it is owing to the steam that surrounds them or to the heat of the water or to the nature of the dress or to all three causes together, they look so flushed and so frightful that we always turn our eyes another way. Fanny Burney is amazed at the public exhibition of the ladies in the Bath. It is true their heads are covered with bonnets, but the very idea of being seen in such a situation by whosoever pleases to look is indelicate.

My lady, probably without a guide, now walks about the Bath, listens to the music, and exchanges jests of a Rabelaisian kind. In an hour's time she calls for her chair (hermetically sealed if she is old, ugly, or prudish, and artistically penetrable if she is finely formed) and returns home to her lodgings. Then she reappears in the Pump Room (still in dishabille, be it noted) to drink the waters, talk scandal, and quiz the dress and appearance of the motley, untidy-looking crew.

Hard by the Pump Room is a coffee house for the ladies,

but young girls are not admitted inasmuch as the conversation turns upon politics, scandal, philosophy, and other subjects above their capacity.

Daily service at the Abbey, dinner in the afternoon, a stroll about the city. Fine avenues of trees, fish ponds, and bowling greens; clipped yew hedges, terraces and flights of steps enlivened with beautiful stone and lead vases and garden sculpture. It is beautiful and wonderful throughout. The hills are built up and down and the vales so stocked with trees and houses that in some places from the ground floor of one side of a street you cross over to your neighbor's attic. In brief, yet in truth, it looks like a city of palaces, a town of hills, and a hill of towns.

Virtuosos go to hear Linley's music, poets seek inspiration on the banks of the Avon, and sentimental damsels and lovers seek the silence or sleep which Wordsworth assures us is to be found among the lonely hills.

Other charming places of resort are the booksellers' shops where novels, plays, pamphlets, and newspapers may be perused for so small a subscription as a crown a quarter, and in these offices of intelligence all the reports of the day and all the private transactions of the Bath are first entered and discussed. (News from Bath fill more space in London newspapers than is devoted to news from the American colonies or from Europe.) From the bookseller's shop we make a tour through the milliners and toymen and commonly stop at Mr. Gills, the pastry cook, to take a jelly, a tart, or a small basin of vermicelli. If we have ample time, we perhaps pay a visit to Sally Lunn's famous bunshop in Lilliput Alley or sit down and write to our grandson or cousin. Then if we are poetasters, we repair to Sappho Miller's at Batheaston (Miller, fair, fat, and forty, rather vulgar, somewhat affected, but truly kind), where in a stiff garden so landscaped as to frame a glimpse of the London road, the plump Queen of the Muses, fresh from the grand tour, holds her fair of Parnassus and crowns the conqueror with myrtle. (Proceeds devoted to the Bath charities.)

Visits in the evening after tea and the day winds

up, as in London, with cards, dancing, or the playhouse.

Mornings at the Bath—"How d'ye do?" The rest of the day—"What trumps?"

The great scenes of entertainment at Bath are two public rooms where the company meets alternately every evening. They are spacious, lofty, and when lighted, striking. They are generally crowded with well dressed people who drink tea in separate parties, play at cards, walk or sit or chat together, just as they are disposed. Twice a week there is a ball, the expense of which is defrayed by a voluntary subscription among the gentlemen and every subscriber has three tickets. We shall find here beauties of all ages who come to show off their charms, young girls and widows in quest of husbands, and married women who seek solace for the unpleasant ones they possess, actors, musicians, gamesters, dupes, sharpers, rustic greenhorns, and would-be beaux. Scotch peers elbow St. Kitts mulattoes, a Colonel dances with a Southwark ironmonger's daughter, and a Wapping landlady stares quality out of countenance. A paralytic attorney nearly trips up the Lord Chancellor, and the Master of Ceremonies mistakes a countess's waiting maid for a great lady.

"Do you dance, sir, tonight?" "No, ma'am, I do not."
"I don't wonder at all, 'tis suffoking hot."

All is hubbub and impudence. The only persons lacking in the gallery are invalids—or if these appear they have none of those illnesses which spoil enjoyment.

Society at Bath is like one united family. Every one meets everybody else every day. People who in London find themselves in totally different cliques mix on a footing of perfect equality, and it is not at all necessary to know people on the Mall because one has perhaps exchanged courtesies with them in the Bath. In fact two persons who live in the most intimate correspondence in Bath or Tunbridge shall in four and twenty hours so totally forget their friendship as to meet in St. James's Park without betraying the least token of recognition. Take George Selwyn for instance. Happening to be at Bath when it is nearly empty, he is induced for the mere purpose of killing time to cultivate the acquaintance of an elderly gentleman he is in the habit of meeting in the rooms. In the height of the following season, Selwyn encounters his old associate in St. James's Street. He endeavors to pass unnoticed but in vain. "What! do you not recollect me?" exclaims the indignant provincial. "I recollect you perfectly," replies Selwyn, "and when I next go to Bath, I shall be most happy to become acquainted with you again."

Religion like friendship is not of much consequence to the visitors of Bath. They go to church daily, it is true, but hardly take the trouble to disguise the fact that it is in order to see their lovers, make assignations, and pass billet doux.

Neither is their main object of stay to do a cure by bathing or taking the waters. The real reason of their visits is pleasure in all its forms. In addition it is a matrimonial market for such slightly tarnished goods (what the French style *Pêches à quinze sous*) as have not succeeded in finding purchasers elsewhere. Fortune hunters flock hither in search of a wife, maids in search of a husband. It is all done and arranged above board. Even Dr. Johnson writes to Mrs. Thrale that Bath is a good place for the initiation of a young lady, and many marriages are regularly brought about as a result of an annual visit to Bath.

But to intrigue, gallantry, and moral licence, the watering place is even more favorable than to marriage. Never does Love behold his empire so flourishing as here. Those who have been attacked by him before coming there feel their ardor redoubled, and those who seem the least inclined to the passion lose all their austerity and become different beings.

> See with joy my Romeo comes
> He conducts me to the rooms,
> There he whispers not unseen,
> Tender tales behind the screen.

UNCORKING OLD SHERRY:

Young men come here to take a course in profligacy. 'Prentice John after practising in accordance with a carefully drawn up program at Astrop, Bury, Epsom, Scarborough, and Tunbridge, considers a season at Bath the last training necessary before approaching London.

> I am a decay'd Macaroni,
>   My lodgings up three Pair of Stairs,
> My cheeks are grown wondrously bony,
>   And grey, very grey, are my hairs.
>
> My landlady eyes me severely,
>   And frowns when she opens the door,
> My tailor behaves cavalierly,
>   And my coat will bear scouring no more.
>
> I'll hasten, O Bath! to thy springs,
>   Thy seats of the wealthy and gay,
> Where the hungry are fed with good things,
>   And the rich are sent empty away.

More remarkable than these visitors is a small coterie of very old men who love country dances and breakfast on hot rolls and butter. They live to an immense length of days merely by leading the same kind of life that is prevalent at this place, and they dance with as much vigor at the Balls as if they had not flourished in a courant at Charles the Second's restoration. To be more particular: here is a Brocas, for instance (now in his 97th year currente anno), who avers he never was sick in his life, nor ever paid a groat for a pennyworth of physick, which athletic constitution he attributes to an utter inattention either to the cares of the public or the various fortunes of his private friends. He thanks heaven he always has a clean pair of gloves and a neat pair of pumps at command, and therefore it is of little consequence to him who is King of England, or which of his relations are married or hanged. But the less he regards public affairs, the more he attends public places. He is at Bath in May, at Tunbridge in July, at Bath again in

September, and every day during Parliament time. The pale faced girls are fond of him, and they are sure to be well touzled when he leads up to the Kissing Dance. Do not imagine from hence that he is a generous or a poisonous animal. No, he is perfectly harmless. Mothers trust him with their daughters alone in the dark. The virgin plays with him, and the married woman takes his advice in laces and tippets. Some envious persons call him a dangler and maliciously whisper in his ear—

> A Dangler is of neither sex,
> A Creature born to tease and vex, &c., &c.

Such is the society at Bath. The courtyards of the Bear, the White Hart, and the Three Tuns still clatter with arrivals and departures. Scrace's livery stables still assist elopements, and Gill the confectioner still shelters constant—and inconstant—couples.

Bath is at once an epitome of London and a rehearsal of it. Both permeate Sheridan's whole career. His plays are founded on its experience, his wit trained in its assemblies, his fortunes decided by its events. Bath breathes in all his characters. *The Rivals* is Bath humorised, *The School for Scandal* is Bath satirized (though London is its nominal scene), there is a whiff of Bath in *The Duenna*.

They are all about in these lively streets—the scandalmongers nodding their heads together, the officers now and then arranging a duel, and Lydia Languish ransacking the circulating libraries. Mrs. Malaprop deranges her epitaphs, Sir Lucius is always ready with his pistols, and the little waiting maid trips about the scene with Delia's letters and Broken Vows under her arm. Doubtless Sheridan often strolls about the fashionable promenade among the bucks and beaux and sees and hears all that is going on.

But at this moment he is rapt in wonder at how far the linnet transcends Miss Waller as she sings "Mad Bess" from Purcell, which concludes the mixed performance.

CHAPTER 4

SYLVIO AND LAURA

A ROMANTIC COMEDY
in Four Acts and Five Scenes

ACT I. ELOPEMENT

ACT II. DUELS

Scene 1. London—Mathews' Doorstep
Scene 2. Hyde Park and Castle Tavern. A May Evening
Scene 3. Bath. A Grotto
Scene 4. Miss Linley's Bower
Scene 5. Kingsdown Hill. July.
Three o'clock in the Morning

ACT. III. RETREAT

ACT IV. MARRIAGE

Time: A Romantic Age
Place: The Continent, Bath, and London

DRAMATIS PERSONAE

Men

The Hero—Richard Brinsley Sheridan
The Villain—Captain Mathews
The Roman Father ("Old Surly boots")—Thomas
Sheridan (Author of *Plan of Education for the
Nobility and Gentry)*
"Old Marplot"—Thomas Linley, Musician
Charles Surface—Charles Sheridan
Seconds, Surgeons, Friends, &c., &c.

Women

The Heroine—Elizabeth Linley (Beauty in Distress)
Accomplices—Alicia Sheridan
     Elizabeth Sheridan
     The Linleys, &c., &c.

The Characters of the Persons

ALICIA (LISSY) SHERIDAN. A girl of nineteen, two years younger than Dick, romantic and ardent. She worships her younger brother. Next to him in her affection rank the two Elizabeths—Elizabeth, her sister and junior by five years, and Elizabeth Linley, whom she adores.

ELIZABETH (BETSY) SHERIDAN. Equally fond of the linnet's sister, Mary or Polly Linley (afterwards Mrs. Tickell). Of all the family she is the tenderest towards her father. In the stricken years of his age she sacrifices the flower of her youth to his tyrannical megrims with an unselfishness that verges on heroism.

CHARLES SHERIDAN. A pattern of prudence and precision—suave, grave, amiable, and good-looking, but always a superior person. He is "Surfaceish." He is not all this in his early days; his future prosperity develops his worst side. He marries a beautiful heiress, through his brother enjoys a lucrative office, yet when most affluent he is least generous. He stints his peevish old father who once writes to him: "You are the only treasure I have on earth and if that were gone, I know nothing in this world worth living for." He stints his sister before her marriage; he stints his poor old Aunt Chamberlaine in her widowhood. He stints his uncle and haggles with his brother. As he waxes fat he coddles his health almost as much as his purse. His father, who falls out with all his children eventually, quarrels with Charles, and this breach with his best beloved rankles deep when that with Richard has been healed. So much for the Sheridans.

THOMAS LINLEY. Tall, handsome, commanding. Father of twelve children. Affectionate though he is, and sensitive, experience has hardened him till he regards his talented children as so many pet lambs with golden fleece. His wife Maria is at once the treasure and plague of his life. Though she has now been married for twenty years, she is still comely, but her chattering tongue and pinching fingers never rest. In her eagerness to save for a rainy day she spares even the candle ends. She loves two penny whist, feeling herself bereaved indeed when she loses. Though she rules her husband with a brazen voice, she loves and respects him. Respectful she is to excess—indeed incurably vulgar in her deference to rank and wealth. Money is the main object of her match-makings. . . . But for all their weaknesses the Linley couple preserve something idyllic. Long afterwards the daughters describe their parents as Baucis and Philemon.

The villain of the piece still remains to be characterized.

The Bath papers of early October, 1770, announce the arrival of a Mr. and Mrs. Mathews, fresh from their honeymoon. At Bath they stay over two winter seasons. There they entertain and are entertained, for they are popular with many. Wilkes is among their guests in 1773, and at a Dr. Delacour's they are the standing dish. Mathews, of a good family, has held a commission in the militia. Although he never seems to call himself "Captain," other people do so to the end of his life. He is a lady killer; indeed he can select from his list of conquests a fair specimen of every degree of rank from the duchess to the spouse of the squire. (Ladies are ever apt to set their hearts on scarlet, and the lively linnet has long set her heart on Mathews.)

With the early months of 1772 our drama begins.

ACT I. ELOPEMENT

THE CURTAIN RISES on the following situation: Old Sheridan absent in Dublin where he has gone to produce his play *Captain O'Blunder,* the young Sheridans and Linleys in close alliance, and Mathews importuning the girl he has mesmerized from childhood. When Elizabeth Linley sings and smiles, she trembles with fears which she can scarcely reveal to her parents who would laugh at them as the dreams of a Romantic Miss. Halhed is in Calcutta, Charles Sheridan has withdrawn to a farmhouse near Bath, and Dick's growing passion is as yet held in secret. Not a syllable of love passes his lips, though Miss Linley soon guesses the state of his affections. Friendship now is their watchword and of friendship she stands sorely in need. Her open association with Mathews has attracted notice. He has long so wound himself about her heart that she feels powerless to repulse him. Nor are her eyes yet opened. She still fancies him the victim of a passion as delicate as it is fruitless. He seems adoring and she pities him. His hints of despair and suicide alarm her. With sighs he resigns her, promises to see her no more and then shortly afterwards forces an interview—draws out a pistol, utters horrible imprecations, and swears that if she does not see him again, he will shoot himself before her face. This dastardly menace is followed by threats to injure her character if she persists in her refusal. At length Miss Linley begins to be undeceived.

She unburdens her heart to the Sheridan sisters and through them to the brother. Alicia never doubts that her brother is designed by nature to act the part of a knight errant. And Miss Linley too hails him as such.

Worn out with the strain of the last two years, she longs for repose and seclusion. Publicity has brought her insult, and this maid of seventeen, who has lived through a short lifetime, resolves to retire. Devoted to her father, she wishes to indemnify him for the loss of her voice, and so she surrenders her share of the fund which was old Long's compensation. The father remonstrates and tenderly entreats her to see the hypocrite Mathews no more. She promises, and Sheridan is employed as a go-between. The result is an unexpected letter from her tormentor, honoring her wishes and praying for her happiness. Melted by Mathews' behavior she half regrets her deceiver when suddenly he reappears on the scene, brandishing a pistol before her and insisting on a renewal of their friendship. He scares her into compliance. The unhappy girl, thus sore beset, now thinks of suicide.

It is Sunday and the family is at church. Wrought into a frenzy, she draws up a will, sits down with a bottle of laudanum on the table, and drinks part of its contents.

Suddenly Sheridan enters, sees the phial, dissuades her from pursuing so fell a purpose and beseeches her to wait till he returns with tidings that will set her mind at rest. He promises to stop Mathews' pursuit, and he at once fetches Dr. Harrington, who arrives only to find the girl stupefied. Then he hurries off and returns with a letter to him from Mathews which proves the utter unworthiness of the man for whom she is thus ready to sacrifice her life. The letter runs that she has given him so much trouble that he has the greatest inclination to give her up, but his vanity will not let him do that without gaining his point. He therefore is resolved the next time he meets her to throw off the mask. He will then sufficiently revenge himself for all the trouble she has given him, but if she changes her mind and will not see him, he is resolved to carry her off by force. The moment she reads the letter she faints.

She has long been weary. She is now panic stricken. To stay at Bath seems impossible. To Sheridan she is well inclined, but her passionate love for him comes afterwards. With Sheridan's sister they are now in conference.

The upshot is a scheme worthy of the trio's years, which

united do not amount to more than fifty-seven. The notion of seeking the temporary shelter of a convent originates with Miss Linley herself. Alicia then suggests that some friends at St. Quentin will offer asylum till the French convent is found. Her brother can act as her preux chevalier, returning when once she has been safely bestowed. And thus she will at once bring her parents to reason and escape the terrors of her situation. To disarm slander, Sheridan arranges an escort in the shape of a waiting woman.

Nightfall of March 18. All are in anxious expectation. The Linleys, father, brother, and sister, are performing at the Bath rehearsals and the home is empty. Elizabeth has excused her absence on the plea of illness. She stands waiting with Alicia who has helped her pack her clothes. At last Sheridan comes, and half fainting she is carried in a chair to the post chaise. Before Sheridan can follow, he meets Mathews who is going to his house. He frames some excuse and begs Mathews to go to his sister's and wait there till he sends for him, as he has an affair of honor on his hands and perhaps shall want his assistance. By this means he gets rid of him—and dashes to Miss Linley. The coach starts and in a cloud of dust they whirl along the lovely and winding road, past the Castle Inn, through Savernake forest, on, on to Newbury, and thence over the fearsome heath of Hounslow. Day breaks before they reach Maidenhead thicket, and by nine of that spring morning they drive through London.

Sheridan at once introduces Miss Linley as a rich heiress to his kinsman, Richard Chamberlaine, then in London, and attempts to borrow money from him on the strength of his supposed expectations. But Chamberlaine does not favor his scheme, and at nightfall they betake themselves to a fresh acquaintance, Simon Ewart, son of a respectable brandy merchant in the city. He suggests the idea of their sailing from the port of London to Dunkirk, to which place his father has a vessel ready to sail immediately. This plan, as making pursuit more difficult, is immediately adopted, and the "old" gentleman accompanies the young couple on

board ship and recommends them to the care of the captain as if they were his own children. The captain, however, proves to be a surly, ill-behaved fellow and uses Dick and Miss Linley shamefully. They are detained by a contrary wind, and there is not a morsel to eat or drink on board. Finally they sail. The passage proves stormy, but they arrive safely at Dunkirk and proceed to Lille. En route they stop at Calais, and this is the occasion for a scene—two French officers eyeing Miss Linley in a theatre, Sheridan glaring at them with arms akimbo, and neither of them varying their dumb show by a word of English or French.

In the neighborhood of Calais they go through some form of marriage. The contracting parties are both minors, and neither of them imagines that the ceremony is legally binding. But Sheridan hopes to attach the linnet more firmly to himself and also to protect her more effectively from Mathews. His course is human—

> Gentle Maid, ah! why suspect me?
> Let me serve thee—then reject me;
> Canst thou trust and I deceive thee?
> Art thou sad—and shall I grieve thee?
> Gentle Maid, ah! why suspect me?
> Let me serve thee—then *reject* me?

As for the linnet, the suffering as well as the romance appeal to her. (Perhaps the woman hired to accompany Miss Linley stays in London. Every place they put up at, Sheridan requests the landlady's company, and takes care to have Miss Linley constantly provided with a bedfellow.)

On April 15 Sheridan breaks his silence by writing to his brother. "Everything on our side has at last succeeded. . . . You will soon see me in England." He meets an old schoolfellow who recommends Miss Linley to a convent and there she remains. But so much has the agitation of the past month told on her that a Dr. Dolman, an English physician of York, is called in to prescribe. He wishes to have her more immediately under his care, and so his wife invites her to their house. Miss Linley leaves the convent while Sheridan remains at a hotel on the Grand Place.

At home Bath is all excitement. Sheridan has left a letter, addressed to the heroine's father, which shows up his antagonist's conduct in a glaring light. The news spreads like wildfire. Newspapers turn into two hostile camps. Reflections on Miss Linley vie with reflections on Sheridan. In both cases they compromise the lady. Mathews calls the morning after they have vanished and never ceases calling. He swears horribly and curses his past in a pitiable manner. Two of his messages are conveyed to Linley who listens to neither, saying that he has been deceived once and will not trust him more—and that if they meet he will not answer for the consequences. A friend counsels Mathews to quit Bath forever. This he solemnly promises to do, but his promises are not to be trusted.

He does no such thing. On the contrary he spreads conflicting reports. And in addition declares that Sheridan and Miss Linley will never show their faces again in England, that her protector does not deserve the treatment of a gentleman. Moreover he swears to have Sheridan's life. Nor is this bombast. In his fury at being bested, he goes further. Failing to receive his enemy's letter from the continent, he publicly posts "Mr. Richard S*******" in the *Bath Chronicle* of April 9, 1772, as "a L*** and a Treacherous S***********. And as I am convinced that there have been many incendiaries concerned in the propagation of this infamous Lie, if any of them, unprotected by *age, infirmities,* or profession, will dare to acknowledge the part they have acted, and affirm to what they have said of me, they may depend on receiving the proper reward of their villainy, in the most public manner—Thomas Mathews." (It will be noticed that in his anger Mathews appends the wrong number of asterisks to two of his capitals.)

But before Sheridan's return Mathews beats a retreat to London. He ascertains Sheridan's address and writes abusive letters to him. Sheridan replies in a spirited manner—he shall thank the villain as he deserves. In his absence Alicia constitutes herself his champion. She sees Mathews after the libel, calls him to severe account. Thereupon he has the insolence to assert that her brother Charles is privy to the affair. Charles is greatly shocked. True he is displeased with his brother, but is incapable of countenancing such base conduct. Nothing but Mathews quitting Bath at the time prevents his taking up the matter in a very serious manner.

Mathews' advertisement diverts public opinion from his own treatment of Miss Linley to Sheridan's. Is Sheridan her deliverer or debaser—gentleman or sneak? Sheridan has accused Mathews, and Mathews now vilifies Sheridan. All Bath is in turmoil. The Pump Rooms agitate the questions. Newspapers fly to Sheridan's defense or flay him mercilessly. Miss Linley is forgotten. The sorrows of Helen are merged in the siege of Troy.

On April 24 Linley arrives at Lille. After a private talk with Sheridan he is quite reconciled to his daughter. But he insists on her returning to England with him to fulfill several engagements. The whole party sets out the next day. Together they travel and together they all reach London. At nine o'clock on the night of Wednesday, April 29, they drive to the same hotel, and there for the nonce, wearied and overwrought, we leave them.

CHAPTER 5

ACT II. DUELS

Scene 1. MATHEWS' DOORSTEP. Conklin's in the Crutched Friars, London. Midnight. A young man battering loudly at the door and in a passion demanding admittance. Naturally he is told to go away, but he persists. Mathews comes down, tells him he shall be admitted, and retires to rest again. The invader of his peace continues the siege. Then the young man is told that the key of Mr. Conklin's door is lost. Still he persists, and there he stands for more than an hour battering and shouting till the sober neighborhood curses his presence. By two o'clock he gets in, but when he enters he finds a being different indeed from the anticipated fire-eater. Mathews dresses, calls Sheridan "his dear friend," one with whom he should be particularly unhappy to have any difference. He complains of the cold, endeavors to get heat into him, and forces Sheridan to sit down. No sooner does Mathews espy two peeping pistols than he is not a little alarmed. He behaves in a dastardly manner. Finding that the *Bath Chronicle* has not been scrutinized, he assures his visitor that the whole affair has been quite misrepresented, that the advertisement was an expedient which the Sheridans sanctioned, that he has never meant to quarrel, and that the real offenders are his brother Charles and another gentleman, Brereton. Nothing can be more peaceable, and Sheridan is calmed. Mathews' behavior is so condescending that Dick lets him off with a very small concession to be made in the Bath papers. Mathews then promises to publish a *full* explanation; its wording is discussed and several drafts are proposed. In any case Bath is to be enlightened and the slanderer to recant.

[79]

Sheridan protests himself more than satisfied, and long past dawn, when the milkmaid goes her rounds, he departs, trusting in Mathews' word. He has come like a lion, gone like a lamb, and he now returns under the morning sun to an excellent breakfast.

On Saturday, May 2, he accompanies the Linleys to Bath. His first visit is to the office of the *Bath Chronicle* where Cruttwell, its proprietor, shows him the text of the incriminating libel. Nor does Cruttwell fail to disillusion Sheridan as to Mathews' sincerity in the promised explanations. The kind of apology that Mathews has proffered proves to be no concession at all. He has turned an apology into the mere consequences of an explanation. Sheridan's blood boils. He rushes off to his brother Charles who expresses horror at being involved as an accomplice. Charles agrees that quibbling can no longer avail; it is impossible to put up with these public and private insults. Others are consulted, and all indorse this opinion. Everything is at stake. Unless Dick properly resents such treatment, he can never show his face again in Bath. Charles does not hesitate. Though he has just been appointed Secretary to the Legation in Sweden and is making the necessary preparations, he, the head and hope of the family, will attend Dick in his mission.

Thus allied the pair hasten to their expectant sisters, disclose nothing of what has transpired, and chat cheerfully. Yet on that very night the brothers jump into a post chaise and rattle over the long levels of the Bath road to London. The dewy chill of a May night does nothing towards cooling their hot blood.

Great is the consternation next morning on finding them flown. It is rumored that high words were heard overnight and that a duel is in train. Alicia at once makes her way to Crescent to learn what Miss Linley knows. Miss Linley swoons more than once; Alicia and her sister faint. They wait for news.

It is now Sunday. Once more in London the brothers lose

no time. Brereton's town lodgings are visited, and they next drive to Ewart's Thames Street abode, when the young son consents to act as second. That evening Charles carries his brother's challenge from Brereton's to Mathews. The budding diplomatist tries hard to prevent an encounter. For two hours he argues with Mathews, but in vain. No further concessions are forthcoming, and as Sheridan's object is an unqualified retraction, there is nothing left but the duel. It is appointed to take place at six o'clock on Monday evening in Hyde Park. Mathews decides that the weapons shall be swords though pistols are to be brought also. His uncle, Captain Knight, is to attend him.

Scene 2. Hyde Park, May 4, about six in the evening. Sheridan and Ewart meet Mathews and Knight at the rendezvous. A chaise and four stands in waiting at the Park gates by the turnpike. They immediately walk to the Ring. Sheridan again tries to make his adversary recant but to no purpose. Then he chooses his ground for the encounter. Mathews objects to it as uneven and appeals to his second. The four of them now cross the Ring and proceed to a plateau at the back of a building. Sheridan has taken his stand and drawn his sword when his second descries an observer. Accordingly the combatants withdraw to a seemingly convenient place. Mathews continues to raise objections. This time he in his turn complains of some onlookers. Thereupon he proposes that they retire to the Hercules Pillars at Hyde Park Corner till the coast is clear. After a space they return, and again Sheridan draws his sword. Mathews then demurs to an officer who seems to be watching them, but Ewart gives his word that nobody shall intercept those who may need the chaise. Mathews, however, remains obstinate and actually proposes to defer the duel till the following morning. Sheridan now remarks that this is trifling work. He will brook no delay and accosts the officer who politely retires. Meanwhile his opponent has gone back to the gates. Sheridan and Ewart then call to Knight and the three readjourn to the Hercules Pillars. Finally they engage a room at the Castle Tavern.

It is now dark. Ewart takes up the lights and the combatants set to work in grim earnest. (Mr. Smith present as surgeon.) This half-lit scene: the flash of crossing swords, the sudden rush, the altercations of the angry group, going on by the light of the flaring candles while the ordinary bustle of the tavern proceeds peacefully below.

Sheridan strikes Mathews' point so much out of line that he steps up and catches hold of his wrist or the hilt of his sword while he points his own at Mathews' breast. Knight runs in and catches hold of his arm, exclaiming, "Don't kill him!" Sheridan struggles to disengage his arm and says Mathews' sword is in his power. Mathews calls out twice or thrice, "I beg my life." The combatants are parted. Knight immediately remarks, "There, he has begged his life, and now there's an end of it." Ewart answers that when Mathews' sword was in Sheridan's power, as he attempted no more, Knight should not have interfered. Knight replies that he was wrong, but that he had done it hastily and to prevent mischief—or words to that effect. Mathews then hints that Sheridan was rather obliged for Knight's interposition. Knight now declares that before he intervened both the swords were in Sheridan's power. Mathews still seems resolved to give it another turn and observes that he never quitted his sword. Provoked at this, Sheridan then swears that Mathews shall either give up his sword and he will break it, or go to his guard again and renew the contest. Mathews refuses, but on Sheridan's persisting, he flings it on the table. Sheridan breaks it and throws the hilt to the other end of the room. Mathews exclaims at this. Sheridan takes a mourning sword from Ewart, and presenting Mathews with his, gives his honor that what has passed shall never be mentioned by him.

Mathews remarks, "I shall never draw a sword against the man who has given me my life," but he still exclaims against the indignity of breaking his sword. Ewart offers him the pistols, and an altercation passes between them.

Mathews—"I can never show my face if it be known that my sword was broken. Such a thing has never been done. It cancels all obligations—" etc., etc.

Finally it is agreed that the affair is not to be mentioned at all. This is settled. Sheridan then asks Mathews whether it does not occur to him that he owes him another satisfaction. As it is in his power to do it without discredit, he supposes Mathews will not hesitate. This Mathews refuses unless conditionally. Sheridan insists on it—he will not leave the room till it is settled. After much altercation and with much ill grace, Mathews gives an apology which afterwards appears in the *Bath Chronicle*. "Being convinced that the expressions I made use of to Mr. Sheridan's disadvantage were the effects of passion and misrepresentation, I retract what I have said to his disadvantage and particularly beg his pardon for my advertisement."

But Mathews later claims that he never begged his life, that Sheridan broke his sword without warning, and that the apology was a mere point of generosity yielded because Sheridan ceased to require it.

Worn out with their labor, the brothers present themselves at King's Mead Street on Tuesday afternoon. Sheridan shows the apology with pride to his sisters and at once despatches it to the printer.

All Bath rings with the battle. The newspapers make most of the sensation. Everything is falsified. The duel took place two days before it really happened. Sheridan has been run through the body. Mathews and Knight have fled to France. This is promptly contradicted in the *Bath Chronicle*. On all sides the victor is applauded. And when Mathews returns en route for Wales he is scouted and shunned.

In the midst of this hubbub the Roman Father returns. If he has misliked the elopement, he is disgusted at the duel. But Charles convinces him that Dick's action has been honorably quixotic and its London sequel a sheer necessity. Family honor has been satisfied. But two things permanently vex him. First: honor cannot be vindicated gratis and bills begin to pour in—not all these for chaises and ammunition. Second: the firebrand's affair with Miss Linley. And so the green room takes to picking a quarrel with the orchestra. Old Sheridan thinks his social standing more exalted than that of a musician. In his *Plan of Education,* published in 1769, he has remarked that music "often draws persons to mix with such company as they would otherwise avoid." He therefore attempts to erase the Linleys from his visiting list and forbids Dick to see Miss Elizabeth Linley. But the lovers meet and correspond often, if in secret.

Scene 3. A grotto across the meads by Purdie's gardens, shaded by a willow and approached by winding footpaths. Moss grown seats and names carved on the barks of trees. Sylvio(Dick) and Laura(Elizabeth) discovered. Laura in tears.

SYLVIO (*sings*):
> Dry be that tear, my gentlest love,
> Be hushed that struggling sigh,
> Nor seasons, days, nor fate shall prove
> More fixed, more true than I.
> Hushed be that sigh, be dry that tear,
> Cease boding doubt, cease anxious fear,
> Dry be that tear.
>
> Ask'st thou how long my love will stay,
> When all that's new is past?
> How long, ah, Laura, can I say
> How long my life will last?
> Dry be that tear, be hushed that sigh,
> At least I'll love thee till I die!
> Hushed be that sigh.
>
> And does that thought affect thee too,
> The thought of Sylvio's death,
> That he who only breathed for you,
> Must yield that faithful breath?

> Hushed be that sigh, dry be that tear,
> Nor let us lose our Heaven here—
> Dry be that tear."

LAURA (*sings*):
> Thinkst thou, Sylvio, I'd forego
> This tender luxury of woe,
> Which better than the tongue imparts
> The feelings of impassioned hearts;
> Blest if my sigh and tear but prove
> The winds and waves that waft to love.

SYLVIO: Hushed be that sigh, be dry that tear,
> Cease boding doubt, cease anxious fear,
> Dry be that tear.

LAURA: Can true affection cease to fear?
> Poor is the joy not worth a tear!
> Did passion ever know content?
> How weak the rapture words can paint!
> Then let my sighs and tears but prove
> The winds and waves that waft to love.

SYLVIO: Dry be that tear, be hushed that sigh,
> At least I'll love thee till I die!
> Hushed be that sigh.

LAURA: The Cyprian bird with plaintive moan
> Thus makes her faithful passion known;
> So Zephyrus breathes on Flora's bowers,
> And charms with sigh the queen of flowers!
> Then let my sighs and tears but prove
> The winds and waves that waft to love.

SYLVIO: Hushed be that sigh, be dry that tear,
> Nor let us lose our Heaven here—
> Dry be that tear.

UNCORKING OLD SHERRY:

Scene 4. Laura's Bower. Midnight. Laura discovered at her desk writing—and repeating aloud. "Though I parted from you so lately and though I expect to see you again so soon, yet I cannot keep my fingers from the pen but I must be plaguing you with my scrawl. Oh, my dearest love. I am never happy but when I am with you. I cannot speak or think of anything else. When shall we have another happy half hour? I declare I have not felt real joy since I came from France before this evening. Perhaps now while I am writing and amusing myself by expressing the tender sentiments which I feel for you, you are flirting with Miss W. or some other handsome girl. I do not believe any such thing, but give me leave to doubt that I may with greater pleasure be convinced to the contrary. No, my life and Soul, I love you to such a degree that I should never bear to see you (even in joak) show any particular attention to another. Judge then by my writing if I doubt your constancy. When shall I hear from you? Let me have that satisfaction at least, although it is impossible to see you so often. . . .

"I really think Charles suspected something this evening. He looked amazingly knowing when I came down. Duce take his curious head. I wish he would mind his own business and not interrupt us in our stolen pleasures. Is it not amazing, my dear Love, that we should always have so great an inclination for what is not in our possession. . . .

"Let me see, what have I more to say?—Nothing but the same dull story over and over again—that I love you to distraction and that I would prefer you and beggary before any other man and a throne.

"I will call you Horatio—that was the name you gave yourself in that sweet poem. Write to me, then, my dear Horatio, and tell me that you are equally sincere and constant.

"My hand shakes so at this moment I can scarce hold the pen. My father came into my room this moment and I had just time to stuff the letter behind the glass. 'Twas well he did not take much notice of me, for I was. . . . Goodbye. God bless—I. . . ."

(With many titles to esteem and praise Miss Linley is as lacking as many of her female contemporaries in the minor virtue of dating her letters or of spelling correctly.)

In another tone. "You unconscionable creature to make me sit up this time of the night to scribble nonsense to you, when you will not let me hear one word from you for this week to come. Oh, my dear, you are the Tyrant indeed. Yet do not fancy I would do this if it was not equally agreeable to myself. Indeed, my dearest love, I am never happy except when I am with you or writing to you. Why did you run away so soon tonight? Tho' I could not enjoy your conversation freely, yet it was a consolation to me that you was so near me. I gave up my cards the moment you left me, as I could not play with any patience. . . .

"My mother and me called on Miss Roscoe this evening, when we talked a great deal about you. Miss R said she was sure you and I should make a match of it. Nay, she said the whole world was of the opinion that we should be married in less than a month. Only think of this, bright Hev'ns! God bless you, my dear, dear love. I am so weary I must go to bed. There is but one thing that could keep me awake and that is your company. . . . once more adieu. . . .

"Upon my knees, half nacked once more I am going to tire you with my nonsense. I could not bear to see this little blank without filling it up. Though I do not know with what, as I have almost exhausted the Budget of news which I have collected since our long absence. I do insist that you write to me, you lazy wretch, can't you take so small a trouble? I can receive your letter by the same method. My sister is very impatient that I don't come into bed, but I feel more happiness in this situation, tho' I am half froze, than in the warmest bed in England. . . ."

Meanwhile the villain of the drama is not idle. He sends the younger man insulting messages, and on a sudden, appears in Bath. He comes attended by a Welsh neighbor William Barnett, who urges him to wipe out the disgrace by a fresh duel. Barnett bears the preliminary challenge to Sheridan and produces for his signature a paper which contains Mathews' version of their previous meeting. So far from signing it, Sheridan indignantly rebuts it in a letter to Captain Knight, and this rejection compels the duel. It is finally arranged for the morning of Wednesday, July 1, 1772.

The coast is clear. Old Sheridan is in London equipping Charles for his Swedish journey. Miss Linley is away, performing at Chester, Cambridge, and Oxford. She renews her lover's complaints—"I have not been out since I came here. I shall be very happy when I am once more in Bath. I cannot tell how much I long to see you to ask you a thousand questions. Oh, my dear Horatio, I have had many perplexing thoughts since I have been absent, but I will return, I shall be content. It is much if I am not with you as soon as this letter. Till then receive my tenderest affections and let me find you constant as I left you. If my prayers are granted, I shall once more embrace my Horatio and convince him how sincerely I am his Eliza."

(In keeping with the spirit of the comedy, this very letter is in Sheridan's pocket on that summer dawn when he sallies forth to meet his enemy. He also wears her miniature.)

Scene 5. White Hart Inn and Kingsdown Hill. July 1, three o'clock in the morning. Sheridan accompanied by Captain Paumier, a young and inexperienced officer, meets Mathews and Barnett at the White Hart Inn whence they drive in post chaises to lonely Kingsdown Hill. Mathews desires the arms to be pistols whereas Sheridan insists on swords. The reason that Mathews gives for his preference is that he fears a repetition of the ungentlemanly scuffle of the former encounter. To this Sheridan angrily retorts. In the end swords are chosen.

Mathews draws first. After three passes with alternate advances and returns they close. Sheridan repeats his previous manoeuvre, charges Mathews, and endeavors to lay hold of his sword. Mathews receives him on its point and in the melée his sword snaps. Mathews then clutches Sheridan's sword arm, trips up his heels, and they both fall. At first Sheridan has the advantage and bends his sword by thrusting at Mathews, but as they roll on the sloping ground, the older and stronger finds himself on top. He hits at Sheridan's face with the hilt and hacks at his neck with the six or seven inches of his broken blade, which eventually sticks in the earth. He then holds the point over Sheridan and orders him to beg his life. The youth indignantly refuses. He manages to disengage his bent sword from Mathews' grasp, lunges at, and slightly wounds his belly. Now comes the crisis. Sheridan's sword breaks in its turn, snapping within four inches of its hilt. It breaks against some hidden armor which Mathews wears. Sheridan raises his right hand both in token of his plight and as a means of defence. It is dreadfully cut. Paumier tries to interpose, but Barnett refuses his assent. Then Mathews suddenly draws his own jagged weapon from the earth and begins to stab him ferociously no less than twenty or thirty times. (His oaths and curses are horrible to hear.) Not more than five of the thrusts take effect. These are chiefly flesh wounds in the neck, for Sheridan manages to ward off the rest with his hand, so that they only penetrate his coat. One thrust shatters the frame of Miss Linley's picture which is found in a pool of blood; another injures his stomach. The affray is unequal, and at length the seconds realize that something must be done.

Captain Paumier calls out, "My dear Sheridan, beg your life, and I will be yours forever." Barnett also desires him to ask his life. Sheridan replies, "No, by God, I won't." Barnett decides not to wait for these punctilios and asks Paumier to assist him in taking them up. Mathews and Sheridan surrender their swords and both get up. Mathews makes the best of his way to London and thence to France.

"I have done for him," is his last word, enhanced by an oath. Sheridan is conveyed in a parlous state to the White Hart Inn. Captain Paumier absconds. Both seconds are censured for their strange behavior and are cut forever afterwards.

(Prompter's version: Aside. Sigmond, who edits Sheridan's plays, tells a different story. According to him, Sheridan is in "a high state of excitement from potations deep." The night before the duel he is invited to sup with Mathews and the seconds. He remains at the table drinking claret until the time of appointment. When he leaves it, he walks up Milsom Street, reels into Mathews' chaise, insists upon the seconds following him, and drives off.

(Again: Lord John Townshend goes to Bath for the purpose of getting acquainted with Mathews and making inquiries about his affair with Sheridan. Mathews describes the duel as "a mere hoax—in fact it was no duel at all," and says that Sheridan came drunk and that he could have killed him with the greatest of ease if he had chosen.

(Even Sheridan himself confesses that the account he has given is "highly exaggerated and malicious." Mathews' second, Barnett, draws up a report which he sends to Captain Paumier who agrees that it is "true and impartial," differing from his own opinion in "a few immaterial circumstances only." After a few recriminations Sheridan accepts the account given by the seconds.)

Mathews is regarded as a would-be assassin. "Were he to appear in the streets of Bath," writes old Sheridan, "he would be stoned to death. If ever he should show his head here again, he will be shunned as one infected by the plague." Yet time is a great healer, and at Bath Mathews dies, whistplaying and popular, fifty years afterwards. His wife, that strange and silent figure in the background, survives her husband by a couple of years and inherits from him "everything of every kind without the exception of the most trifling article."

None are really pleased but the journalists. They make most of the sensation to the amusement of young Dick scanning the daily papers in bed: "I wish to know whether I am alive or dead."

The *Public Advertiser* says: "Mr. Sheridan junr., who fought a duel with Captain Mathews about the Maid of Bath, is entirely recovered of his wounds, but has lost the use of his right arm from receiving a shot between the bones of the joint."

Indeed the gossips of Bath have good cause to swear with Bob Acres, "Odds hilts and blades, odds flints, pans and triggers."

When the news reaches Miss Linley, she is dreadfully affected. "My husband, my husband!" she blurts out, which startles all who are present, but is set down to her excitement and distress, and presently forgotten. She pens tender billets to him. "Believe me, I have not been in my senses for two days, but the happy account of your recovery has perfectly restored them. Oh! my dearest love, when shall I see you? I will not ask you to write, as I am sure it must hurt you. . . . Oh! my Horatio, I did not know till now how much I loved you. Believe me, had you died, I should certainly have dressed myself as a man and challenged Mathews. He should have killed me, or I would have revenged you and myself. . . . God in heaven bless you, my dearest Horatio, and restore you once more to health, to happiness, and the arms of your Eliza."

But the spell is broken. The fathers decide to end the match, Mr. Linley to secure himself the advantage of his daughter's talents, Mr. Sheridan from a high spirit of honor. He is averse to his son's forming a connection with a person whose name has been so much the subject of public discussion. The truth is: Old Sheridan is outraged that his son should marry the daughter of a fiddler, Linley furious at the thought that his daughter should be allied to the son of an actor.

The lovers' position is plain. They are to meet as mere acquaintances. Linley shortly afterwards exacts a promise from his daughter never to marry Sheridan while Sheridan senior binds his son not even to correspond with her. Then follows a fresh engagement for the actor at Dublin Theatre, and all his family must be dragged forsooth with him. Eliza harbors horrid thoughts of her Dick's going to Dublin. (It is midnight when she takes up her hasty pen.) "How beautiful at this moment does that bright moon appear! . . . I feel I love you every day more tenderly. I cannot support the idea of a separation. . . . Oh, my loved Horatio, what will then become of your Eliza?"

Then suddenly old Sheridan changes his mind again. He is sick to death of those Linleys. His daughters shall find asylum with his old friends at St. Quentin; the incorrigible Dick shall attend them across the channel. The actor's plans shift with his temper and he changes once more. The incorrigible Dick shall not go. He is unworthy of such a change. He is unworthy to prove a guardian to his young and virtuous sisters. Then Dick's meetings, letters, and poems are discovered. Dick is proscribed and excommunicated. He shall go to the Bar; he shall repent in sackcloth and ashes. He shall swear to write to her no more, scarcely to speak of her, much less to speak to her. Exile shall be his portion. The decree is peremptory. He is banished to a farm near Waltham Abbey in distant Essex under the charge of their respected friends the Parkers—far from his Goddess, far from his sisters. "Let him study and reflect; let him be punished, sir." And the angry parent sets off to toil alone for them all in Ireland.

CHAPTER 6

ACT III. RETREAT

"I HAVE PASSED TWO DAYS in excessive melancholy," Sheridan writes to his friend, Thomas Grenville, from Farm Hill, Waltham Abbey, "and I am perfectly convinced that that unfortunate being called a lover, if a true one, could better bear a separation from her he loves in a desert than a paradise. Place me in the first, and I am surrounded with one plain, absolute, and evident wretchedness. There is no image round me to remind me of her, none which I can join with her idea; nay, by heaven, I should feel supremely happy that she was not there to partake of my hardships. But in the other, when I see a pair, blest in peace, let me say, 'Why am I shut out from this forever?' and 'tis torture! Let me sit in a beautiful scene, and exclaim, 'What would her presence make this?' and 'tis worse than a wilderness. Let me hear music and singing, 'I cannot hear her sing and play,' and the notes become the shrieks of the damned. In short I cannot find a place either so perfect or so abominable as not to admit the idea of this torturing comparative improvement. . . . I am sick and without society. My love is almost the only feeling I have alive. *Amo, ergo sum,* is the confirmation of my existence: I love, therefore I am," and so "there is nothing for it but to sit down and write Hymns to Patience." But he keeps his resolution not to reply to Miss Linley's letters.

He reads widely and thinks. He becomes absorbed in astronomy, mathematics, mensuration, and navigation. He purposes to learn Italian. His Waltham tutor is a Mr. Adams, a self-taught and poverty stricken man blest with great merit and a wife and family. With him he works like the devil in Milton, "oar and sail." And he writes dutiful letters to his father—with his tongue in his cheek.

But his penitentiary is not quite so black as he paints it. "I wish you could on any pretense come and spend a fortnight in Essex," he writes to Grenville. (Betsy speaks of Grenville as an "angel." There is no cant or condescension about him.) "You shall hunt and shoot and study in the prettiest rotation imaginable. At night you shall go on stargazing parties, and with the ladies too, and conclude the day with wine and pipes, if you choose them."

Sheridan is a Pierrot. He does not yearn for a union with Miss Linley without some previous interludes. A Mrs. Mary Lyster, the flighty wife of a neighboring surgeon, sets her cap at him, while the uncertain Miss C——y complicates the tangle. Moonlight meetings ensue. Mrs. Lyster repents and Miss C——y, violently in love, returns to Bath bristling with jealousy and scandal.

Eliza herself is no longer the entirely trusting and patient adorer of Horatio. Tales reach her of his making love to these ladies. Though she is gentle, she is never tame, and the spirit of the Linleys now flames out—"I have been so deceived by you and by everyone that it has almost deprived me of my reason, but I have paid too, too dear for my experience ever to put it in your power or anyone's to impose on me again. I did not expect you would attempt to vindicate your conduct. You cannot to me. Think! oh! reflect one moment on what I have suffered and then judge if I can again consent to risk my life and happiness. For God's sake, S——n, do not endeavor to plunge me again into misery. Consider the situation I am in. Consider how much your persisting to refuse my letters will distress me. Reason, honour, everything forbids it. This is not a sudden resolution, but the consequence of cool, deliberate reflection. You are sensible it is not from caprice, but when I tell you I have lately had some conversation with Mrs. L.—— and Miss C——y, you will not suppose I will be again deceived. Farewell! If you value my peace of mind, return my letters."

Indignant Eliza well nigh resolves on a marriage of convenience. Rumors of an intended proposal reach Sheridan, and his former passion revives. The happy man is alleged to be Sir Thomas Clarges, a friend of Grenville's. Grenville reassures Sheridan: Clarges has never proposed. (As a matter of fact, he has already been rejected.) Sheridan is beside himself. In his jealousy he even sounds Grenville as to his own feelings—a suspicion which he afterwards explains away. He tracks his Eliza's every movement. She is off to Winchester, to Gloucester; she is back at Bath. Heavens! she is actually in London, within a ride of Farm Hill, and under an engagement to sing at the oratorios of the season. "Eliza," he tells his friend Grenville at the close of February, "is within an hour's ride of me, and must have been for some time, yet, upon my honor, I have and do industriously avoid knowing the particular place that is blest with her inhabiting. I was obliged to go to London the other day, and I protest to you, no country girl passing alone through a churchyard at midnight ever dreaded more the appearance of a ghost than I did to encounter this (for once I'll say) *terrestrial* being."

Miss Linley still presses for her letters. Sheridan refuses to surrender them till she gives her word that she prefers another. Even while she upbraids him, she cannot forsake him. She is indeed miserable, watched and worried. "You are sensible," she writes in supposed farewell, "you are sensible when I left Bath I had not an idea of you but as a friend. It was not your person that gained my affection. No, S——n, it was that delicacy, that tender compassion, that interest which you seemed to take in my welfare, that were the motives which induced me to love you." She passes to the letters, his resolve never to surrender them. "Do not distress me so much as to continue in that resolution. Believe me, I am incapable of loving any man. They [the letters] cannot be of any use to you. Do not think I shall alter my resolution or that I am to be terrified by your threats. I will not think so basely of your principles as to suppose you meant anything by them. There are unsurmountable obstacles to prevent our ever being united, even supposing I could be induced again to believe you! . . . My father has this minute left me. He knows I am writing to you, and it was with the greatest difficulty I pacified him. He was going immediately to your lodgings. He has given strict orders to Hannah to bring every letter to him. You will make me eternally miserable if you persist after what I have told you. Be assured I will not open any letter of yours, nor will I write again. If you wish me to think my happiness is dear to you, return my letters. If not, I cannot compel you, but I hope your generosity will not permit you to make an improper use of them. For God's sake, write no more. I tremble at the consequences."

But Sheridan writes again and again and she warmly responds.

> Oh, had my love ne'er smiled on me,
>   I ne'er had known such anguish;
> But think how false, how cruel she,
>   To bid me cease to languish;
> To bid me hope her hand to gain,
>   Breathe on a flame half perish'd
> And then, with cold and fix'd disdain,
>   To kill the hope she cherish'd.
>
> But days like these with doubting curst
>   I will not long endure;
> Am I despised?—I know the worst,
>   And also know my cure.

ELIZABETH ANN LINLEY
AND HER BROTHER TOM
by Gainsborough

THE SECOND MRS. R. B. SHERIDAN
(HESTER JANE OGLE)
WITH THEIR SON, CHARLES BRINSLEY
by Hoppner

CHAPTER 7

ACT IV. MARRIAGE

(In the last act the interest flags)

Miss Linley is reaching the summit of her professional successes. The town rings of no other name for a month. She alone engrosses all eyes, ears, hearts. Still she earns large sums nightly, and only four days before her marriage sings privately at Buckingham House before the King and Queen who are "particularly affable." The King presents the father with a banknote of £100 while he profusely compliments the daughter and ogles her "as much as he dares to do in so holy a place as an oratorio and at so devout a service as Alexander's Feast." She and her sister sing in the chapel of the Foundling Hospital, and the announcement of the performance requests that gentlemen should come without swords and ladies without hoops.

The breach in Miss Linley's affections has been healed. Ewart has acted as mediator. And Sheridan, in disguise, acts as hackney coachman to drive her home from concert and theatre.

Linley makes a sudden about face. Finding it hopeless to sever his daughter's connection, he consents to her wedding. But first Sheridan renews his promise never to touch the £1200 which Linley has been allowed by his daughter to retain from the settlement made on her by Long. Such an undertaking pleases the man who wants a wealthy suitor and has early protested that he would rather see his daughter dead than married to one so extravagant as Sheridan.

But Sheridan makes no doubt that he will carve a career, and on April 6, 1773, he is duly entered at the Middle

Temple. Just a week later, he is married by licence in Mary-lebone Church in the presence of Thomas Linley and John Swale, with whom, a month later, the bridegroom settles all expenses, observing that for a *friendly* bill, it is "pretty decent."

With nothing in particular to live upon, it is quite in order that the young husband who has no trade should waive off all offers of employment for his wife who has one. He decides never to turn those liquid tones into gold. George III offers him the post of Director of Oratorios. This he refuses. During his honeymoon, Arnold, the impressario, tempts him to let Elizabeth sing at the Pantheon, but this also he refuses. And shortly afterwards no less than £3200 for various appearances are declined.

"He resolves wisely and nobly," exclaims Dr. Johnson of the quixotic bridegroom. "He is a brave man. Would not a gentleman be disgraced by having his wife singing pub-licly for hire? No, sir, there can be no doubt here."

But she does sing at Oxford after her marriage on the occasion of the installation of Lord North as Chancellor of the University, at which time degrees are being con-ferred *honoris causa*. And Lord North tells Sheridan that he deserves one *uxoris causa*.

She sings also at the Worcester Festival, the profits of which go to charity. Mrs. Sheridan's fee is a banknote of £100 which she puts in the plate at the Cathedral.

After this superb gesture, she never sings again in public. Her husband is equally determined that she shall not be invited to private houses as an unpaid performer. Sir Joshua Reynolds asks them to dinner. Expecting that she will enter-tain his guests, he buys a new pianoforte and invites a large company. To his mortification, when he hints that a song by Mrs. Sheridan would be received as a great favor, her husband replies that *with his assent* she has resolved never to sing again in a public company. This polite rebuke angers Sir Joshua who enquires next day from James Northcote, "What reason could they think I had in inviting them to

dinner unless it was to hear her sing?—for she cannot talk."
But Sir Joshua is soon mollified and becomes one of their
greatest friends.

Sheridan's father receives the unwelcome tidings in Ireland. When the blow falls, nothing can exceed his fury. He
curses Dick with bell, book, and candle, and swears that he
has no other son than Charles. The estrangement is not
healed for three years and then for a time only. For the
nonce old Sheridan vents his rage upon his daughters who
are forbidden all access to the turtledoves.

The latter spend their honeymoon in a rose-covered
cottage at East Burnham. "I feel myself absolutely and
perfectly happy," writes Sheridan to Grenville. "As for the
little clouds which the peering eye of prudence would
descry to be gathering against the progress of the scene,
I have a consoling cherub that whispers me that, before
they can threaten an adverse shower, a slight gale or two
of fortune will disperse them. But when a man's married
'tis time he should leave off speaking in metaphor." . . .

The sole rift in his lute is his father's anger, which, Mrs.
Sheridan says, is the wrath of a *"damnatum obstinatum
mulio."*

Amid all his transports Sheridan devises Schemes, and
he goes now to Morden, now to London. During one of
these absences, he vents his feelings—

> Teach me, kind Hymen, teach—for thou
> Must be my only tutor now—
> Teach me some innocent employ
> That shall the hateful thought destroy
> That I this whole long night must pass
> An exile from my love's embrace. . . .
>
> .   .   .   .
>
>   What bard, O Time, discover,
>   With wings first made thee move?
>   Ah! sure he was some lover
>   Who ne'er had left his love!

UNCORKING OLD SHERRY:

For who that once did prove
    The pangs which absence brings,
        Tho' but one day
        He were away,
Could picture thee with wings?

Mrs. Sheridan is not slow in replying—

How dull and heavy are the hours!
    How slowly wastes the day!
Those once-loved scenes, those favorite bowers
    Appear no longer gay.

But now forlorn and sad I stray
    No longer these delight!
With joy I see the settling ray
    Yet dread th' approach of night.

Ah, Sylvio, dost thou now bestow
    A thought on Laura's pain?
Will thy fond heart in transport glow
    When here we meet again?

For then each anxious care shall cease,
    All jealous doubts remove;
And virtue shall detain sweet peace
    To dwell in Burnham Grove.

CURTAIN

CHAPTER 8

APOLLO'S NURSLINGS

THERE IS SOMETHING unusually attractive about the Linleys. They are all musicians, all graceful, all handsome, all artists. When Tom Linley is found playing his violin in the nursery and is asked whether the little man too is going to distinguish himself like the rest, he replies, "We are all geniuses here, sir."

Tom will become a great musician, Mozart predicts when he meets him in Florence. Both of the younger brothers are also unusually gifted. Ozias—so christened after the artist Ozias Humphry—studies metaphysics as well as music and remains all his life as odd and absent-minded as he is clever. After graduating at Oxford, he takes holy orders, holds a Norfolk living, and then becomes organist fellow of Dulwich College. William makes his fortune in the service of the East India Company, is educated at St. Paul's and Harrow, writes plays and poems from childhood and sings admirably, and retires in 1796 from active service to cultivate literature and the arts. As for the sisters, they are Apollo's nurslings indeed, and when Mary and Elizabeth blend their voices, the effect is ravishing.

The children begin work when they are little more than babes. For Ozias Humphry, the painter, who lodges with the Linleys, little Elizabeth at eight years old sings sweetly all the songs in *Thomas and Sally*, *The Chaplet*, and *Love in a Village*, seated at the foot of his easel and looking up at him with such heavenly features as prevail upon the motley visitors of Bath when she gracefully holds up her little basket with her father's benefit tickets at the door of the Pump Room. Thomas Linley père has married young, and he is not yet thirty-five when in 1767 he leads Elizabeth, something over twelve, and Thomas, something under eleven, upon the concert platform at Bath, the girl to sing, the boy to play the violin.

That Tom is the trickiest and most engaging of Pucks may easily be believed by anyone who studies Gainsborough's picture of him. His roguish yet wistful eyes look out beneath his thick curly hair. The dimple of a smile hovers at the corner of a sensitive yet determined mouth. Even when at twenty or so he has grown into the pale, trim, somewhat satisfied young gentleman of his later portrait, with the curls all brushed down into powdered smoothness, his cravat up to his chin and a smart cocked hat under the arm of his smart red coat, the look of Puck still lingers in his eyes and the hint of a smile still hangs about his lips, close pressed now and firm almost to hardness.

Of Maria, also a great favorite, "beauty, innocence, wit" are attributed to her, and the last looks more like real knowledge than conventional compliment. She is described as

> Sweet as opening buds,
> Mild as the hours of May,
> Bright as the sunbeams on the floods,
> And constant as the day.

In other words, Maria, like the rest of the family, is exceedingly attractive.

The father loves all of them not only because they are his own, but because they love music.

They have an invariable knack of attracting the interest of interesting people. They early possess themselves of Gainsborough's affections. How, indeed, can he fail to be enchanted by them?—he who adores beauty and music almost equally. He paints the father, he paints Tom and Sam; he paints Elizabeth and Tom together, Elizabeth and Mary together; Elizabeth alone, twice, if not three times; Mary alone, Mary's husband and Elizabeth's husband, and Elizabeth's son. He also on two occasions models and colors a head of Elizabeth in clay. (What would we not give for either of these models?) But alas! each in turn is broken by some zealous maid in the course of dusting. Finally when he and they alike move to London and all are prosperous together, he adopts a little boy of three years old for the avowed reason that he looks so like the Linleys.

But the fates play havoc with the Graces. The young Linleys begin to die. The Linleys who stand for poetry, music, and laughter, and who bring beauty into life. Tom drowns August 5, 1778, and Sam dies of a fever in December of the same year. Death creeps a fraction closer. George Frederick dies in childhood, Thurston and William Cary, also in childhood, Charlotte in early womanhood; Jane Nash dies at thirty-nine, Elizabeth before she is thirty-eight, Mary Tickell before she turns thirty, Thomas when he is twenty-two, and Samuel when he is twenty-one. William Linley, the youngest, lives longest. He and Ozias Thurston are the sole inmates of this nest of linnets who survive the summer of their days while some of them barely attain springtide.

Maria, the sweet singer, goes to play in an old black bonnet and her own common clothes, and a man's great coat over all. The poor pretty creature never has time to outgrow these little eccentricities. She is taken ill in Bath of brain fever and dies in a few days. In her delirium, shortly before her death, she sits up in her bed and says, "I know that my Redeemer liveth" with all the beauty of voice and expression that mark her singing when in full health.

After Maria's death it is melancholy for his pupils to sing to Mr. Linley, whose tears continually fall on the keys as he accompanies them. And if in course one of them is obliged to practice a song which he has been accustomed to hear his lost daughter sing, a similarity in manner or voice so affects him that he is frequently forced to quit his instrument and walk about the room to recover his composure.

The two sisters, Elizabeth Sheridan and Mary Tickell,

regard themselves as a club apart. An adoption into it is considered a privilege. Their little language is even tenderer than Swift's to Stella—"God thee bless," "Comfort 'ee up," "don't be angry wig us, madam," "tumfy" for comfortable, and "sickirts" for sick. And Mrs. Tickell has her own names and phrases for things and people: "to bepuppy" for to scold, and "Signior Wisky Wosky Something" to hit off a diplomatist. Their correspondence dates from the late summer to the opening of 1787, the year of Mrs. Tickell's death.

We view the whole environment of the Court "Tabbies" and country misses, their balls and card parties in which Mary Tickell is usually picked to the bone, their expectations, too, of being honored by the company of the great, Fox as a friend of Sheridan, George Selwyn, with his freshest bon mot, and the Norths, Townshends, Hobarts, and Fawkeners with whom they consort. There are the Court ladies—flaunting Miss Jeffries and boring Miss Boss ("the tender virgin" she styles her), who are pet aversions, for Mrs. Tickell is an excellent hater. Often and often they drive to town for the sights and theatres, for snug oyster suppers in Drury Lane box office, for much needed medical advice, for the comfort of the old parents, Baucis and Philemon, in Norfolk Street. They witness the wonders of Blanchard's balloon, the debut of Mrs. Jordan, who enchants the town with her boyish slimness and irresistible laughter, the triumph too of Mrs. Siddons, who seems Kemble in petticoats, and the fluctuations of the theatre, now in the skies, now in the depths. Impulsive Gainsborough, the family worshipper, steps in and out of the scene, cheering old Linley, regarding all his offspring as pictures, and retouching his portrait of the two girls, the light of whose faces irradiates the dark, mysterious grove around.

For Mrs. Sheridan there is nothing that her sister Mary will not suffer or do. Her circumstances may be narrow, but her heart is wide. When their father gives her money, she begs to surrender it. When Elizabeth journeys in the winter, she sends her the cosiest sabots to protect her feet from the cold. She implores her to abate the racket of late hours and to cease turning night into day. She fears for her health at every turn. She is always, as it were, feeling her pulse and taking her temperature. She cannot gaze at a lovely landscape near Norwich without wishing that Sheridan and his wife were near to share her pleasure.

She loves and quizzes each member of her family, she befriends and houses them all. Now it is poor Maria, rebelling against routine, dressing herself in a man's surtout and sleeping out at her friend Miss Troward's. Now it is Jane whom she counsels and consoles, with whom she reads, and for whom she schemes and matchmakes. Now it is the philosopher and star gazing Ozzy who fancies that he met the ghost of Charles I under the Hampton Court arches. As for the old parents, Baucis and Philemon, Phillis and Corydon, they are perpetually under her roof, he with music to last a fortnight and she poring over accounts and newspapers.

Mrs. Linley, indeed, is a trial, stinting even the mourning when Maria dies, furious over the mounting of the theatre, "cribbaging" everything that her careful hand can clutch, scolding and scandalizing, yet loyal withal and courageous. Even bereavement cannot abate her foibles or slake her thirst for cards. Down she swoops on Hampton Court in her blue poplin, "determined to play whist though I told her she won't have the least chance with the Tabbies."

Constant sorrows mellow the passionate and unbending father. His gloom deepens as one by one his children fade from him, but he finds solace in the loving care of Mrs. Tickell and Mrs. Sheridan. We see him sitting melancholy in his own room attired in his worsted nightcap and Persian robe, happy at length to have received a letter from Sheridan. Once the two sisters ramble together as far as Devonshire. When they reach Exeter at nightfall, they hear suddenly that their father is there. In a moment they resolve to surprise him. They are told that he will be returning from a friend's house through a lane under the moonlight. They stop their chaise, change their clothes and voices, and accost him in loud and forward tones. To his shocked surprise and eventual joy, he finds that the supposed minxes are his own dear daughters.

Mary Tickell's sprightly humor and sweet gaiety are always welcome in Sheridan's household. An instance is afforded outside these letters by her brother William. In 1781 she and he join a New Year's jollification at Bruton Street. After supper Sheridan proposes that every guest shall epigrammatise on some new book or topic. Hayley's *Triumphs of Temper* has just appeared, and Mrs. Tickell at once strikes off the following—

> With female patience here's to do,
> Serene and her trials three!
> Now, I have *read the poem through*
> What d'ye think of me?

The sadness of her premature death is deepened by such memories.

That end approaches too soon. She has long been ailing and concealing her malady. Mrs. Sheridan recounts the slow stages of the treacherous disease, the tragic progress to the Hot Wells, the tenderness of both husbands, her resolve never to disclose the hopelessness of the case, her own struggles to be resigned. Even then Mrs. Tickell tries to cheer her sister, and when her hand can scarcely obey her will, she sends her a pathetic note from her deathbed—"Mrs. Tickell presents her compliments to Mrs. Sheridan, and thinks it would be no ill use of her time if she copied the above for her improvement after breakfast." Under this Mrs. Sheridan writes, "The last lines written by her dear hand a few days only before her death, to prove to me that she was still able to write to me."

Four years after she has passed away that heart-broken sister thus commemorates her in the pathetic lines which preface the letters that she treasures—"On the 27th of July, 1787, she ceased to suffer, and I forever lost the friend and companion of my youth—the beloved sister of my heart whose sweet and amiable qualities endeared her to all who were so happy as to know her. She died in the twenty-ninth year of her age, universally regretted and lamented and was buried in the Cathedral at Wells. where she spent her infancy and where she enjoyed happiness in poverty the first year of her marriage. In less than two years afterwards Mr. Tickell married again a beautiful young woman of eighteen!!! [When Mary dies, Tickell believes himself inconsolable and desires to inscribe on her tombstone the impossibility of his marrying again. From this intention he is judiciously dissuaded.] The dear children remained with me till that time. The boys were then taken down to their father. The girl—the dying legacy of her ever dear and lamented mother—is still mine and constitutes all my happiness. E. A. S., August, 24th: 1791."

There are tears in these voices. She weeps for her sister and will not be comforted, and when she revisits the spot near Brandon Hill where each of them has spent her schooldays, she breaks down and sobs aloud. She wears her miniature by Cosway next to her heart till her dying day, and bequeaths it to the niece whom she has so fondly cherished. Her epitaph on Mary Tickell still remains among the Sheridan papers—

> You who have mourned the sister of your heart,
>   The dear companion of your youthful years,
> Pass not regardless. Drop ere you depart
>   On this sad spot your tributary tears.
> For here the sweetest friend forever lies,
>   The best, the kindest, loveliest and beloved,
> Whose cheerful spirit brightened in her eyes
>   And graced those virtues which her life approved.
> Modestly wise and innocently gay,
>   She lived, to my grieved Heart a blessing given,
> Till God approving, from its beauteous clay,
>   Called the pure spirit to its native heaven.

CHAPTER 9

GEORGIANA

A THRONG of noble admirers pays court to St. Cecilia, a bevy of fair ladies—Georgiana, Duchess of Devonshire, Lady Duncannon (afterwards Lady Bessborough), Mrs. Crewe, and many others—flutter round Sheridan. They are the fashion, they are the rage.

From their abode in Orchard Street, Portman Square, they advertise that concerts will be given "twice a week to the nobility and gentry." Fashion flocks to the parties for which the music room at the back of the house is fitted up. No money is taken at these performances. Mr. Linley supplies the furniture. (When Sheridan is scolded for living beyond his means, he replies, "My dear sir, these are my means.")

The ascent to Olympus is by no means unencumbered by obstacles. There is some hesitation before the doors of Devonshire House are opened to them, and so late as 1785 Mr. Windham spends the morning with Mrs. Legge, and their chief topic of conversation is the reasons for and against being acquainted with Mrs. Sheridan.

But Sheridan immediately captivates Georgiana and her sister Harriet, Lady Duncannon. Georgiana is seventeen and has just married that marital iceberg, the fifth Duke of Devonshire, regarded as the first match in England. She effaces all without being a beauty, but her youth, figure, flowing good nature, sense, and lively modesty make her a phenomenon. She is neither regular in features nor faultless in form, but she is fascinating. She is tall, divinely fair, with deep blue eyes and reddish hair. Her good humor is unceasing—her lips ever laughing, parted over a splendid set of teeth—a rare attribute in these days. Her character speaks out in her countenance—it is as open as her heart. She is sweet, easy, charming; indeed the last epithet has been coined for her.

She is an *esprit*. Both she and her sister prattle prettily with the Muses. If she enters a minister's room, she will startle his underlings by abrupt snatches of French, soliloquised for the occasion. She delights in the society of persons of talent and numbers among her friends Charles Fox and George Selwyn. She is seen hanging on the sentences that fall from Dr. Johnson's lips and contending for the nearest place to his chair.

She loves to surprise and defeat expectation. She is the fairy queen, not of poesy, but of transformation. Her moods are as varied as the months which display them. Now she is scholar, now coquette, by turns quick-witted and hesitant, rake and recluse, gambler and innocent. When she returns from Ranelagh it is to moralise in verse while she unlaces a corsage so tight that it has made her swoon. Wherever she goes, she scatters verses, French, Italian, and English, in her wake. Her poem on crossing the St. Gothard is read throughout England. Wherever she moves, men and women turn her slaves. Marie Antoinette, when the Duchess visits Paris, proves no exception. Philosophers, poets, statesmen, succumb to her spell. The Prince of Wales, whom she upbraids for falsehoods, is madly in love with her and jealous of young Grey whom he fancies her favorite. These are no exceptions. Those who know Georgiana Cavendish love her, and she never loses their affection.

Her passionate friendship with Lady Betty Foster eclipses the ravings even of their pet Rousseau. "All, all my possible hopes of friendship," she writes to her from Venice, "are concentrated in you. Without you the world is nothing to me. If you could forsake me, I would not bear to live, or living, should never think of any other creature."

But sense alternates with sensibility. She is an excellent mother, tending and training her children not only with discrimination but with humor. When she believes herself dying in 1790, her last words to her little son are, "Be brave, always speak the truth." She is a devoted daughter and writes almost daily to her mother, who in truth is her mother confessor. She vows to reform, to retrench, to retire. She weeps over every trouble that her escapades occasion.

Yet still she dines at seven, summer as well as winter, goes to bed at three, and lies in bed till four; she has hysterical fits in the morning and dances in the evening; she bathes, rides, dances for ten days, and lies in bed the next ten. She continues to lead the fashion for several years, famous in politics, in pleasures, and in painting. It is so much the rage to possess her portrait that all the prints of the famous picture of her are seized upon instantly, and her little foibles, even the effects of her illnesses, are imitated by the zealous.

Her greatest faults are youth and high spirits. The first she grows out of; sorrow cures her of the second. Her love of dress is another subject of criticism. She does not invent plumes. But she wears feathers which are larger than the feathers ever worn by any other woman. This surprising feat makes her immediately famous; it makes her notorious, and it excites the bitter pens of Grub Street pamphleteers and the far bitterer tongues of other ladies of quality who seek to set the ton. Her success is thus complete. "Nothing is talked of now so much as the ladies' enormous dresses more suited to stage or masquerade than for either civil or sober societies," writes Mrs. Delany. Friends are invited from abroad to come to London and admire their plumes—"we sweep the skies." Heads become higher than ever with feathers *en rayons de soleil* and *le jardin anglais*—roses, fruit, turnips, acorns, and potatoes, the gowns trimmed the same way. A lady looks like a walking house, but on the whole it is pretty. Lord Stormont gives the Duchess an ostrich plume an ell long. It is long enough to arouse a spirit of frantic emulation. But where can feathers of such a size be found? Rivals of Georgiana search London in vain until an undertaker is induced to sell the huge waving plumes from the top of his hearse. From six feathers the number rises to eleven in one coiffure, and by degrees the hair is raised on cushions from ten inches to a yard above the forehead. Under Queen Anne a lady's headdress rises and falls thirty degrees. Now under Queen Charlotte it is growing as rapidly as the Tower of Babel.

All this happens years after 1774, but even now Georgiana is chafed into caprice by a listless and cold husband. He is wholly incapable of strong emotion and can only be roused by whist or faro from a sort of mortal lethargy.

The Duke belongs to a family silent and retiring. Once the Duke and his brother, Lord George Cavendish, are traveling to Yorkshire and at one inn are shown into a three bedded room. Two of the four-poster beds are for the brothers; the curtains of the third bed are drawn. Each brother in turn walks across the room to the bed, peeps between the curtains, and then goes to bed. During the next day's journey, one brother says to the other, "Did you see what was in that bed last night?" "Yes, brother," is the laconic reply. The bed contained a corpse.

This attitude towards life is partly natural and partly acquired. It is bon ton to be tranquil.

The Duke does not lack intelligence. He is a classical scholar of considerable attainments, a sort of oracle at Brooks's when disputes arise about passages from Roman poets or histories. While to know Shakespeare as well as the Duke of Devonshire is a byword among his acquaintances. But there is no incentive urging him to take his true place in society. He has no ambitions. Decorated with a green sash of a noble order, his only remark is that a green coat would be of more use to him.

He is not a man without a certain kind of affection. He is by no means insensible to the seduction of female charms. He certainly is insensible to the charms of his beautiful and engaging wife.

No wonder then that Georgiana grows restive and hungry after distraction. No wonder that her glamour gains such a hold on the Sheridans when at length she condescends to become their friend and patroness.

Georgiana's sister, Lady Duncannon, with whom Sheridan grows more intimate, is nearly as fascinating and far more ungovernable. Her interests are wide. She plays with art, literature, and politics. She is very sensible and very frivolous. To a certain extent the same applies to all the great ladies who cross the threshhold of Devonshire House. They are not all angels or all fiends. But whatever they do, good or bad, right or wrong, they do with enthusiasm. And their energy is extraordinary.

Lady Duncannon is courted, followed, flattered, and made love to *en toutes les formes* by four men. She has a good heart, if a very weak head. She loves much and for those whom she loves she is ready to dare all things and fail in most.

The sisters, Countess and Duchess, share in all good and evil things, and they share Sheridan. He is a welcome guest at Devonshire House—that rendezvous of all the wits and beauties of fashionable life, where politics is taught to wear its most attractive form and sits enthroned, like Virtue among the Epicureans, with all the graces and pleasures for handmaids.

Not only incomparables like these, but Lady Lucan, Lady Cork, the Coventrys and the Harringtons extend their friendship to the brilliant pair. Music, wit, and ability rivet the bond. Butcher and milkmaid, however, are not to be propitiated by titles, and so Sheridan works with a will to support the needs of the small household in Orchard Street.

Besides an additional incentive is provided by the birth of his first born, Tom, a child, who, before he is nine months old, astonishes "everybody by his vivacity, his talents for music and poetry, and the most perfect integrity of mind,"—an infant prodigy whose progress is so rapid "that one may plainly see the astonishment the sun is in of a morning at the improvement of the night."

For the nonce Sheridan engages in essays and reviews. He wields a tomahawk—this hack's thoughts are "all borrowed," his derivations "trite," his style "puerile." He sharply criticizes Lord Chesterfield's *Letters* and answers

Dr. Johnson's *Taxation No Tyranny,* a defense of the royal prerogative against the American Colonies. He dismisses the burly Doctor as "an eleemosynary politician who must yield the miserable quit rent of an annual pamphlet. . . . Men seldom think deeply on subjects on which they have no choice of opinion. They are fearful of encountering obstacles to their faith (as in religion), and so are content with the surface." Fortunately this essay remains unpublished.

He writes a crude fragment, *The Drama of Devils,* and composes a lyric ode on *The General Fast,* satirizing the solemn fast day that has just been proclaimed. "Sire," he begins, "to dedicate to the throne without permission first obtained, may be called insolence and audacity by the weak and uninformed, but those who are acquainted with the routine of business at St. James' will know that to ask a reasonable request is, in effect, to solicit a refusal. A plain man, and à loyal subject, wanting because he is plain and loyal the necessary recommendations, must announce himself, and tell his Sovereign a truth which his courtiers, his *friends,* as they are falsely called, have either too much ignorance to discover, or too little honesty to reveal. This truth, Sire, which every schoolboy in political knowledge could confirm, is, simply, that the American War, founded in injustice, and carried on by folly, must end in irretrievable disgrace or in absolute destruction."

He girds himself for Utopian ideas. He sends to the press a book which he thinks will do him "some credit if it leads to nothing else." *The Sanctuary* is a chimerical essay on the education of women, inscribed to Queen Charlotte. When the Queen is approached, she discountenances a work French in origin and revolutionary in ideas. An academy is to be formed on the model of Mme. de Maintenon's at St. Cyr, and Sheridan presumes the Queen will surrender Hampton Court or some other place for the purpose. She is to be made Chancellor of this woman's university, and the first ladies of the land are to be its sub-chancellors. He insists on equality. "The classes are to be distinguished by age, none by degree. The instructors should be women, except for the languages. Latin and Greek should not be learned. The frown of pedantry [observes grave three and twenty] destroys the blush of humility. The practical part of the sciences should be taught. In history they would find that there are other passions in man than love."

And then comes a diatribe against the realistic novel. Women are to be schooled by more chivalrous characters than the cold, courtly worldlings who "are so clipped and rubbed and polished that God's image and inscription is worn from them, and when He calls in his coin, He will no longer know them for his own." As for recreations, they should ride and walk. Prizes are to raise a spirit of emulation in dances and concerts, and the French petits jeux are to enliven the winter. "As to the moral duties and love of the heart, there should be a clergyman of uncommon character for their curate. . . . They should be taken into life by degrees. Above all a knowledge of economy and the management of a house should be inculcated as by the nuns in France. The want of this has hurt matrimony more than can be expressed. . . . I hate women link-boy-like."

Finally, thinking perhaps of adorable Georgiana and desirable Lady Duncannon, Sheridan remarks, "The dispute about the proper sphere of women is idle. That men should have attempted to draw a line for their orbit shows that God meant them for comets and above our jurisdiction. . . . The influence that women have over us is as the medium through which the finer arts act upon us. In savage countries where the pride of man has not fixed the first dictates of ignorance into law, we see the real effects of nature. The wild Huron shall, to the object of his love, become gentle as his weary reindeer. He shall rob the birds for feathers for her hair, and dive for pearls for her neck; her look shall be his law, and her beauties his worship. It is the destiny of man to be ruled by women."

CHAPTER 10

THE RIVALS

ON THE NIGHT of Tuesday, January 17, 1775, the first performance of Sheridan's *The Rivals* is given at Covent Garden Theatre. It is announced anonymously, though the author is known, and succeeded by a new pastoral masque and a pantomime. It attracts a crowded and brilliant house. But the social success of the Sheridans has provoked some envy, and a claque is organised both in and outside the house against the play. A whole chorus hisses disapproval, a faction is ejected from the gallery, and even the boxes witness a challenge. Only the epilogue escapes, but that is given out to be Garrick's. The play itself is damned. Its blemishes—length, exuberance, drawnout sentiment—are fair game, but its very beauties are belittled as second hand. On the whole nothing can content the journals. It is all a bungle. It is voted insufferably tedious. Its naturalness is resented. It is immature. Point and polish may mend it, though it can never save it.

The clamor is directed almost as much against the actors. Quick, lightest of comedians, plays Bob Acres, a part which, it is alleged, "betrays him into farce." An old stager, Mrs. Green, bears the full brunt of Mrs. Malaprop's unpopularity. (Sheridan has borrowed the character of Mrs. Malaprop from his mother's *A Trip to Bath*.) Lewis, who enacts Faulkland, only receives praise because "he struggles with a difficult character." Mrs. Bulkley, the Julia, is applauded, but mainly on account of the epilogue which she recites. Shuter, who plays Sir Anthony Absolute, forgets his words, and Woodward, who plays the hero, is assured that he has often appeared to greater advantage. The sever-

est rebuke, however, is reserved for Lee, who as Sir Lucius
O'Trigger deeply offends the Hibernian portion of the audience. During the violent opposition in the fifth act, an apple
hits him. Whereupon he steps forward and exclaims in a
rich brogue, "By the powers, is it personal? Is it me or the
matter?" It cannot be the matter, for his representation is
declared to be "an affront to common sense . . . and so far
from giving the manners of our brave and worthy neighbors that it scarcely equals the picture of a *respectable
Hotentot* [sic], gabbling in an uncouth dialect, neither
Welsh, English, nor Irish." On the second night the part
is transferred to Clinch, and Sheridan, who in despair has
thoughts of throwing the piece overboard, is induced by
Harris the manager to withdraw it for cutting and revision.

He substitutes for the original prologue, a somewhat
flat dialogue between a sergeant-at-law and an attorney, a
new prologue spoken by Mrs. Bulkley. The actress pointing
to the figure of Comedy at the side of the stage, tells the
audience to—

> Look on her well—does she seems formed to teach?
> Should you expect to hear this lady preach?
> Is grey experience suited to her youth?
> Do solemn sentiments become that mouth? . . .
> Must we displace her? and instead advance
> The Goddess of the woeful countenance—
> The sentimental muse!

In fact the play has been damned largely by the con-
servative section of the audience who regard it as an unwar-
rantable departure from the sentimental comedy in vogue.

Sheridan is disappointed but not depressed. He feels
the play must succeed if he reshapes it. His wife is greatly
relieved. "My dear Dick, I am delighted. I always knew
that it was impossible you could make anything by writing
plays, so now there is nothing for it but my beginning to
sing publicly again and we shall have as much money as we
like." High offers, in fact, are immediately renewed for
her performances, but on all these Sheridan again lays his

embargo. "No," says Sheridan, "that shall never be. I see where the fault was. The play was too long, and the parts were badly cast."

The revised *Rivals* appears on the evening of Saturday, January 28, in association with a new musical entertainment called *The Two Misers*. It meets with marked success, and the journals change their tone. Thus the play which limps at first runs fourteen or fifteen nights before the close of the season. Sheridan's dramatic reputation is established, his pockets replenished, and by mid-February commendatory verses appear in the newspapers.

The author is grateful to the actor who by taking the part of Sir Lucius O'Trigger has saved the situation. Clinch is greedy and his family large. A benefit performance is arranged, and the playwright resolves to make it a success. In forty-eight hours he produces his short farce of *St. Patrick's Day or the Scheming Lieutenant*, which is acted on May 2, 1775, with Clinch as Lieutenant O'Connor, the Irish lover and soldier. It is five times repeated before the summer begins.

All through that summer Sheridan works hard at a comic opera, the music of which is selected and composed by his wife and his father-in-law Linley. Linley resents the dictation of a young spark who does not know a note of music while his artistic feelings are outraged by the use that is made of other people's compositions. But in the end he submits.

Several of the songs are adapted from Scottish and Irish airs, and it is in singing ballads of this kind that Elizabeth excels. The hand is the hand of Richard, but the voice is thus the voice of Elizabeth.

The Duenna is performed at Covent Garden on November 21, 1775, and succeeds beyond the author's wildest expectations. It has an unprecedented run of seventy-five nights, thirteen more even than that of *The Beggar's Opera* nearly half a century before, and it is acted with universal applause. It not only adds to the author's laurels but to his purse. It does more than run, it gallops— the only respite being a few days at Christmas and the Fridays in every week—the latter on account of Leoni (Don Carlos), who, being a Jew, cannot act on those nights. (In Leoni "the playhouse goes snacks with the synagogue." He is cantor at the synagogue in Bevis Marks under his own name of Meyer Lyon and is permitted to appear at the theatre so long as it does not interfere with his duties.)

The Duenna is a new departure. The previous operettas by O'Hara, Bickerstaffe, and others have been a tinkling farrago of dull dialogue and forced songs. *The Duenna*, on the other hand, is a coherent whole, and the songs which Sheridan introduces are his own love lyrics fraught with the romance of his courtship. The refrain of his duels runs through the romping prose of *The Rivals*, that of his elopement haunts the measures of *The Duenna*.

He troubles himself remarkably little about character and local color; it is enough that his dialogue is brisk and witty and his songs graceful and tuneful. Certain it is that he sets no great store by the book of the opera. He never takes the trouble to revise any of the printed editions. Many years afterwards, Kelly, the musician and singer, leaves a printed copy of *The Duenna* on his table after looking over the part of Ferdinand which he is to perform that evening. On his return home, he finds Sheridan reading it and correcting it as he reads. "Do you act the part of Ferdinand from this printed copy?" Sheridan asks. Kelly replies in the affirmative and adds, "I have done so for twenty years." "Then," says Sheridan, "you have been acting great nonsense," and corrects every sentence before he leaves the room.

A five act comedy, a two act farce, and a three act comic opera are not a bad year's work. At the beginning of 1775 Sheridan is an unknown literary tyro, at its close the leading dramatist of his time.

The results are far-reaching. In the first place they reconcile the Roman Father. Then they bring Sheridan a fresh olive branch. Dr. Johnson praises him. For some time Sheridan has been a favorite with Sir Joshua's circle, and his

name is among the signatures to the round robin beseeching
Johnson to revise his epitaph on Goldsmith. Besides he has
turned a neat compliment to Savage's biographer at the revival of that poet's drama, *Sir Thomas Overbury*. The Doctor's kindness now does not stop at praise. None can be
more jealous than he of the Literary Club, which meets
now in Gerrard Street, now in St. James's, and numbers the
choicest spirits of the day. He honors the young playwright
by proposing him, and Dick Sheridan is elected on March
14, 1777. Gibbon and Garrick, Burke and Reynolds are of
the company, and Charles Fox presides when Sheridan takes
his seat at the round table.

Sheridan makes the acquaintance of Fox shortly after the
debut of his first comedy. They profess themselves mutually
enchanted, and the acquaintance soons ripens into friendship. Gibbon first makes him known. A piquant picture:
the dumpy and unsavory savant introducing the dramatic
wit to the political Alcibiades. Thus Sheridan's dramatic
successes pave the way for his political career.

They influence his future in other directions. Garrick,
like Johnson, though at loggerheads with the father, favors
the son. And as Sheridan has complimented Johnson in a
prologue of 1777, so now in an epilogue he compliments
Garrick. The actor is highly pleased and warmly espouses
Sheridan's claims as his successor. Thus the three plays
have at length put Drury Lane and even Parliament within
Sheridan's reach.

Then too they advance him socially. He at once becomes celebrated and recherché, and the Duchess of Devonshire is now justified in her choice. This very spring her
friend, Mrs. Crewe, gives a famous ball—a ball so famous
it is embalmed in verse—and Sheridan attends.

Amoret, as she is called, now shows the zenith of her
charms, both mental and physical. She is a quick wit and
an unparalleled beauty—the handsomest of her set. She
uglifies everything near her. She is not only beautiful but
also exceedingly intellectual. In this day every woman of
quality writes verse. Mrs. Crewe is no exception. Making

[119]

verses is become almost as common as taking snuff. Literature is in her blood. Her mother has written an ode as well as an unfinished novel. Mrs. Crewe writes verse and journals. But her association with learned ladies, bluestockings, tinge her conversation with the slightest trace of pedantry. She enjoys the company of Edmund Burke and may have caught some of his ponderous mannerisms. Mrs. Crewe, as has been said, is very beautiful, exceedingly witty, certainly intelligent. She is also warmhearted, impulsive, and indiscreet. She chats, gossips, laughs, talks incessantly, never waits for an answer—all bustle and joy and grievance and anxiety.

There is something childlike about her that draws men to her side more powerfully than a bolder charm. Without seeming to wish it, she melts them into obedience. She does so with Sheridan. And for some years his heart is under her sway.

He attends Mrs. Crewe's fête during his wife's absence at Bath. A bouquet of beauties adorns it. Georgiana of Devonshire, Isabella of Rutland, the Countess of Jersey, and the erratic Lady Craven. It is rumored that Sheridan is courted and caressed. But he sends his wife a poem in which Sylvio assures his Laura that it cannot be spring because she is not there. Laura retaliates by a longer one which betrays her misgivings yet ends with a blissful reassurance.

The gay, the young, the fair throng round him. Majestic Stella (the Duchess of Rutland) moves to claim the prize, but he catches the look of Myra (the Duchess of Devonshire). The remaining beauties defile before him. Then comes Mrs. Crewe to whom he presents a pansy—

> With gentle step and hesitating grace,
> Unconscious of her power, the fair one came;
> If, while he viewed the glories of that face,
> Poor Sylvio doubted—who shall dare to blame?

But Laura will not doubt him, and as she looks on the grotto where their vows were plighted, she is confident of his love—

But where does Laura pass her lonely hours?
Does she still haunt the grot and willow tree?
Shall Sylvio from his wreath of various flowers
    Neglect to cull one single sweet for thee?

'Ah, Laura, no,' the constant Sylvio cries,
    'For thee a never-fading wreath I'll twine,
Though bright the rose, its bloom too swiftly flies,
    No emblem meet for love so true as mine.

'For thee, my love, the myrtle ever-green
    Shall every year its blossoms sweet disclose,
Which when our spring of youth no more is seen,
    Shall still appear more lovely than the rose.'

'Forgive, dear youth,' the happy Laura said,
    'Forgive each doubt, each fondly anxious fear,
Which from my heart, for ever now is fled—
    Thy love and truth, thus tried, are doubly dear.

'Each anxious doubt shall Laura now forego,
    No more regret those joys so lately known,
Conscious that tho' thy breast to *all* may *glow*,
    Thy faithful *heart* shall *beat* for *her* alone.'

CHAPTER 11

EXIT DAVID GARRICK

THE BRITISH ROSCIUS is taking his last shattering farewell of the public who can hardly let him go. There is a rush from all parts to see his performance as Don Felix in *The Wonder*. From floor to ceiling the theatre is crowded by admirers of all ranks, all nationalities. Never does he play with more fire and energy, more lightness and animation. When Mrs. Centlivre's wit is done and the curtain has shut out that Don Felix forever, there comes a moment of suspense and even awe. The great stage is now empty, and then the departing actor is seen to come forward, very slowly. Behind stage fills with groups of the players eager not to lose anything of the solemn situation. Not a sound is heard. There is a solemn pause. His face is seen to work as he tries to speak, and with an effort he says—It has been customary on such occasions to address friends in a farewell epilogue. He intended following the practise, but when he came to attempt it, he found himself quite as unequal to the writing of it as he now would be to its delivery. The jingle of rhyme—the language of fiction—would but ill suit his present feelings. The moment is a terrible one for him, now parting forever from those who have lavished on him such favors and such kindness; and upon the very spot where all these favors were received, he is now—here he is utterly overcome and cannot go on, till he is relieved by tears. Recovering himself he merely adds that he shall never forget their goodness, and though his successors may have more ability, they cannot surpass the pains he has taken to win their support, nor the deep gratitude he feels. On this he retires slowly—up—up the stage, his eyes fixed on them with a lingering longing. Then he stops. The shouts of applause from that brilliant amphitheatre are broken by sobs and tears. "Farewell, farewell," echo a hundred voices. Mrs. Garrick in her box is in an agony of hysterical tears. The wonderful eyes, still brilliant, are turned wistfully again and again to that sea of sympathetic faces, and at last with an effort he tears himself from their view.

Though an afterpiece is to follow, it is not suffered to be played, nor can the actors find enough spirit to perform it.

Exactly a fortnight after Garrick's retirement, Sheridan signs the contract which makes him part proprietor and chief controller of the historical theatre. Much mystery is made of how a young author of twenty-five could raise the funds for so large a purchase. Sheridan's contribution is £1300 in ready money, one twenty-seventh of Garrick's half share in the property, totally valued at £70,000. When the subject is broached, Sheridan laughs, murmurs "the philosopher's stone" and rushes out of the room. The touchstone, however, is merely the dull flint of mortgages and annuities which prove a dead weight.

Despite some natural jealousy Sheridan's advent is welcomed at Drury Lane. But the slipperiness of his rule contrasts painfully with Garrick's orderly foresight. Sheridan trusts to the turn of the wheel and his own power to retrieve disaster at the last moment.

Even experienced stage folk would have hesitated to shoulder such responsibility, knowing the anxiety and risk involved. Sheridan does not see the risk or simply does not care. He slips into a situation bristling with difficulties, complications, and demanding business acumen, tenacity, a level head, and great nicety of judgment—qualities he has shown no signs of possessing.

The season perforce starts with Garrick's remnants, several of them tragedies resembling comedies and the rest, comedies with a tragic ending. Not till the beginning of 1777 can Sheridan choose for himself. But during the interval he is engaged on *The School for Scandal,* polishing it again and again till it shines like a burnished table.

Obsequious Cumberland—blundering, unforgiving, unforgetting Cumberland, master of the sentimental school—calls, hat in hand, with one of his eternal tragedies. He sees Sheridan yawning over the fifth act, hears his excuse of sitting up for two nights in succession, and artlessly ascribes the yawn to dissipation.

Actors are always in revolt, shaming sickness or clamoring for a raise in salary. Or still worse flaunting their conceit. The conceit of an author is proverbial. But what is that to the conceit of an actor? A wart to Ossa. An author after all is but vain upon one point; an actor is vain upon all. Sheridan can scarcely persuade the most crooked varlet that ever presents himself at a stage door for examination that he is not "the glass of fashion and the mould of form," or many a hound that yelps out his notes that he is not a second Rubini.

There are other sources of trouble. Prompter Hopkins grumbles over delayed scenery, over the postponed pantomime, and the mischances of *Much Ado About Nothing.* Moreover an old rent charge, which has hung over the theatre, is revived by the Walpole family. The crown of Drury Lane, never an easy burden, proves heavy indeed for its new king, but luckily Mrs. Sheridan is its Queen. She keeps the accounts, reads the plays, helps the songs, and smooths the difficulties.

Sheridan himself freely corrects and condenses several pieces. A play called *The Picturesque Incidents* becomes *The Artist or Love in a Garret,* and the names of some of the characters are altered. Thus Sir Gregory Greylove becomes Sir Lionel Latelove. A soliloquy by Sir Lionel with the stilted opening, "It is a thousand pities that I should not have felt sweet Love's influence sooner. Summer is gone, etc." is made by Sheridan to begin, "Rather late in the day to be sure for both of us. Summer is gone." In another opera he notes, "The young soldier Albert wants a horse to go three miles in search of his mistress! Make it longer."

But while he performs the function of dramatic reader he devises a makeshift for the boards. He turns to Vanbrugh and produces a version of *The Relapse,* which he names *A Trip to Scarborough,* changing the play to please the delicate ears of his audience. It is first acted on February 24, 1777, and greeted with the accustomed volley of carping comments and a few hisses. But it is performed ninety-nine times and realizes over £1400.

A humorous prologue banters ladies' coiffures. The Duchess of Devonshire promptly appears in a box with an enormous tuft of pink ostrich feathers on her head to convince the world, notwithstanding what is advanced in the prologue, that her Grace's headdress is the true bon ton. This action raises the pyramid of hair, gauze, and feathers several stories. Such labor is employed to rear the fabric that night caps are made in proportion to it, covered over the hair, and kept by long black pins. Twenty-four large pins are by no means an unusual number to go to bed with. And in driving to the performance at Drury Lane, stools placed in the bottom of the coach are provided for ladies the height of whose head-dresses does not allow them to occupy the regular seat.

The second Congreve no longer inhabits Orchard Street. His father's fluctuations between affluence and penury have taught him to regard money as a rare blessing, to be enjoyed when possible and not to be hoarded. And so he removes to Great Queen Street, in the neighborhood of Drury Lane. There he stays till shortly after his election to Parliament three years onward. Then he transfers himself to the more fashionable Grosvenor Place. Mrs. Sheridan dislikes Grosvenor Place and they next migrate to a large house at Heston, near Hounslow. By the close of 1781 they take another at Harrow, and then after a brief trial of Lower Brook Street, they install themselves in Bruton Street, Berkeley Square, near Charles Fox in South Street and not far from the Duchess of Devonshire. There they long remain till Sheridan in one stroke leases a house in Grosvenor Street, a mansion at Isleworth, and a large cottage at Wanstead. Householding is his mania, but he is soon driven from place to place—Hertford Street, Jermyn Street, George Street for a considerable time, and later on Wimpole Street, Cavendish Square, George and Great Queen Streets again, and finally two houses in Savile Row and a villeggiatura at Barnes.

At Great Queen Street two plays never produced absorb his energies—*The Statesman,* a satirical piece by John Dent, and *The Foresters,* a fantastic drama, Ossianic and sentimental, which reveals Sheridan's innate romanticism.

Thus pass the months before *The School for Scandal* is perfected. Garrick warmly interests himself in the work as it develops from two to five acts, and Colman also reads it aloud to Burke and Reynolds. There is no lack of speculation as to its contents. All London stands on tiptoe to hear and see him.

The play narrowly escapes postponement. Petty politics intervene. A city election for the office of Chamberlain is in progress, and Wilkes is the anti-ministerial candidate. He is opposed by the vulture Hopkins, not the prompter but a merchant, who is charged with practises similar to those of one broker in lending money to minors. The government is apprehensive that a satire on usury may favor Wilkes, and a license is stopped at the last moment. Sheridan, however, at once sees Lord Hertford, the Lord Chamberlain, who laughs at the affair and accords permission.

Then again the play is announced before the copy is in the prompter's hands, and the last scenes have to be dashed off currente calamo. On the last leaf—
"Finished at last. Thank God.
R. B. Sheridan"
"Amen!
W. Hopkins."

CHAPTER 12

HYDRAS

WE ARE IN the noisy streets of London on a foggy night. A few flickering lamps have already appeared in Pall Mall, but our way to Drury Lane is lit by the cloudy light waved about by shouting linkboys. Gorgeous chairs are brought to the doors of the theatre by liveried porters, but fashion is seen alighting more generally from hackney coaches. The play is drawing a gay and colorful throng. Securing our slip of paper for the pit we abandon ourselves to the mad rush for front seats. There is no center aisle so we must scramble over the benches and be thankful that they have no backs. Women are shrieking for fear their brains will be knocked out, and the behavior of many a surly looking Britisher, all elbows and knees, gives cause for their fears. Hardly knowing how, we find ourselves suddenly planted upon a hard bench not far from the stage.

Pit, gallery, boxes are crowded. The noise and bustle are tremendous. Frantic yells like a congregation of wild geese, with roaring sometimes like bears, mows and mops like apes. And catcalls, whistles, hisses, whoops, and horse laughs.

Dub-dub-dub—"Throw him over"—"Won't ye ha some orange chips, ladies and gentlemen?"—"Bottled port and cider"—"Shut the door"—"There's room by the pow'rs"—"Pray, ask that gentleman to sit down"—"Boxkeeper, where's my fourth row on the second circle?"—"Take off your hat"—"Be Quiet"—"What an overflowing house, methinks I see"—'Turn out that blackguard"—"Zounds, how you squeeze; what do you think one is made of?"—"Oh, and is that your mode, honey?"—"Keep down your elbows or you'll break my

ribs"—"Is this your wig?"—"No, it's that there lady's"—
"Come, come out, my dear and give me satisfaction"—
"There's Alderman Cramp, a gouty, rich old citizen with
his young bride"—"No room? Give us back our money,
robbers"—"Madame, you're a charming spouse, so neat in
limb"—"Sir, I don't understand you"—"What say, dove?"—
"I'll pull your nose, faith, you coward and"—"Nothing, my
duck. I'd only dropped my glove"—"Tomorrow, at the fruit
shop"—"I'll shillally you through the lobby!"—"Will you
come? At twelve o'clock"—"Lord, sir, how you presume"—
"You shan't shove my wife"—"I shove her? A good joke"—
"Here, boxkeeper, are these my places? No? Then I'll go
back"—"You can't"—"You can," she fibs.

The ladies and gentlemen of fashion stroll in. The former
come in to show themselves, spread their fans upon the
ledges, make curtsy to their acquaintances—then talk and
laugh as loud as they are able. Peers, poets, nabobs, belles,
and 'prentice beaux fill the side boxes. The pit is occupied
by critics who to denote their capacity smear their upper
lips with snuff—

> Ye belles and ye beaux
>   Who adorn our low rows,
> Ye Gods who preside in the high ones;
>   Ye Critics who sit
>   All so snug in the pit—
> An assemblage of clever and sly ones. . . .

We glance around. The gorgeous blaze of a thousand
candles in the lustres. Throngs in brightly tinted holiday
frocks, waistcoats embroidered with gold and silver, plumed
bonnets and powdered wigs. Mrs. Crewe, the Devonshires,
and the Lucans beaming from the boxes. Mercurial Garrick
in blue and portly Dr. Johnson in black.

A green haze of curtain with the classic muse of comedy
and a waterfall in a glade veils the mysterious world of
wonders. Along the front edge a row of fiddlers and swell-
cheek blowers add superfluous animation to a noisy crowd.

SHERIDAN AT THIRTY-SEVEN
after the pastel by John Russell
(National Portrait Gallery, London)

SHERIDAN LATE IN LIFE
from a contemporary engraving
in the British Museum
Artist unknown

Cries of "Cider, spruce, and ginger beer" come from the balconies. Near us a trimly dressed matron politely suggests "Choice fruits and bills o' the play." Our red-faced neighbor picks out an apple to match his cheeks and ostentatiously pays his penny. For the same amount we secure a sheet of coarse paper, a foot long and half a foot broad, blotchily exhibiting all the printer's fonts—especially the largest. A glance informs us that tonight, May 8, 1777, will be performed the comedy of *The School for Scandal*, that it is written by Richard Brinsley Sheridan, and that it is acted for the first time this season. The names Mr. King (Sir Peter Teazle), Mr. Smith (Charles Surface), and our pet actress, Mrs. Abington (Lady Teazle) are almost lost in a jumble of other performers.

Our fingers, we are startled to discover, are smudged with the greenish black ink of our bill, and our clothes with the ink of our neighbor's. But our hardships are soon forgotten. Our watches say half-past six. The play is to begin.

An actor steps from the wing to speak the prologue written by Mr. Garrick.

> A School for Scandal! tell me, I beseech you,
> Needs there a school this modish art to teach you?
> No need of lessons now, the knowing think;
> We might as well be taught to eat and drink.
> Caused by a dearth of scandal, should the vapours
> Distress our fair ones—let them read the papers;
> Their powerful mixtures such disorders hit;
> Crave what you will—there's *quantum sufficit.*
> "Lord!" cries my Lady Wormwood (who loves tattle,
> And puts much salt and pepper in her prattle),
> Just risen at noon, all night at cards when threshing
> Strong tea and scandal—"Bless me, how refreshing!
> Give me the papers, Lisp—how bold and free! *(Sips.)*
> *Last night Lord L. (Sips) was caught with Lady D.*
> For aching heads what charming sal volatile! (Sips.)
> *If Mrs. B will continue flirting,*
> *We hope she'll Draw, or we'll UNDRAW the curtain.*
> Fine satire, poz—in public all abuse it,

But, by ourselves *(Sips)*, our praise we can't refuse it.
Now, Lisp, read you—there, at that dash and star":
"Yes, ma'am—*A certain lord had best beware,*
Who lives not twenty miles from Grosvenor Square;
For, should he Lady W. find willing,
Wormwood is bitter"—"Oh! that's me! the villain!
Throw it behind the fire, and never more
Let that vile paper come within my door."
Thus at our friends we laugh, who feel the dart;
To reach our feelings, we ourselves must smart.
Is our young bard so young, to think that he
Can stop the full springtide of calumny?
Knows he the world so little and its trade?
Alas! the devil's sooner raised than laid.
So strong, so swift, the monster there's no gagging:
Cut Scandal's head off, still the tongue is wagging.
Proud of your smiles once lavishly bestow'd,
Again our young Don Quixote takes the road;
To show his gratitude he draws his pen,
And seeks this hydra, Scandal, in his den.
For your applause all perils he would through—
     He'll fight—that's write—a cavalliero true,
Till every drop of blood—that's ink—is spilt for you.

The curtain rises. Lady Sneerwell discovered at her toilet;
Snake drinking chocolate.

> LADY SNEER.   The paragraphs, you say, Mr. Snake, were
> all inserted?
> SNAKE.   They were, madam; and, as I copied them my-
> self in a feigned hand, there can be no suspicion
> whence they came.
> LADY SNEER.   Did you circulate the report of Lady
> Brittle's intrigue with Captain Boastall?
> SNAKE.   That's in as fine a train as your ladyship could
> wish. In the common course of things, I think it must
> reach Mrs. Clackitt's ears within four-and-twenty
> hours; and then, you know, the business is as good
> as done.
> LADY SNEER.   Why, truly, Mrs. Clackitt has a very
> pretty talent, and a great deal of industry.

SNAKE. True, madam, and has been tolerably successful in her day. To my knowledge, she has been the
cause of six matches being broken off, and three sons
being disinherited; of four forced elopements, and as
many close confinements; nine separate maintenances,
and two divorces. Nay, I have more than once traced
her causing a *tête-a-tête* in the *Town and Country
Magazine,* when the parties, perhaps, had never seen
each other's face before in the course of their lives.

LADY SNEER. She certainly has talents, but her manner
is gross.

SNAKE. 'Tis very true. She generally designs well, has
a free tongue and a bold invention; but her coloring
is too dark, and her outlines often extravagant. She
wants that delicacy of tint and mellowness of sneer
which distinguish your ladyship's scandal. . . .

and on and on in triumph. Every variety of scandal presented—from its butterfly to its wasp. From the votaries like
Mrs. Candour who kill time and reputation at once to
villains who trade on it. Here and there some carpers vary
the monotony of acclaim. Wit Jekyll murmurs—"Why don't
all these people leave off talking and let the play begin?"
Scholar Warton objects to chance characters disconnected
with the plot. But the mirth of the audience gets stronger
and stronger each set. Journalist Reynolds, passing the
theatre at about nine o'clock, hears such tremendous noise
over his head that he fears the building is ready to collapse
and runs for his life. He finds the next morning that the
noise did not arise from the falling of the house, but from
the falling of the screen in the fourth act—so violent and
so tumultuous were the applause and laughter.

Some time later Cumberland brings his children to a performance of the play. They thoroughly enjoy it and laugh
uproariously, but Cumberland keeps pinching them and
exclaiming audibly—"What are you laughing at, my dear
little folks? You should not laugh, my angels; there is nothing to laugh at. Keep still, you little dunces."

Sheridan remarks of Cumberland that his envy is gross

ingratitude since *he* heard his tragedy and laughed at it heartily from beginning to end.

Old Surlyboots is also in a censorious mood: "Talk of the merit of Dick's comedy, there's nothing in it. He had but to dip the pencil in his own heart and he'd find there the characters both of Joseph and Charles."

However, Thalia, discrowned, has been restored to her reign. Dick knows his audience wants to be amused and he amuses them right royally. Night after night the theatre overflows, and for a space even the American War of Independence is forgotten in the sensation of the moment. It runs twenty nights in its first season and sixty-five in its second. It continues to be acted regularly three nights a week and damps the new pieces. It realizes nearly £15,000. In the provinces it meets with the same favor. It creates a furore in Bath, and Sheridan comes down on purpose to superintend the rehearsal. Soon it crosses the Atlantic and becomes the favorite play of George Washington. It becomes the standard by which other comedies are measured.

On the night after the first performance Sheridan is so drunk in the street that he is nearly taken up by the watch.

Congreve is a spectator, standing aloof and eyeing his creations like a connoisseur. He is an intellectual Petronius; his wit is an icicle. Sheridan never keeps his characters at a distance; he laughs with and at them. Besides while Congreve never errs, Sheridan heightens his effects by mistakes. Compared with the Restoration dramatist, Sheridan is warm and sociable; compared with Goldsmith, however, he is cold.

(As one scholar suggests, Sheridan in writing *The School for Scandal* has made an excursion into the Restoration, his purpose being to write a neo-Restoration high comedy of manners. What is the basic conflict that keeps the world of Restoration comedy spinning? The answer is the struggle between the socially elect and the parvenus—some are to the manner born and some are not.

The School for Scandal expresses this conflict of the parvenu class versus the elect. The scandal motif is an almost inevitable one in a comedy of the haute monde. The preoccupation with scandal and intrigue is one of the specialized functions of a leisure class—"At ev'ry word a reputation dies." Forbidden to occupy itself in the earning of sustenance, there are monotonously few things to occupy the days and hours—except the jockeying for social position and the pursuit of sex adventure.

But scandal has nothing to do with the Teazle plot. That story is one of domestic conflict. Lady Teazle is misled not by gossip but by vanity—the country girl gone giddy with city fopperies. The scandal group is just the frame and is perilously close to being separable from the main action. As a matter of fact Sheridan drafted two plays, *The Slanderers* and *The Teazles* and joined them with poor carpentry. The scandal plot and the Teazle plot never achieve final union.

One of the most typical conceits of Restoration comedy —that love and marriage are incompatible—goes overboard. The Charles Surface—Maria affair is shockingly heretical in that its intent is not seduction but marriage. Even Joseph is impeccable in that respect.

The play is remarkably free from offense—there is no bawdy in the dialogue, and none of the evil in action is accomplished. The playwright's task is simply to turn a comedy of manners into a vehicle of Addisonian didacticism. It is a deliberate attempt to recapture the tone of the preceding age. And the play does indeed restore the wit, the bustle, the brilliance of the high tide of English comedy.)

In spite of the complete triumph of *The School for Scandal* there is still a good deal of uncertainty about the fortunes of Drury Lane. Garrick is at first sanguine. "This is but a single play," observes a critic, "and in the long run will be but a slender help to support the theatre. To you, Mr. Garrick, I must say the Atlas that propped the stage has left his station." "Has he?" says Garrick. "If that be the case, he has found another Hercules to succeed him."

But soon afterwards, on July 13, 1777, we find him writing to King: "Poor old Drury! It will, I fear, very soon be in the hands of the Philistines." And Mrs. Clive, though long retired from the stage, is evidently well posted in theatrical news, for she writes the following year, "Everybody is raving against Mr. Sheridan for his supineness. There never was such a contrast as between Garrick and Sheridan. What have you given him that he creeps so?"

To make matters worse: Old Sheridan, whom in an evil hour his son has appointed stage manager, contrives through his self-importance to pick a quarrel with Garrick who writes indignantly, "Pray assure your father [Tom O'Bedlam, as Garrick names him] that I meant not to interfere in his department. I imagined (foolishly indeed) my attending Bannister's rehearsal of the part I once played, and which your father never saw, might have assisted the cause without the least offence. I love my ease too well to be thought an interloper, and I should not have been impertinent enough to have attended any rehearsal had not you, sir, in a very particular manner desired me. However, upon no consideration will I ever interfere again in this business nor be liable to receive such another message as was brought to me this evening by young Bannister." This letter is written in October, 1778, and by January 20, 1779, David Garrick is dead.

He is buried in Westminster Abbey, his pall borne by noble peers, thirty-four mourning coaches in all the panoply of woe following, while the streets are lined with groups of spectators falling in with the train as it reaches the Abbey.

Sheridan is called on to indite a monody. His *Verses to the Memory of Garrick*, dedicated to Lady Spencer, recited at Drury Lane by Mrs. Yates as the Tragic Muse, and afterwards set to music by Linley, is a polished performance. Polished but not good. It lacks strong personal feeling. It is not so much an elegy on the life of a friend as an epilogue to his plays and fame.

Johnson utters a windy phrase: "I am disappointed by that stroke of death which has eclipsed the gaiety of nations and impoverished the public stock of harmless pleasure." These words Mrs. Garrick causes to be engraved on her husband's monument in Lichfield.

Sheridan's pen lies idle. Many people are angry with him for his indolence, but *The School for Scandal* continues to draw good houses, and Shakespearean revivals are of frequent occurrence. At last he resumes his activity and sets to work on *The Critic.*

It is announced and talked of long before its completion. Then it is sent to the theatre in detached scenes. Finally a definite date is fixed for its appearance—the 30th of October. But when the 28th arrives, the work is still incomplete. Linley begins to get nervous, and the actors are absolutely *au désespoir*, especially King, who is not only the stage manager but has to play Puff. However, the combined intelligence of King and Linley are equal to the occasion. Linley decoys Sheridan down to the theatre, and King whispers to Sheridan that he has something particular to communicate and begs him to step into the green room. Accordingly Sheridan goes and finds there a table with pens, ink, and paper, a good fire, an armchair at the table, a dish of anchovy sandwiches—and, of course, two bottles of claret. The moment he gets into the room, King steps out and locks the door, and Linley comes up and tells the author that until he has written the scene, he cannot get out. Sheridan laughs cheerily, eats the anchovies, finishes the claret, and writes the scene.

Sheridan now insists on choosing a certain Mr. X for the part of Lord Burleigh, a densely stupid man, but of "looks profound." Having done this he maintains that the actor cannot go wrong, and a friend lays a bet that Mr. X will make some blunder. Sheridan not only accepts the bet but refuses to allow Mr. X to rehearse. He is merely to get his instructions by heart, which runs as follows—"Mr. X as Lord Burleigh will advance from the prompter's side, proceed to the front of the stage, fall back to where Mr. G.

stands as Sir Christopher Hatton, shake his head and exit."
Mr. X does not literally fall back as Sheridan for a moment
fears. But instead of shaking his own blundering head he
takes that of Sir Christopher within his hands, shakes it
long and manfully, and then walks off with a look of exultation at having so exactly complied with his lesson.

The play is a huge success and once more fills the coffers
of Drury Lane. It is a laughable farce and has many good
things—its retort on critics, its ridicule of pomposity, its
thrust at windy tragedies. Cumberland is hit off to the
life. Incidentally the first act contains Sheridan's valedictory
remarks on sentimental comedy which he has killed by the
success of his own plays. In 1781 Wilkie publishes the play
with the author's graceful dedication to Mrs. Greville,
arbitress of literary taste and mother of Mrs. Crewe. Edition
follows edition.

With the dancing mirth of *The Critic* Sheridan's literary
and dramatic career comes practically to an end. Fugitive
verses, patch-work pantomime, adaptations and impromptus
employ him in the future, but these contributions are of
little consequence. From dramatic authorship of a more elevated character he recoils.

"You will never write again," Michael Kelly says to him
one day. "You are afraid to write."

Sheridan fixes his penetrating eye on Kelly and asks,
"Of whom am I afraid?"

"You are afraid," Kelly retorts, "of the author of *The
School for Scandal.*"

CHAPTER 13

ELECTION TO PARLIAMENT

ALL ALONG SHERIDAN intends literary
fame to be merely a stepping stone to political renown. The
stage of the House of Commons appeals to a larger audience
than that of Drury Lane, and he hopes to supplement the
revenue of the theatre by the salary of office. It is an age
of political adventurers, mostly Anglo-Irish, and the prospects of the Whigs seem rosy. Lord North's star is obviously
setting under the disasters of the American War, Pitt's has
not yet risen, and the liberal opposition headed by Charles
James Fox is confident of a speedy return to office. Everything combines to urge Sheridan to lay down his pen and
mount the hustings.

But before he does that he collaborates with Fox in
The Englishman, writing the first two numbers and Fox the
third. They espouse the American cause, attack Lord North
and the War Minister, Lord Germain. The three penny
newspaper has a great sale, but the authors grow lazy, and
the Saturday number does not appear sometimes till Tuesday. Mr. O'Beirne, afterwards Bishop of Meath, undertakes
to have a Saturday issue always ready. Delighted to be
relieved of their labors, Fox and Sheridan write no more,
and *The Englishman* falls to the ground. "Ay, ay," says Fox,
"I knew what would come of it. Our d——d punctuality
would be the ruin of it."

Sheridan now fixes his gaze on St. Stephen's. A general
election during the autumn of 1780 affords him a chance.
Two seats are suggested, but Sheridan finds both prospects
hopeless. Finally at Devonshire House he meets Lady Cork,
who offers him an introduction to her brother Edward

Monckton, already one of the two members for Stafford. Lord Spencer (the Duchess's father) and the Crewes control much of that borough's interest. So Sheridan goes down under the combined auspices of the Moncktons, Devonshires, and Spencers, and is well received. Hundreds of cards are presented—

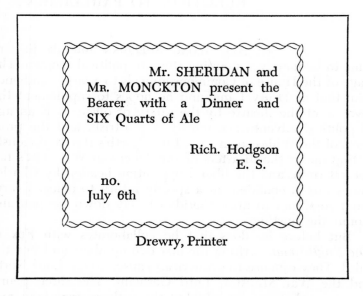

Mr. SHERIDAN and Mr. MONCKTON present the Bearer with a Dinner and SIX Quarts of Ale

Rich. Hodgson
E. S.

no.
July 6th

Drewry, Printer

and on September 12 after endless beer drinking, swearing in freemen, buffeting, junketing, processions, and the expenditure of £1,000, Richard Brinsley Sheridan is duly returned for the city, which he represents without a break for twenty-six years.

After the poll is declared, he steals away from dinner and walks alone dreaming rapturously of the future. The die is cast.

BOOK THREE

POLITICS

CHAPTER 1

VIGNETTES:
WHIGS AND TORIES

AFTER ALL BURKE is a damned wrong headed fellow through life—always jealous and contradictory. He has a sort of feudal turn of mind. Fox says that he is a most unmanageable colleague—that he will never support a measure, however convinced he may be in his heart of its utility, if it has been first been proposed by another. In company he is vulgar, either haughty or overbearing or mean and cringing. This vulgarity is felt by others. Wilkes says that as the Venus of Apelles suggests milk and honey so the Venus of Burke occasionally suggests whiskey and potatoes. The toast, "Perpetual war and universal adultery," given by Burke to his friend Dr. Lawrence to wish him success in his calling, certainly shows a coarseness absent from the broadest specimen of Sheridan's wit. Tarleton boasts of having butchered more men and lain with more women than anybody. "*Lain with,*" says Sheridan, "what a weak expression. He should have said *ravished*—rapes are the relaxation of murder."

But Burke is a pure bred Irishman, and the Irish never understand the literary effect of understatement. His blemishes are all Irish—luxuriance of expression, vehemence, impetuosity, a tendency to excessive gesture. He is never unwilling to begin to talk nor in haste to leave off. He does not do himself justice as a speaker. He is always hurried and always in a passion. His friends sometimes hold him down by the skirts of his coat to restrain the outburst of his anger. He speaks with a burning brain and quivering nerves. And as he speaks his head is continually in motion, now rising and falling, now oscillating from side to side in a very singular manner, according to his nervous excitement.

His voice is harsh, his brogue strong, his delivery execrable. His large spectacles, his tight and ill fitting brown coat and the little bob wig with curls excite the derision of the dandies from White's and Brooks's. His speeches are often drowned by coughing, cracking of nuts, and sucking of oranges. He empties the House—he is the Dinner Bell. Once as he rises with papers in hand, a rough hewn country gentleman who has more ear for the melody of the hounds than for political discussion, exclaims with a look of despair, "I hope the honorable gentleman does not mean to read that large bundle of papers and bore us with a long speech in the bargain." Burke is so swollen and suffocated with rage that utterly incapable of utterance he runs out of the House. It is on this occasion that George Selwyn remarks: he never before saw the fable realized—a lion put to flight by the braying of an ass.

While Fox passes at once from Parliament to a night of dissipation at Brooks's, Burke returns from debate jaded, irritated, soured. He is not an orator; his speeches are all writings. They are full of episodes and digressions, of excessive ornamentation and illustration, of dissertations on general principles. They are far better suited to a patient reader than an impatient hearer. Erskine once is so bored with a speech of Burke's that in the middle of it he skulks out of the House as invisibly as he can. But when a print of the speech reaches him in the Isle of Wight, he wears it to tatters in the rereading.

Burke's eloquence may be compared to the roar of an ocean thunderstorm or to the procession of a Roman triumph, exhibiting power and riches at every step—occasionally mingling the low Fescennine jest with the lofty music of its march, but glittering all over with the spoils of the whole ransacked world. Sheridan says to Rogers: "When posterity reads the speeches of Burke they will hardly be able to believe that during his lifetime he was not considered as a first rate speaker, not even as a second rate one."

Examine Burke's motives, he is a patriot; look to his opinions, and with all his powers, he is a bigot. He starts with the sublime and beautiful, and it appears that his ideal is the figure of a narrow minded queen and the symbols of a narrow social caste. He begins as a philosopher and finishes as something not very far from a snob. His life work is wrecked because his intellect is always at the mercy of his emotions.

He inveighs against the crimes of Hastings with acrimonious exaggeration. The flagrant immorality of the French nobility, the notorious infidelity of the French clergy, the levity and frivolity of the Queen of France find in him not a lenient and equitable judge but a passionate advocate. He conjures up a vision of political virtue, of moral purity, of social harmony which have no existence in the society of the French monarchy. The overthrow of religion, the execution of the King and Queen, the massacres of the nobles, the violence and ferocity of the mob of Paris, the insults offered to women—all these things completely unsettle his mind and drive him into a state of frenzy in which all control from reason is lost.

His prejudice is on the side of law and order. He calls good order "the foundation of all good things." Liberty is worthless except in an orderly community, and at bottom it does not seem possible to him that the interests of order can clash with those of liberty. Reform should be timely, temperate, and should not attempt completeness. Finally the change must not be incurred except when the existing evil is patently excessive.

One of the altars that he sets up in his mind is the British Constitution. He loves its very faults; he will not part with a jot or tittle of it. He invests it with Miltonic grandeur. He must keep the Constitution free from the stain of corruption, but also safe from the experiments of a meddling generation. So he discriminates between one reform and another. Economic reform is the removal of a blot on the Constitution, but parliamentary reform is a detestable innovation. Is a new pension to be granted on the Irish Civil List? Burke will rush into the fray, calling all history to witness the new fangled abomination. Is some rotten Cornish borough to be disenfranchised? Only over his dead body will the suffrages of past generations be snatched away.

His desire is to preserve, not to progress. His conception of government is oligarchic, its basis class distinctions. People of great families and hereditary trusts and fortunes are to his eye great oaks that shade a country and perpetuate their benefits from generation to generation. In his thought man is a creature bearing the taint of original sin. Frowardness, pride in self, and lust after innovation came into being with Lucifer, prime father of Jacobins. Society is divinely ordained, and its workings are subject to the immediate rule of Providence.

He becomes at last such an enthusiastic admirer of kingly power that he cannot sleep comfortably on his pillow if he does not first think that the king has a right to carry it off from under his head.

It is objected that his Toryism is largely emotional. To the famous passage in *The Reflections,* beginning—"It is now sixteen or seventeen years since I saw the Queen of France, then the Dauphiness, at Versailles, and surely never lighted on this orb, which she hardly seemed to touch, a more delightful vision. I saw her just above the horizon, decorating and cheering the elevated sphere she just began to move in—glittering like the morning star, full of life and splendor and joy. Oh! what a revolution! And what an heart must I have to contemplate without emotion that elevation and that fall!" etc., etc. All this, according to Sir Philip Francis, is "downright foppery." But Philip Francis is full of spite and envy, thinking how much better he could have managed the impeachment of Hastings.

Fox pities the downtrodden because he is a man of warm and generous feeling; Burke pities them because he is interested in the study of humanity. One procures admirers, the other possesses friends.

Burke shortens his life by the frequent use of emetics. He is always tickling his throat with a feather. He complains of an oppression of the chest which he fancies emetics will remove.

2.

Fox looks like a landlord of a public house. His frame is stout, and he has a swarthy complexion, shaggy eyebrows, and black hair. But in his veins flows the blood of the Merrie Monarch. His very names Charles and James remind him that he is a Stuart. Half royal and half radical he frolics with the Prince of Wales and is fervent for Robespierre.

From his childhood he is courted for his gaiety, originality, and genius. He is perfectly good natured, eager, and unselfish. With great natural abilities, a singular quickness of apprehension, and a retentive memory, he combines the habit of doing all things with his might. He is, as he says, a very painstaking man, and even when secretary of state he writes copies for a writing master to improve his handwriting.

He delights in literature and art; his critical faculty is acute and his taste cultivated. The habit of scholarship comes to him easily and pleasantly, and he never loses it. When someone in his presence disputes the authenticity of a line in the *Iliad* because it is in a measure unknown to others, Fox disconcerts him by quoting twenty others to match it. He is indeed capable of conversing with a Longinus on the beauty, sublimity, and pathos of Homer, with an Aristotle on his delineations of man, and with a pedagogue on his dactyls, spondees, and anapests. Works of his favorite authors, Greek, Latin, English, French, Italian, and in his later years, Spanish, never fail to afford him refreshment and consolation. Poetry is to him "the best thing after all," and he declares that he loves all the poets. Statesmanship may be a respectable calling, but poetry claims seven of the Muses and oratory none.

[145]

He can speak French as fluently and as correctly as his mother tongue. The only men who criticise his diction are Napoleon and Talleyrand. And his knowledge of Italian is almost as perfect. He can rise from the fluctuating delights of the faro table to spend a quiet hour with Dante, Ariosto, and Tasso, or drudge his way through Guicciardini and Davila. *Orlando Furioso* is his favorite Italian poem. "For God's sake," he writes his friend Fitzpatrick, "learn Italian as fast as you can to read Ariosto. There is more good poetry in Italian than in all other languages, I understand, put together. Make haste and read all these things, that you may be fit to talk to Christians."

He waits upon Voltaire at his villa by the lake of Geneva. The old man is very gracious, treats his guest to chocolate, and does him the easy favor of pointing out some of his writings which have a tendency to counteract the influence of religious prejudice. "Voilà," says the patriarch, "des livres dont il faut se munir."

He is fond of exercise, and even after he becomes very fat continues his activity. He takes pains to excel as an amateur actor and retains his love for this amusement for some years. His father, Lord Holland, has brought up his children without the least regard to morality. Unfortunately this teaching is not thrown away, and Fox early acquires extravagant and dissolute habits. In his younger days he is an outrageous fop and leads fashion among the macaronies. After his visit to Italy he and his cousin post from Paris to Lyon simply in order to choose patterns for their waistcoats. He appears in London in red-heeled shoes and blue hair powder, and sometimes, at least, wears a hat and feather in the House of Commons.

For four years he plays constantly for high stakes. Although his horses are generally beaten on the turf, his bets are judicious, and in 1772 he wins £16,000 on a single race. Nor is he a loser in games that require skill such as whist and piquet. He is ruined by his losses at hazard, and it is tolerably certain that the "immoderate, constant, and unparalleled advantages" gained over him at the gaming table are the result of unfair play. In order to pay his gambling debts he has recourse to Jewish moneylenders. He has a theory that money is a commodity, and that like any commodity it can always be procured if a sufficient price is paid. In carrying this theory into practise he finds that the price he has to pay makes him a beggar. In the summer of 1773 his difficulties induce him to put faith in an adventuress, Mrs. Grieve, who promises to procure him a wife with £80,000. She informs him that Miss Phipps, a West Indian heiress, is in love with him. Being told that Miss Phipps dislikes a dark-haired man, he consents to have his hair and eyebrows powdered white. The heiress is a myth. In the same year the wife of his elder brother bears a son, and the money lenders refuse to give him further credit. "My brother Ste's son," he says, "is a second Messiah, born for the destruction of the Jews."

But whether he wins or loses, his jest, his appetite, his sleep are as spontaneous as ever under circumstances such as would drive other young sparks to suicide. In 1781 he wins £70,000 in partnership with others at hazard, loses it all at Newmarket, and is £30,000 "worse than nothing." He is often in need of the smallest sums, and in 1781 his books are sold under a writ of execution. He bears his losses with great equanimity. Immediately after a run of ill luck that leaves him penniless, he is found quietly reading Herodotus. At other times he will at once fall sound asleep. His embarrassments render his faithfulness to his party especially praiseworthy. His opposition to the American War is sworn, and the emoluments of office cannot tempt him to be false to his principles.

No man likes popularity more than he does, but he scorns to gain it by unworthy means. Yet his modesty is almost excessive. When the entire audience of the first theatre in Paris rises to do him honor, he shrinks with the diffidence of a girl from acknowledging the compliment. Mme. de Récamier, the greatest beauty of her day, has much difficulty in persuading him to take a drive with her in order that the Parisians may see the distinguished Englishman who divides with her the adulation of the hour. And one night at Vauxhall he is much annoyed by being followed about as a spectacle from place to place. On such occasions he is not shy but gauche.

He practises oratory in the House. It is in fact his debating society. He records that he spoke on every evening that he was present, "except one, and I regret that I did not speak on that night too." His distinguishing trait is spontaneity—words never fail him. He delivers his speeches without previous preparation and avoids the flowers of rhetoric. He is vigorous, plain, clear, never strays from the matter in hand, never rises above the level of his hearers' understanding, is never obscure, and never bores the House. At the commencement of his discourse he is almost unintelligible, sputtering it like a roasting apple. His actions are ungainly, and he does not become fluent until he warms with his subject. Then his style becomes nervous and eloquent. On great occasions he seems like the Pythian priestess "to labor with th' inspiring Gods" and to dissolve in floods of perspiration.

In the summer of 1788 he goes abroad with his mistress Mrs. Armistead. During the whole tour he never opens a newspaper except once to see how his bets have been decided at Newmarket, and as he leaves no address, he has no news from England.

During the period of his unpopularity he is cheerful and unsoured. There is nothing small in his nature. His letters to his nephew, whom he loves as a son and who is then travelling on the Continent, are full of the pleasure he derives from the society of Mrs. Armistead, the fine weather and the beauties of St. Anne's Hill, of the pictures that pleased him most in Italy and of his reading. He would have Lord Holland take note in the Pitti of Titian's "Paul III, the finest portrait in the world." Titian's masterpiece he holds to be his "Peter Martyr" at Venice, and he speaks of his delight in the pictures of Guercino at Cento and so on. He is fairly at ease about money, for in 1793 his friends subscribe £70,000 to pay his debts and buy him an annuity.

Two years afterwards he marries his mistress. Mrs. Fox is plain and fat, but her manners are pleasing and gentle-womanlike.

During this period also, he leads a quiet and regular life, spending much of his time reading. He carries on a literary correspondence with Gilbert Wakefield. The four finest compositions of the century are, he says, the *Isacco* of Metastasio, Pope's *Eloisa*, Voltaire's *Zaire*, and Gray's *Elegy*. Burnet he holds to be a master of the historical style, he delights in Dryden's works and thinks of editing them. Milton's prose he cannot endure, and he does not admire Wordsworth. Everything is to be found in Homer. He reads that poet through every year, enjoying the *Odyssey* more than the *Iliad*, though admitting that it is not so fine a work. Euripides he prefers to Sophocles. "I should never finish," he writes, "if I let myself go upon Euripides." The *Aeneid* he reads over and over again, dwelling with special pleasure on the pathetic passages. He begins his *History of the Revolution of 1688;* he makes very slow progress with it, writing drop by drop. He reads much to Mrs. Fox and even now never wearies of her society. He is extremely anxious that everyone shall do her honor, and it is said considerations of this sort weigh too much with him. He enjoys shopping with her, and Sir Gilbert Elliot marvels to see them setting off together to buy cheap china and notes that they are both very economical.

One visitor finds him on the grass teaching the birds to think he is dead. Love in a cottage at fifty comes as naturally to his appetite as Newmarket, Parliament, and the faro table with no time for bed at twenty-five.

Gibbon says that Fox possesses the powers of a superior man blended with the softness and simplicity of a child. Adding that perhaps no human being has ever been more perfectly exempt from the taint of malevolence, vanity, or falsehood. But the greatest tribute comes from Burke who describes him simply and sufficiently as "a man to be loved. . . ."

Opinions vary. Sir Walter Farquhar talks with George

Selwyn, and the latter says: "Genius is an indefinite term. I never think a man really an able man unless I see that he has attained the object of his pursuits, whatever they may be. I try Charles Fox by that test. He has had three favorite pursuits—gambling, politics, women. He addicted himself to play and thought himself a skilful player, but lost an immense fortune almost before he was of age. Power was his grand object, yet he has never been able to keep possession of it, scarcely for a twelfth month. He was desirous of shining as a man of gallantry and he married a whore."

3.

Politics are not a matter of ability, nor even a matter of votes; they are founded on corruption and patronage. Since 1688 the government of England has been in the hands of great Whig families who regard power as little more than a means of providing for themselves and their relations. Son succeeds father much as though the office were a tailor's business. Posts and places are handed out if possible on a family basis, and if necessary as a bribe.

Indeed there are no great parties, only splinters of them in the shape of gangs for and against the King attached to this or that political patron. If Chatham had never got the gout, there would probably have been no American War. But Chatham's gout gives all the atoms a chance, and they shoot hither and thither, either towards the Court or the paying families. Unless a political aspirant is a King's man, he must be a Grenvillite or a Rockinghamite, a Grafton's man or a Richmond's man, a dependent of the Rutlands or of the Bedfords, a nominee of the Bentincks or the Cavendishes.

Two of Chatham's early lieutenants emerge, the one Lord North, the King's friend, amiable, agreeable, conciliatory, the other Lord Shelburne.

The secret of North's power as a minister is not his subservience to the King but his extraordinary tact in managing the House. Nothing can be more coarse or clumsy or ungracious than his outside. Two large prominent eyes that roll about to no purpose (for he is utterly shortsighted), a wide mouth, thick lips, and inflated visage give him an air of a blind trumpeter. But within that rude casket are enclosed many useful talents. He has wit, good humor, and strong natural sense. His greatest fault is indolence, his most serious shortcoming irresolution. He is just as undecided in a party of pleasure as in any other party. Yet he is a welcome guest everywhere.

The word gentleman is never applied to any person in a higher degree or more generally than it is to Lord North and to all he says or does in the House of Commons. He deprecates the too great readiness to take offence which then seems to possess the House. "One member," he says, "who spoke of me, called me 'that thing called a minister.' To be sure," he continues, patting his large form, "I am a thing. The member, therefore, when he called me a thing said what was true, and I could not be angry with him; but when he added, that thing called a minister, he called me that thing which of all things he himself wished most to be, and therefore, I took it as a compliment."

While sitting in the House, he frequently holds a handkerchief to his face. Once after a long debate, someone says to him, "My Lord, I fear you have been asleep." "I wish I had," he replies.

These good natured sallies drop from him constantly. On his resignation he should have retired. Many things which may be defended cannot be applauded. The coalition between his lordship and Mr. Fox is of this description.

Chatham's titular successor is Lord Shelburne, a philosopher statesman of less genius but of greater insight than Burke. In practise he is the worst of cabinet colleagues, cursed by a reputation for insincerity and duplicity which obtains for him the nicknames of "Malagrida" and "Jesuit of Berkeley Square." What is the reality? Shelburne is a great nobleman who lives magnificently and gives splendidly. He peoples his house with the first brains of the time—Price, the financial theorist, Priestley, Bentham. All that is best worth patronizing he patronizes. His ability is matched by his industry. He keeps his own staff of clerks at Lansdowne House to analyze and examine the public accounts. He is a government department in himself. His manner, however, is partly responsible for his evil reputation. He is a little too anxious to please, he protests his candor overmuch—in a word he is smooth. Nothing he does not know, except possibly the rules of faro. Among the bloods of Brooks's he appears incongruous and alarming. He will be opening his private despatches from Paris at an hour when Fox and Sheridan are half seas over. He is not a good fellow, not at all clubbable, always a little outside the pale. This aloofness not only estranges his colleagues and perplexes his sovereign; it also prevents his ever finding a party or enlisting any real support.

The hope of the old Whigs on the other hand is Rockingham, and he also is the hope of the new. He is gentle, blameless, rich, and receptive. He offers a clean slate for Burke to write on. Only his amiability holds the Whig household together, a household which comprises Shelburne, its family lawyer, Fox, its spendthrift heir, Sheridan, its boon companion, and Burke, its dominie.

The August returns of 1780 worst and baffle the Northites. The Prime Minister finds both his health and his forces failing. He wants to make peace with America; the monarch thwarts him. Dutch and Indian affairs threaten; with the best intentions he is powerless. But for the King's insistence, he would gladly have resigned earlier in the year. Now the Gordon riots against the Catholics deal a fresh blow to his tottering government. At one moment his majority sinks to ten; later on it sinks to less. He is worried to death. All his adherents, anticipating his downfall, clamor in crowds to pick the bones of the carcass. The Foxites redouble their energies. But the end of North's long reign is not yet. When it comes, the jumble of political grouping shows itself in three successive ministries within eighteen months.

4.

George III is now forty-two years of age and has reigned twenty years without popularity. He aims at being a patriot king but is singularly unfortunate in his means. In his first speech to Parliament he makes a bid for the affection of his people. "Born and bred in this country," he says, "I glory in the name of Briton," in pointed allusion to the German upbringing of his two predecessors. But unfortunately the appeal falls flat, largely owing to the use of Briton instead of English. Nor is his marriage of a nature to awaken any romantic enthusiasm. In the early days of his reign he is attracted by the beauty and unconventional charm of Fox's niece, Lady Sarah Lennox, and even makes a clumsy attempt at a proposal of marriage. However, the influence of his surroundings overcomes his passion, and he chooses as his wife a lady of no special beauty or charm, Charlotte of Mecklenburg, consoling Lady Sarah by assigning to her the post of bridesmaid. But even his marriage is overshadowed by his partiality for the unpopular Scotsman Bute. And it is not till 1784 that monarch and multitude are brought together.

He wishes to rule not to reign. He is not a genius nor a prophet but is a king every inch. His courage is conspicuous. He cannot bear, he once says, that any of his family should want courage. He dislikes show and pretence. He sets an example of simplicity to his subjects and relies on the household virtues. Affable to the crowd, he is yet a stickler for pedigree. In his eyes nobody is a gentleman who cannot show three generations, and he flatly refuses to appoint any but such "gentlemen" to the bishoprics. Even his antipathy to Fox is tempered by the admission that he is a gentleman, and to this extent "not disagreeable in the transactions of business." But he inherits some of those

[153]

characteristics which have not recommended the House
of Hanover. Alexander Pope has thus satirized George's
father—

> Heav'n spread o'er all his family
> That broad, illustrious glare,
> Which shines so flat in ev'ry eye
> And make them all stare.

> God send the Prince that babe of grace,
> A little whore and horse,
> A little meaning in his face,
> And money in his purse.

Like his predecessors he has to contend with his own
superstitions. He believes in divine right fully as much as
the Stuarts. For him America rebels against God when she
defies the Lord's anointed. So does France, and he is ready
to fight and make England fight for monarchy. He is anti-
Romanist fully as fierce as Cromwell. His main fault is
ignorance.

Above all he has to wrestle with the Whig oligarchs to
whose dictation he is in thrall. Pitt, whom he admires, enjoys his confidence just because he stands unfettered by
these connections.

5.

On February 26, 1781, the House is debating Burke's
bill for Economical Reform. Mr. Byng, member for Middlesex, urges the young member for Appleby to reply and
appears to understand that he is prepared to do so. Pitt,
however, has decided in his mind not to take such a chance
and does not realize that Mr. Byng has told his friends
around him to expect his intervention. When therefore the
previous speaker sits down, the member for Appleby to his
surprise is assailed by cries of "Mr. Pitt! Mr. Pitt!" Every

eye is directed to Pitt alone. He has to accept what is the challenge of destiny.

A tall, slim man rises. Not by a gesture, not by a hesitation does he betray what he feels. At once there is revealed in him that Parliamentary manner, in him a manner inborn. After all Pitt belongs to the fourth generation of fathers and sons who make the House of Commons their home. To him the House is as familiar as his fireside.

To this perfect poise is added a voice clear and musical. The speech arouses the deeper astonishment because it is delivered ex tempore. The sentences are accurately constructed. The phrases are precise. The argumentation is to the point; he is lucid, cogent, complete. From that moment he takes his place among the illustrious who have addressed the chair. He sits down amidst loud and prolonged cheering, again and again renewed. Lord North, the leader of Pitt's political opponents, says at once that Pitt has delivered the best first speech he has ever heard. When someone says to Burke that here is a chip of the old block, Burke replies, "He is not a chip of the old block; he is the old block itself." And Fox, anticipating no thorn in his side, hurries from his front bench to Pitt's less prominent seat and warmly congratulates him.

An old member joins the two young men. "Aye, Mr. Fox," says he, "you are praising young Pitt for his speech. You may well do so, for excepting yourself there is no man in the House can make such another, and old as I am, I expect and hope to hear you both battling it within these walls, as I have heard your fathers before you."

Fox is disconcerted by this allusion to the dissensions among the Whigs of a previous generation. He stands silent. But Pitt is equal to the occasion. "I have no doubt, general, you would like to attain the age of Methuselah!"

There are many who recognise that Pitt like his father is a ready made orator who has made a famous speech. But it needs more than one speech to establish him as "the first man in the country." To hear Pitt a second time becomes the desire of a curious House. On May 31, 1781,

[155]

the members are debating a financial matter and he rises.
Fox rises at the same time but at once gives way. Pitt
repeats his earlier success. "Mr. Pitt," says a member to
Fox, "seems to be one of the first men in Parliament."
Without a touch of jealousy, Fox replies, "He is so already."
(Such a parliamentary honeymoon does not last forever).

Indeed Pitt, with his "d----d long obstinate face," the
fine forehead, the keen eye, the conspicuous nose, soon
commands the assembly. He excels in sarcasm and uses it
freely. When he begins to speak, many a frightened member
seems to express by his looks, "I fear the thunder will fall
on me." That it falls somewhere is evident from his frequent converting so many a premeditated No into a willing
Ay.

Fox's oratory is impassioned; Pitt's is calculating, correct.
Fox persuades his hearers; Pitt commands their assent. His
undeviating circumspection tends to obtain for him from the
considerate and grave a confidence which they deny to his
rival.

To the end of his life he remains a celibate of the strict-
est variety. This draws Pete Pindar's ridicule of an under-
graduate virtue which repels the flower girls in Cambridge
who come fresh from the country and who only endeavor
to sell to the young gentlemen their roses and lilies. He
is no less rigid in other indulgences. Neither play, turf, or
theatre can allure him. But he swallows at times a whole
bottle of port in tumblerfuls before going down to the
House. He enters it with a stiff bow and advances up the
floor with a quick and firm step, his head erect and thrown
back, looking neither to the right nor to the left, nor favor-
ing with a nod or glance any of the individuals seated on
either side. He is unbending. His nose, says Romney, is
turned up at all mankind. Fox enters the House every inch
of him the good fellow—spontaneous and ample. He has
some pleasantry to exchange with everybody. "I know the
coldness of the climate you go into," writes Shelburne to
one who is to have an interview with Pitt, "and that it
requires all your animation to produce a momentary

thaw." Like an Alpine peak Pitt is cold, solitary, lofty, and inaccessible.

He omits to patronize arts and letters. Neither Porson as a scholar, nor Gibbon as an historian, nor Johnson as a lexicographer obtains a farthing from the public purse. To Pitt literature like linen and steel is a commodity, the price of which must be fixed by supply and demand.

Dundas tells Lady Anne Barnard his feelings about Pitt: "I often envy that rogue. While I am lying tossing and tumbling in my bed and cannot sleep a wink for thinking of expedeshons and storms and bauttles by sea and laund there does he lay down his head in his bed, and sleep as soond as a taup."

6.

The House of Commons consists of five hundred and fifty-eight members. Like the House of Lords it is included in the Palace of Westminster. The chamber is oblong—a mere box, with narrow galleries at the side but none at the ends, and a plain roof. Behind the speaker's chair are windows which are of little use during the climaxes of debate in the small hours of the morning. What lights the House is a vast chandelier hung from the ceiling.

There is little provision for the public. Parliament is an intimate affair. The members, knowing one another, do not need to know anyone else. They comprise an exclusive assembly of purple-nosed bon viveurs, with powdered hair, elaborate waistcoats, knee breeches, and glittering shoe buckles. They sit in serried ranks, as if debate were a levée. They do not applaud, for applause is of the hands. But the collective voice of the Commons: "Aye—No—Hear! Hear!— Oh! Oh!—" Laughter. Most eloquent are the silences.

On the one hand it is the best club in Europe; on the other a talking or debating society.

CHAPTER 2

FLORIZEL AND COALITION

SHERIDAN IS HEART and soul for fulminating Fox. In a word he is a "new Whig" a modern Radical. He is appointed sub-chairman of the Westminster Association for Reform and presides over a mass meeting in Westminster Hall to press the cause of universal suffrage and even of annual Parliaments. "Once a year," say some, "and oftener if need be." Sheridan belongs to the "oftener if need be's."

Fox brings him into the Whig sanctuary, Brooks's, and the House expects much from his fame. On November 29, 1780, he delivers his maiden speech on a charge of bribery and corruption against the sitting members for Stafford, himself and the Honorable Edward Monckton. He is heard with particular attention, the House being uncommonly still while he is speaking. But when he sits down, Rigby, Paymaster of the Forces, rises to make him the target of coarse and insulting abuse, and Fox is forced to protect him. The House meanwhile is disappointed. He speaks again on the alleged necessity for employing troops against the Gordon rioters. This speech draws from publisher Woodfall the remark, "Parliament is not your line." Sheridan leaning his forehead on his hand replies, "It is in me, and by God, it shall come out."

On March 20, 1782, "the noble Lord in the blue riband" laughs himself out of office, and the King, hard pressed but anxious to be popular, sends for Lord Rockingham. George III does not yield without a struggle. Twice he summons Lord Shelburne, but Lord Shelburne owns that he cannot stand without Lord Rockingham, whereas Lord

Rockingham can well stand without him. And when at length the Whig is inevitable, he actually refuses to see him until he kisses hands and transacts all preliminaries through Shelburne, who is appointed one of the Secretaries of State and a Knight of the Garter. Charles Fox, the other Secretary of State, storms and curses, but does not move for North's impeachment as he and Burke have vehemently threatened. Office like charity covers a multitude of sins.

In this mild administration, Sheridan as Fox's henchman receives his reward. He is appointed an Under Secretary of State. He perseveres as a man of business. Like Fox he is now as industrious as he has been idle. He speaks seldom. He devotes himself to routine and takes a keen interest in two problems pressing for solution—peace with America and the Continent, and some sort of Home Rule for Ireland. It is rumored that he has refused a gift of £20,000 from the American government towards the close of the war in 1781.

While the friends of freedom regard American Independence as the dawn of a new era, the old guard sees nothing but humiliation for England. Peace has to be made both with France, Holland and America. The difficulty is how to accommodate the surrender to patriotism.

The ministry is divided. Shelburne declares that the sun of Great Britain will set whenever he acknowledges American Independence. Now voicing the King, he wishes to delay its formal recognition. Fox presses for an instant and separate declaration. Sheridan's fervor for America outdoes even that of Fox. Like Fox he wishes to exclude any clause for American Independence from the French treaty, for if it appears as a stipulated demand on the part of France that America shall be independent, that country will gain fresh credit with the new world.

From the first Fox and Shelburne disagree about their respective spheres and the conduct of negotiations. In Paris their representatives give contradictory reports on the attitude of the cabinet towards France and the Colonies. When Fox learns of what is taking place, he demands the recall of Shelburne's representative who has committed several indiscretions. But the cabinet refuses to uphold him.

On July 1, 1782, Rockingham dies of the influenza, and the consequence is a reconstructed Whig cabinet led by Shelburne. Fox flatly refuses to remain as Shelburne's colleague, and Burke, Sheridan, Lord John Cavendish (a noble nonentity) and others follow his retreating footsteps. They form the Opposition. Charles and Dick, captain and lieutenant, become more friendly than ever. Their energies are concentrated on Shelburne's overthrow.

His short reign proves but an interregnum. He can satisfy very few of his hangers-on. North is agog to edge in. The Bentincks and Cavendishes await a suitable occasion. The preliminaries of the Versailles Treaty are signed on January 2, 1783. On the twenty-seventh copies of the provisional treaty with the United States are laid upon the table. On February 21 a vote of censure on the Peace is carried by seventeen—and seventeen are enough. Shelburne, eclipsed by the rising young Pitt, flickers out in the socket.

An interval of chaos ensues. (It is due to the King who is always resisting what ought to be and prolonging what ought not to be). For nearly six weeks England is without a government. George implores Pitt to form an administration. Pitt refuses, willing to give Fox from whom he has finally parted, more rope to hang himself. The King then urges North to the rescue. North replies, "The Duke of Portland is ready to come in." The King's comment is, "Then I wish you good night." Finally, under Portland's nominal aegis, oil and vinegar, Fox and North, the unmixed, get together, though Fox has vowed that never while he breathed would he shake hands with such a scoundrel as North. But Shelburne's enormities efface that feud. And as Fox protests in Latin—his enmities are placable but his friendships eternal.

The King is in despair. Portland is not to his taste. Fox is his abhorrence. He sighs, he sobs, he swears, he even threatens a retirement to Hanover. All along he has sought a "comprehensive" ministry, but this is a thing which like the Peace of God "passeth all understanding." North becomes Secretary for the Home Department, Fox becomes Secretary for the Foreign; Burke is Paymaster of the Forces, and Sheridan, with Burke's son, Secretary to the Treasury. Mediocre Lord John Cavendish becomes Chancellor of the Exchequer.

From the first the coalition is unpopular. Both country and closet are against it. Pitt smiles a bitter smile, and the King turns his back when Fox kisses hands, looking for all the world like the shying horse at Astley's just before it kicks off its rider.

And so in a shower of patronage, rained alike on radicals and reactionaries, the Coalition rushes in. It is a freak of clandestine intrigue. It typifies no cause and no necessity. It is a union of talents, not of principles. From the nation's point of view it is a fraud, from the monarch's a monster.

Behind the Coalition lurks another league which nearly ruins the North and Fox administration. This is the secret pact between the Foxhounds (Extreme Whigs) and the young Prince of Wales on whom an income is settled. It is an ill starred alliance and mixes up the party of progress with the extravagance of a royal rake.

George is a young bull charging about in pursuit of pleasure. He is headstrong, licentious, prodigal. His father is a model of decorum and conjugal fidelity. He, on the contrary, is extraordinarily dissolute. His liaisons are notorious. In addition to his five more or less historic connections—Perdita Robinson, Mrs. Fitzherbert, and Ladies Jersey, Hertford, and Conyngham—there are eleven others named, and two others unnamed who are his mistresses—besides many other temporary intrigues.

His first conquest is that of his mother's Maid of Honor. "Well," remarks her Majesty suspiciously, "taking it on the whole, the life of a Maid of Honor is a very monotonous one."

"I perfectly agree with your Majesty," replies the Prince, "it must be dullness itself, for what can be more vexatious to the spirits that to make one of a formal procession through the presence chamber to the drawing room; never to speak but when she is spoken to; to make an occasional one of six large hoops in a royal coach; to make up, at least, two new court suits a year, and to aid the languor of a party at a side box in a royal play?"

"And, George, is there no other act which a Maid of Honor performs?" asks the Queen significantly.

"Oh, yes," replies the Prince, "she goes to plays, concerts, oratorios, etc. gratis; she has physicians without fees and medicines without an apothecary's bills."

"But you have forgotten one very material act," says the Queen.

"Very likely," says the Prince, "the acts of a Maid of Honor form no part of my education."

"Then I will tell you one," says the Queen, "of which you have lately attained the knowledge; and that is, you were right when you said that a Maid of Honor goes to plays and concerts and oratorios gratis—but you forget to add that she also flirts with young Princes and goes to meet them by moonlight—and is that also gratis?"

The Prince can speak French, Italian, and German fluently; he is well read in the classics, and he affects a taste for art and the belles lettres. His taste is not always correct and tends overmuch to the showy and florid, yet in comparison with that of his father, who has no taste at all, it is hailed as perfect. He loves outdoor exercise and shows to great advantage on horseback. He is a good shot, an accomplished fencer and can on occasion use his fists with good effect. He does not lack courage; he can face death boldly. "This is death, my boy," is his salute to eternity. On the other hand, he can never face anything that thwarts his whims. Besides he is not truthful. But the blame for that does not rest wholly with him. "You know, I don't speak the truth," he says once, "and my brothers don't, the Queen having taught us early to equivocate."

To London society wearied by the dullness of the Courts of the early Georgian sovereigns, this young Prince, born on English soil, bred in England, and speaking English with no Westphalian accent, comes as a Prince Charming. There is no doubt that the Prince of Wales is charming—he is tall and finely formed; he has a handsome and manly countenance, though he is not so handsome as the Duke of York who is called the Apollo of the day. Even so late as 1829 Madame du Cayla, the favorite of the last years of Louis XVIII, is astonished at his good looks, his *belles jambes et sa perruque bien arrangée—ses belles manières.* He dances a minuet better than any of his contemporaries. He is the envy of all the beaux. His smile is the desire of all belles and his bow the most princely bow in all Europe.

He is in line with the bucks and dandies. At his first appearance in society, he creates a sensation—he wears a new shoe buckle. This is his own invention and differs from all previous articles of the same kind insomuch as it is an inch long and five inches broad and reaches almost to the ground on either side of the foot. When he takes his seat in the House of Lords, he wears black velvet, richly embroidered with gold and pink spangles and lined with pink satin. His shoes have pink heels and his hair is pressed much at the side and very full frizzed with two small curls at the bottom. A plain coat from its repeated alterations and the consequent journeys from London to Windsor of Davison the tailor often costs £300 before it meets his approbation.

In conversation he is amusing and talkative and passionately fond of gossip. What he most seeks for is deference without awe and a capacity for keeping him amused. He is fond of music, sings well, and will accompany the piano on the violoncello. He holds the balance between the rivals Crosdill and Cervetto, remarking that "the execution of Crosdill has all the fire and brilliance of the sun, while that of Cervetto has all the sweetness and mildness of the moonbeam." He frequents the opera, delights in chamber music, and is a patron of many musical societies. Giardini, the worthy man who says of him that he is a musician among princes and a prince among musicians, must be set down as a flatterer unless, indeed, he is implying with subtle humor that he is.

Erskine, also in spite, says that the Prince is a "cosmogony man" (alluding to the Vicar of Wakefield), for he has only two classical quotations—one from Homer and one from Virgil—which he never fails to sport when there is any opportunity of introducing them.

He has a mania for misplaced hoarding. All the coats, boots, and pantaloons of fifty years are in his wardrobe, and to the end he carries a catalogue of them all in his head and can call for any one of them at any moment. He has five hundred pocketbooks and all contain small sums of money laid by and forgotten. He has countless bundles of women's love letters, of women's gloves, of locks of women's hair.

The reverse side of the picture is dark. He is a dissolute and drunken fop, a spendthrift and gamester, "a bad son, a bad husband, a bad father, a bad subject, a bad monarch, a bad friend." His adventures affect his father more than any of the defeats of the American War. He goes to houses of prostitution, gets dead drunk, and is carried home in that condition. He is often marched off to the watchhouse. He squanders vast sums and is constantly in debt. He falls under the influence of the Duke of Cumberland and the Duc de Chartres; he is so extravagant that he spends £10,000 on his clothes in a year. His I.O.U.'s are snatched up by usurers. Yet mere want of money is never allowed to interfere with his numerous amusements. Faro at Mrs. Hobart's, cricket at Brighton, racing at Newmarket, private theatricals at Richmond, and masked balls at Wargrave engross his attention. Golden sovereigns are swept away in dice playing; others go to purchase fine coats and ruffles, or are exchanged for jewels to sparkle on the fair throats of women who flutter round him.

Still he is his mother's darling, and the Queen reads to him that paper from the *Tatler* which gives an account of a young man of good heart and sweet disposition who is allured by pleasure into a libertine life, which he pursues by habit, but with constant remorse and ceaseless shame and unhappiness. All the mother is in her voice while she reads it and her eyes glisten. But the heir apparent has neither remorse nor shame, and his conduct wears down the love of his mother.

In his bed rolling about from side to side in a state approaching nudity, he gives audience to his friends and receives information of every sort; it constitutes his throne, his cabinet, and his council chamber.

Fox says there are two ways of governing him—by bullying him and by furnishing him with money for his pleasures. He promises the Prince an income of £100,000 and payment of £30,000 on account of his debts. The King is furious. He weeps before the Duke of Portland: he confers with Lord Temple. But Fox steps in, the Prince yields, and the coalition is saved.

2.

The great gamble of Fox's venture begins early in November. For sixteen years the need has been owned of stricter parliamentary control over a close and unscrupulous corporation that administers a revenue of seven millions sterling, commands an army of sixty thousand men, and disposes of the lives and fortunes of thirty millions of their fellow creatures.

India has become the paradise of the fortune hunter. Whoever obtains a post under the company is a made man. A job with a nominal salary of £300 is worth anything up to £50,000 a year. "What is England?" asks Walpole. "A sink of Indian wealth filled by nabobs and emptied by macaronies." Some reform is inevitable and Fox introduces his East India Bill.

In Indian affairs Burke and Fox, master and pupil, are united, but they meet in an opposite spirit. Both can be violent, but Burke's is the violence of an apostle, Fox's that of a mutineer. Both are zealots, but their zeal differs in tensity. Once seized by an idea Burke seems a Dante with an infernal vision spread out before his eyes. Fox is no such idealist; he is cast in an earthy mould. But under his coarser clay heaves a volcanic sympathy that sweeps men off their feet. The two men are agreed: if the system is bad, the man is worse. Warren Hastings must be impaled. If the Crown influences East India patronage, it is a gross abuse of prerogative.

Sheridan's temper and attitude are in the middle course. He is far less abstract in outlook and not so headstrong in bearing. He believes in the purpose of the India Bill, defends it ably and vehemently and afterwards prints his arguments for its superiority to Pitt's both in detail and principle. The dramatic aspect of the problem engrosses him. He melts at the loud cry of "trampled Hindostan" and rejoices to humiliate sleek monopolists gorged with Eastern plunder. But unlike Fox he does not wish to stake his political existence on the mere form of an act of Parliament. And he has little or none of Burke's ideality. Much as he resents injustice, the comedian sees the absurdity in extremes. He is unactuated by revenge and absolutely good tempered. If Parliament checks Indian misgovernment, the mischief is over and there will be no need for the sacrifice of an exceptional governor. If, however, Parliament refuses to remedy the mischief, then Warren Hastings must be impeached. That is Sheridan's view, a view that is neither Burke's nor Fox's. While Burke soars into the clouds and Fox dives into the depths, Sheridan remains a man of the world—his wit and common sense are heartily at their service.

Under the terms of the East India Bill, Fox proposes to create a board of seven commissioners, appointed in the first instance by Parliament and later by the King, to exercise authority over government, patronage, and commerce. Unwisely the seven commissioners nominated in the Bill are all members of Fox's party.

The directors raise an indignant outcry. The Bill is a breach of chartered rights; it strikes at royal prerogative;

all public companies are said to be endangered. It provides opportunities for corruption; it gives the Whigs virtual sovereignty. Country squires shake their heads and curse the rascals. Traders scent theft and swear that Hastings' patriotic exactions pale into insignificance beside it. Pitt prophesies that if it is passed, "no public securities whatever—no public corporation—not the Bank of England—not even the Magna Charta itself—will be secure from the innovations of a ravenous coalition whose harpy jaws are gaping to swallow a patronage amounting to more than two millions of money sterling." Fox is charged with desiring to make himself King of Bengal, Emperor of the East, and by virtue of such influence a despot in the West. He is caricatured as Carlo Khan riding in Leadenhall Street on an elephant (Lord North) led by Edmund Burke.

Honest Marten in the House of Commons wishes for a starling that may din into the ears of its members, "Coalition, Coalition"—and Sheridan remarks that a marten would obviously be apter for the omen than a starling.

Outside the House: "No Grand Mogul, no India tyrant!" hoot the rabble. The freeholders of Middlesex and even of Fox's stronghold, Westminster, protest. The Bill is unjust and violent. It is treason, confiscation, unEnglish, unconstitutional. Everywhere alarm reigns and suspicion for a moment rallies the people round their monarch.

But huge majorities attend the Bill at every stage. Burke and Sheridan speak strongly for it. On the night of December 8, 1783, the supreme moment of the third reading arrives. Fox will brook no delay; the division must be taken. In vain does Major Scott (Hastings' representative) quote Desdemona's prayer (and with the more sting because Fox's complexion matches Othello's)—"Kill me not tonight, my Lord! let me live one day." In vain does Devil Wilkes stigmatise the whole as an imposture. In vain does another member urge that its voice is the voice of Jacob, but its hands are the hands of Esau. The ministers triumph. Only 102 follow Pitt into the lobby; 208 vindicate the Coalition.

Fox, heading a jubilant procession, carries the Bill up

to the Lords where it is ordered to be read a second time and printed. George III now makes a desperate attempt to reassert himself. He gives Lord Temple a paper in which it is stated that "whoever votes for the India Bill is not only not his [the King's] friend, but will be considered by him as an enemy and if these words are not strong enough, Earl Temple may use whatever words he may deem stronger and more to the point."

At Windsor George waits impatiently for the result of the division. On the morning after it occurs, he is according to custom at the early meet of the royal staghounds. But now the King's mind is distracted, and when the hounds draw off, he continues to linger behind as if momentarily expecting the arrival of important news. A horseman at full speed approaches. The letter he bears is handed to the King who eagerly tears it open. He glances at its contents, raises both arms, and cries fervently, "Thank God, it is over; the House has thrown out the Bill!" "So," he adds, "there is an end of Mr. Fox." He sends messengers to North and Fox commanding them to yield up the seals of office, as he will not receive them personally, and on the nineteenth of December he hands them to William Pitt.

The East India Bill has rung the knell of Coalition. Fox, adopting Burke's Eastern imagery, exclaims that a measure framed to emancipate thirty millions has been strangled "by an infamous string of bedchamber janissaries."

The fallen angels have still a future. All is not lost. A first minister daring to govern in the teeth of an enormous majority in the House of Commons is a case that may well inspire hope and redouble their energy. If only they can prevent the King or rather Pitt from dissolving (though this is the constitutional course), they may yet be revenged by making government impossible.

The reins are in Pitt's hands. Dandies in coffee houses and clubs chuckle over his appointment—

> A sight to make surrounding nations stare,
> A kingdom trusted to a schoolboy's care.

Fox himself goodnaturedly laughs at the news. Christmas is about two weeks off; noone expects the ministry can outlast the year. "Well," says Mrs. Crewe, "well, Mr. Pitt may do what he likes during the holidays, but depend upon it, it will only be a mince-pie administration."

Amid all these sneers Pitt goes on his way calmly. He is determined that the mince-pie administration shall last several Christmas seasons.

After the holidays the members reassemble. Pitt lacks a majority; he lacks also the aid of a single Cabinet Minister in the Commons. Friends urge him to advise a dissolution. Fox is on his legs in an instant. He questions the right of the Crown to dissolve Parliament during the business of a session. "James II did so, and thereby put an end to his reign." To this Pitt replies that he will not compromise the royal prerogative or bargain it away in the House of Commons.

A battle begins, one of many months' duration. "It is a battle," says Dr. Johnson, "between George III's sceptre and Mr. Fox's tongue." Day and night the Whig leaders assemble at Burlington House. Sheridan is now the mainstay of his party and monstrously fagged with their nightly consultations.

Party rancor mounts higher than ever. Even great ladies do not mince their words. "Damn Fox," roars the Duchess of Rutland before a full house at the opera. "Damn Pitt," rejoins Lady Maria Waldegrave, and Lady Sefton adds, "This is a great *aria* in the history of England." Surely these are elegant pastimes for a duchess who has just endowed the charity schools in commemoration of her first daughter's birth and vies with Mrs. Crewe in her fancy for Negro pages. But no partisans are more zealous than women. At this time Mrs. Tickell calls Pitt "a poor half-devil that deserves to be scouted."

In the House of Commons the proceedings are stormy. No fewer than sixteen times in the course of the next ten weeks do tellers announce to Pitt a minority. Fox puts forth all his strength to compass Pitt's resignation. To no purpose. Pitt will not dissolve. He is vilified for his youth, his subservience to the King and the trickery which worsted the Coalition. Sheridan calls him "mean and hypocritical." Lord Surrey (afterwards Duke of Norfolk) jumps up every two minutes with an aggressive motion.

Uproar of every description signalises the debates. But Pitt stands his ground and moves to bring in his own India Bill which is rejected. At one time Pitt begins to fear that the game is up, but the King is on his side urging him not to give way. "If you resign, Mr. Pitt, I must resign too."

On January 2 Fox's faithful squire, Coke of Norfolk, moves to censure the ministers. Sheridan braces himself for an effort and makes a powerful speech. Pitt has asserted that he "stood firm in the fortress of the Constitution," but where, urges Sheridan, is the constitutional fortress that is not garrisoned by the Lower House? "The present ministers are laboring to erect a fabric that may shield them against every attack, but they are erecting it on ground that is already undermined; and however strong the pillars may be, however solid and firm the buttresses, however well turned the arches, yet the foundation must be weak when the ground is undermined. Not only the building cannot stand, but the very weight of it will precipitate its fall. Secret influence is what undermined the whole; it constitutes a fourth estate in the constitution, for it does not belong to the King, it does not belong to the Lords, it does not belong to the Commons. . . . The King will have forced upon him an administration which he cannot dismiss." Then Sheridan goes on to defend Fox and attack Pitt—"a king's minion," he calls him. But despite his eloquence, the scales are already turning.

Quickly the nation rallies to the support of its sovereign. Many who have long opposed the Court now become amongst its eager champions. Addresses against the ministers pour in from Middlesex and Westminster. Fox is mobbed; Pitt is mobbed; the Opposition majority is reduced greatly. Masses of people are seen plainly to be with the new ministry. On March 1, Fox has a majority of only twelve in the House of Commons. A week later his majority sinks to a single vote. On the twenty-third Pitt is ready to dissolve.

Burke styles it "a penal dissolution." Georgiana of Devonshire announces the news to her mother with the addition that she is dressing and that "the Duke of Portland and C. Fox" are writing in her room.

The overthrow of the Whigs is complete. At the general election one hundred and sixty of the Opposition candidates (Fox's martyrs) are hewed hip and thigh. But Sheridan has the good fortune to head the poll of Stafford.

His election bill at this contest amounts to over thirteen hundred guineas. Forty pounds are spent in ale tickets, ten for coals, ten in "swearing young Burgesses." The bulk of the whole goes to the 248 Burgesses at large. Five guineas enrich the Infirmary, two rejoice "clergymen's widows," another two, other beneficiaries. Beer covers a multitude of sins and clearly prevails over benevolence—though we learn elsewhere that so much as a hundred guineas are allotted to charity.

But the great event of the year is Fox's historic Westminster election.

CHAPTER 3

THE FOX, THE LION, AND
THE ASS

1.

CHARLES JAMES FOX
Civil and Religious Liberty
The Ancient Families and the Old Nobility!
Liberty of Election!
The Duchess of Devonshire and the Ladies
and the
Freedom of the Press!
HUZZA! HUZZA! HUZZA!
God save the People.

The Duchess of D——re, canvassing for Mr. Fox, asks a
butcher for his vote. "I will give your Grace a plumper,"
says the tradesman, "and procure you five more on a certain condition." "What is that?" "That your Grace will give
me a kiss." "Why then," says Charming Georgiana, "take
one." *

Covent Garden is a veritable saturnalia. Mr. Fox and his
opponents—Lord Hood and Sir Cecil Wray—"the Fox, the
Lion, and the Ass,"—are the spectacles of the hour. For
them the theatres are thinned and the opera well nigh forsaken. Sir Cecil Wray is the would-be imposer of the maid-

---

* In the course of these paragraphs, we have only to caution our readers
that all the abuse and illiberality against the virtuous and lovely D——ss
of Dev——re are taken from an infamous paper, whose slander, however ill
meant, can never take effect with the lovers of truth and those of the
public, who know anything of the editor.

servant tax, "a bounty on bachelors," as Mr. Sheridan tells the House of Commons.

When the D——ss of D——shire is canvassing at St. Albans, as she steps out of her carriage to go into the house of a tradesman, by some accident her shoe is torn, insomuch that it is with difficulty she can keep it on her foot. In this embarrassment the beautiful politician acquits herself with great vivacity and good humor—she kicks the shoe from her and says, "I gladly serve my friends even barefooted."

(When Julius Caesar landed in Africa, as he jumped out of the vessel, he stumbled and fell to the ground. The superstitious soldiery would have been discomfited at so ominous an incident had not Caesar with great quietness turned it into a favorite prognostic. He grasped the earth and exclaimed, *Teneo te Africa*—I hold thee Africa, as if he would conquer in spite of fortune. What an excellent couple Julius Caesar and the Duch——ss of Devon——re would have formed——!)

A certain lady of great beauty and high rank requests that in the future when she condescends to favor any butcher, shoemaker, or other mechanic with a salute that he will kiss fair and not take improper liberties.

Mr. Fox in his canvass, accosting a blunt tradesman whom he solicits for his vote, the man answers, "I cannot give you my support. I admire your abilities, but damn your principles." Mr. Fox replies, "My friend, I applaud you for your sincerity, but damn your manners."

The plump Mrs. Hobart is canvassing for Sir Cecil Wray, but her charms do small execution, for Fox holds all the Queen cards in his hand. Covent Garden Market beholds its flowers eclipsed by a blaze of beauty.

A gentleman who has a vote both for Westminster and Surry being strongly solicited by a certain Duchess to vote for Fox answers, "I am very sorry, madam, but I have made an unalterable resolution neither to vote for Fox or goose."

Good velvet cushions will prevent the ladies who drive

about town on canvassing business from being too much jolted with the motion of the carriage.

Henrietta Street is now become the resort of all the fashionable reps: Perdita attends constantly and throws out Fox's colors. (Perdita seems to have lost her bloom as well as her spirits. Is the Pr—— still insensible?)

Mr. Fox, on asking a saddler in the Haymarket for his vote and interest, is shown a halter with which the latter expresses his willingness to oblige him. "I return you thanks," replies the candidate, "but I should be sorry to deprive you of it as I presume it must be a family piece."

The D—— of D——, on seducing a blacksmith's vote, wins over an Irish laborer who gives her full measure for her kiss. "My lady, your eyes are so bright, I could light me pipe at them."

> Sure Heaven approves of Fox's cause,
> (Tho' slaves at Court abhor him)
> To vote for Fox, then, who can pause,
> Since Angels canvass for him.

The Duchess of Devonsh—re yesterday canvassed the different alehouses of Westminster in favor of Mr. Fox. About one o'clock she took her share of a pot of porter at Sam House's in Wardour Street.

The three seducing Duchesses are indefatigable in their canvass which they manage in a different way. The old Dowager Duchess of Portland attacks with chit chat and voluble persuasion; the Duchess her daughter with mildness and sensible moderation; while the lovely Captivator ensnares with a glance and carries her point by majestic sweetness.

Black Reynard moves everywhere, ready with his retort and making merry over the fact that his enemies always assemble in auction rooms—Christie's in Pall Mall, Suffolk's under the Piazza, and Petterson's in King Street.

The D—— of Dev——re says, at all events, if her friend Charley should be discharged at Westminster, the only borough in her gift is at his service.

The Prince of W——s himself descends into the arena wearing the cockade of a fox's brush entwined with sprigs of laurel. He escorts the Duchess and her lovely train. He unbends to all. His friends, Captain Morris the singer, Sam House the bruiser, and Bate-Dudley, the fighting parson, diversify the proceedings.

When the Duchess of D—— alights at a tradesman's in T—— Street to solicit his vote, the man tells her Grace that her person is charming, her eyes bewitching, her mouth inviting, but as all these make no alteration in the principles or conduct of Mr. Fox, he shall adhere to his former declaration by giving his vote for Sir Cecil Wray.

It is observed of the D——ss of D—— and Lady Duncannon while they are soliciting votes in favor of Mr. Fox on Saturday that they are the most perfect pieces that ever appeared upon a canvass.

The female interest daily making for Mr. Fox only serves to expose the wretchedness of his cause, for the candidate whose sole dependence is on Ladies must be put to his Shifts.

> Say, Duchess, loveliest woman, say
>   Where is your prudence flown?
> Admitting Fox should win the day,
> His consequence will hardly pay
>   For having lost your own.

The Duch——ss of Devon——re commences her canvass at St. Martins Le Grand and concludes it in St. Margaret's parish. This is right. The sun should always rise in the East and set in the West.

Her Grace the D—— of De—— having lately discarded her black hairdresser, perhaps as the sex is fickle, she may soon discard her black patriot.

"I'll lay you five guineas," says a celebrated canvasser, "and stake the money in your own hands, that you will not vote for Mr. Fox." "Done," says the Independent Elector of Westminster, and thus one more vote is procured for the Man of the People.

While her Grace is busied in canvassing the Constituents, her domestic husband is employed in the nursery singing "Hey, my Kitten! my Kitten," and comfortably rocking the cradle.

Irish chairmen, the honest mob, are become the firm supporters of Fox and the Constitution; they are found useful in demolishing ministers and in times of election, they manage a *pole* with great spirit.

The only reason that can be assigned why the women of the town are so much on the side of the popular members is that they are in the habit of obeying the wills of their constituents.

His Grace of D——re has hurried his cara sposa into the country where it is thought she will undergo a pretty severe scrutiny.

If Mr. Fox is no longer the Man of the People, he must be allowed, from the number of females who attend to give him their support, to be at least the Man for the Ladies.

The Westminster firm is Fox, Derby, D——re, Weltjie, House & Co.

A certain beautiful lady of quality, who has for some meets past canvassed on foot for her favorite candidate, meets with such a reception as she may reasonably expect: one man offers 100 votes for one of her favors.

Mr. Sheridan is composing skits and nonsense rhymes, arranging surprises, and attending dinners at the Crown and Anchor where he proposes his favorite toast—"The Liberty of the Press."

Among the female canvassers there is none more formidable from personal charms than Mrs. Sh——dan. Her features seem to meliorate by time and to mellow into an irresistible sweetness.

Three bricklayer's laborers who live in a garret in Long Acre, having polled for a certain candidate, receive a letter of thanks, which not being able to read, they carry to their master, who by this means discovers their infamous transaction.

Considering the frequent visits the Ladies pay to Covent

Garden, it is no wonder that they catch the contagion of party spirit and are so warm in support of their favorite members.

ODE

To The D——— of Devonshire
Hail, Duchess! first of woman kind,
Far, far you leave your sex behind,
    With you none can compare;
For who but you from street to street
Wou'd run about a vote to get,
    Thrice, thrice bewitching fair!

Each day you visit every shop,
Into each house your head you pop,
    Nor do you act the prude;
For ev'ry man salutes your Grace,
Some kiss your hand, and some your face,
    And some are rather rude.

The girl condemn'd to walk the streets
And pick each blackguard up she meets,
    And get him in her clutches;
Has lost her trade—for they despise
Her wanton airs, her leering eyes—
    Now they can kiss a Duchess.

The Duchess of Devonshire retires every Sunday to Chiswick and we hope she takes the opportunity of going to church there to wipe off the transgressions of the week.

It is a miracle if all Mr. Fox's taylor bills have got receipts at the bottom of them.

It is a miracle that Lady⸱ Ar——r's complexion is as blooming and brilliant as it was twenty years ago.

A youth shouting "Fox for ever" was knocked down yesterday by a brute in the shape of a constable. An attempt was made to wreck Fox's headquarters, the Shakespeare Tavern, but in a battle the rioters were beaten off by the inmates.

UNCORKING OLD SHERRY:

It is a miracle that Mr. Sh——dan's creditors have not hanged themselves years ago.

A young man of genteel appearance and a physiognomy expressive of good humor, hilarity, and an honest heart, reels smiling into the lower boxes of Covent Garden Theatre, "hot with the Tuscan grape and high in blood." A gentleman soon afterwards appearing with Mr. Fox's favor in his hat, the disciple of Bacchus vociferates, "Fox forever!" A phlegmatic politician in the opposite interest immediately takes up the matter gravely. "Sir," says he, "do you consider the place you are in?" "Fox forever," exclaims the buck. "Sir, the audience must not be disturbed," rejoins the other. "Fox forever," is the reply. "Sir, you are intoxicated," says the grave man. "Fox forever," reiterates the buck. The grave man now begins to be irritated. "Damn me," says he, "but I wish you were at Calais." "I am half seas over, already," replies the other man. The grave man now rises with an air of the utmost self importance. "Sir," says he, "you have offended the ladies and gentlemen round me and I insist on your asking pardon." "Ladies and gentlemen round me," says the buck with a bright effusion of good humor emanating from his eyes, "if I have offended you, I ask pardon, but as for this vinegar faced curmudgeon," (looking at the grave man with ineffable contempt), "remember I make no apology to him—so Fox forever! and let me see if he will follow me out." Having said this, he withdraws, but the grave man, little expecting such a rebuff, chooses rather to stay quietly till the conclusion of the piece than to accompany his antagonist out of the House.

It is a miracle to hear the Pr—— argue against cuckoldom and fornication.

It is a miracle that L——d N——h has escaped both the axe and the halter.

Item: Mr. John Scott contesting the borough of Weobly in Herefordshire. When Mr. Scott gets to Weobly, he inquires what is the usual mode of proceeding there and is told that he is to go first to the house that contains the prettiest girl in the place and give her a kiss. This he does and then attends the hustings and addresses the constituents. "My audience liked the speech and I ended as I had begun by kissing the prettiest girl in the place—very pleasant indeed." And young Scott not unnaturally heads the poll of Weobly.

Item: From a Westminster Subscriber. "Lord, sir, it is a fine sight to see a grand lady come right smack to us hard working mortals, with a hand held out and a 'Master, how d'ye do' and a laugh so loud, and talk so kind, and shake us by the hand and say, 'Give us your vote worthy sir, a plumper for the people's friend, our friend, everybody's friend'; and then, sir, we hum and haw, they ask after our wives and families, and if that doesn't do, they think nothing of a kiss, aye, a dozen of them. Lord, sir, kissing is nothing to them and it comes all natural."

Note: When Pitt's cousin Grenville, young, genteel, and handsome, visits the poet Cowper at Olney, soliciting his interest, he kisses the ladies in the parlor, kisses likewise the maid in the kitchen, and seems on the whole a most loving, kissing, kind-hearted gentleman. And Grenville not unnaturally heads the poll for Buckinghamshire.

2.

May 14, 1784. The final poll is declared. Two members have to be returned—

Lord Hood 6694
Fox 6234
Sir Cecil Wray 5998

Shouts of triumph rend the air. Fox is chaired in a semiroyal procession led by mounted heralds, surrounded with flags and emblems and brought up by six-horsed coaches conveying their fair Graces of Devonshire and Portland. Carlton House outdoes itself in a *fête champêtre*. Nine marquees are pitched in the gardens and covers are spread in each. There are choice viands, confectionaries, and ices, strawberries, grapes, and fruit. Some of the guests watch the clowns or buffoons who have been brought to antic for their amusement. Four bands disposed at proper distances play music. His Highness and the Duchess of Devonshire are the first couple in the country dances and cotillons. It is Watteau's world come to life on an English May afternoon.

In the evening the company attends a gorgeous ball at Mrs. Crewe's. All Fox's adherents, including the Prince, appear in buff and blue. There is dancing and then the guests descend to an elegant supper. Captain Morris is placed in the chair and a general call ensues for the "Baby and Nurse"; he sings it in his very best style and the fair circle chorus with spirit. The ladies then drink his health. Upon which Captain Morris, after thanking the company, gives as a toast, "True blue and Mrs. Crewe." To which the fair hostess responds, "True blue and all of you." The toasts being drunk, Captain Morris entertains them with a continual succession of droll songs and sings them with a spirit that makes every fair eye in the room dance with delight.

At this ball Sheridan figures with éclat. Not six months ago he has done the honors of Drury Lane to Amoret who turned her chaise back from Crewe Hall on purpose to see her King Arthur. Mrs. Tickell assures her sister that they mean nothing but pure innocence and laughs at the episode. But Mrs. Sheridan writes from Delapré Abbey—"S— is in town, and so is Mrs. Crewe; *I* am in the country, and so is *Mr. Crewe;* a very convenient arrangement, is it not?"

The Westminster paeans are shortlived. It is discovered that the total number of votes is in excess of the total number of voters on the register. Wray demands a scrutiny and the high bailiff concedes it. For months the conqueror lacks his seat and has even to seek a temporary one in the Orkneys. And in this humiliating fashion then the Man of the People scrambles back to the House of Commons.

Lady Hester Stanhope, Pitt's niece, confides to her doctor. "Oh, Lord, when I think of some people who fancy that abruptness is the best way of approaching you—how horrid it is! I received one man, a sensible man too, who came into the room with 'Lady Hester, I understand you are a very good judge of a leg; you shall look at mine. See, there are muscles! They say it is an Irish chairman's, but isn't it the true antique?' Another would enter and begin— 'What a horrid bonnet Lady So & So wears. I have just seen her, and I shall never get over it.' A third would cry on seeing you—'Do you know—Lord Such a One is given over? He has tumbled down from a terrible height and is so hurt!' 'Good God! What's the matter?' 'Why, don't you know? He has tumbled from his government!' And then they fancy that wit! . . .

"A man of some note stops me just as I enter the room. 'Lady Hester,' says he, 'I am anxious to assure you of my entire devotion to Mr. Pitt.' So far he got on well. 'I had always—hem—if you—hem—I do assure you Lady Hester, I have the sincerest regard—hem—God damn me, Lady Hester, there is not a man for whom—hem—I esteem him beyond measure, and God damn me—hem,' and here the poor man who could not put two ideas together, coming to a standstill, the Duchess of Rutland, to relieve his embarrassment, helped him out by saying, 'Lady Hester is perfectly convinced of your sincere attachment to Mr. Pitt's interests.' He had a beautiful amber cane, doctor, worth a hundred guineas that he had sent for from Russia. . . .

"But look at the Princes. What a family was there! Never getting more than four hours' sleep and always so healthy and well looking. But men generally are not nowadays as they were in my time. I do not mean a Jack——— and those of his description, handsome, etc. but of no conversation. They are, however, pleasant to look at. But where will you see men like Lord Rivers, like the Duke of Dorset? Where will you find such pure honor as was in the Duke of Richmond and Lord Winchelsea? The men of the present generation are good for nothing—they have no spirit.

UNCORKING OLD SHERRY:

"And as for the women, show me such women of fashion as Lady Salisbury, the Duchess of Rutland, Lady Stafford. However, I never knew more than four fashionable women who could do the honors of their house, assign to everybody what was due to his rank, enter a room and speak to everybody and preserve their dignity and self-possession at all times. It is a very difficult thing to acquire. One was the old Duchess of Rutland, the others the Marchioness of Stafford, Lady Liverpool, and the Dowager Countess of Mansfield—all the rest of the bon ton were bosh. I have seen Lady Liverpool come into a room full of people; and she would bow to this one, speak to that one, and when you thought she must tread on the toes of a third, turn round like a tetotum and utter a few words so amiable that everybody was charmed with her. But Lady Liverpool was a Hervey and the Herveys, as I told you before, were a third part of the Creation. As for the Duchess of Devonshire it was all a 'fu, fu, fuh,' and 'what shall I do? Oh, dear me! I am quite in a fright!' and so much affectation that it could not be called high breeding. Then there were some with highly polished manners, who would pass along like oil over water, smooth and swimming about. But good breeding is very charming, doctor, isn't it?"

CHAPTER 4

THE RISING ORATOR

HENCEFORWARD in Parliament India, Ireland, and afterwards France take the place of the American War as storm centers. In the summer of 1784, the Indian question reappears in Pitt's India Bill, at first rejected, ultimately carried in triumph. The commercial monopoly and functions of the company are left intact, but its political authority is vested in a Board of Control appointed by the Crown. Fox thunders against the Bill. Burke consigns it to "the abhorrence of Europe and Asia." Sheridan shoots his arrows of sarcasm at Pitt and the Eastern Lords.

Sheridan has already captured his audience. He is emerging as a commanding orator. He has wit, irony, ridicule, fancy, epigram, and cool judgment. Besides he has feminine intuition. He pierces through things rather than dissects them. He sums up a situation lightly and earnestly— "Englishmen, it is true, have not shed their blood, but the honor of England has bled at every pore." He adds living phrases to the language. But one gift he owns which enchants his hearers. His voice, though occasionally tending to thickness, is singularly musical, vibrating to every mood. Fox barks, Burke shrieks, Pitt, always stately and imposing, speaks sometimes as if a ball of worsted were in his mouth. Sheridan has no such drawback; he sings his listeners into attention—he wins by a sort of fascination. Byron afterwards hears him only once, but he likes his voice, his manner, and his wit, and he is the only member of Parliament he ever wishes to hear at greater length.

Sheridan composes his speeches in the same manner that he does the dialogue of his plays. When he has settled the plot and the characters, he can go on with the dialogue traveling, visiting, walking, anyhow, anywhere. The Prime Minister satirizes his eloquence as "an explosion of froth and air," and Gillray the caricaturist drives the application home by his famous cartoon, "Uncorking Old Sherry."

Many of Sheridan's colleagues in Parliament surpass him in several departments of learning. The mathematical problem which Windham finds a pleasant mental exercise puzzles Sheridan as greatly as a sentence in Sanscrit; Pitt is far superior to him as a classical scholar; Fox knows more Greek than Sheridan has ever acquired, while Burke's knowledge is encyclopedic. Yet neither Pitt nor Windham, Fox nor Burke can match Sheridan in representing in dramatic shape any subject upon which he speaks.

During the debate on Pitt's India Bill, at which period John Robinson is Secretary of the Treasury, Sheridan one evening, when Fox's majorities are decreasing, says—"Mr. Speaker, this is not at all to be wondered at, when a member is employed to corrupt everybody in order to obtain votes!" Upon this there is a general outcry made by everybody in the House: "Who is it? Name him! Name him!" "Sir," says Sheridan to the Speaker, "I shall not name the person. It is an unpleasant and invidious thing to do so, and therefore I shall not name him. But don't suppose, Sir, that I abstain because there is any difficulty in naming. I could do that Sir, as soon as you could say Jack Robinson."

Pitt at first imagines that Sheridan is easy game. He sets out to crush an adversary whom he feels to be galling— "There is no man, sir, who admires more than I do the abilities of that honorable member, the elegant sallies of his mind, the pleasing effusions of his fancy, his dramatic turns, and his epigrammatic allusions. If they were only reserved for the proper stage, they would, no doubt, ensure, what his distinguished talents always have acquired, the plaudits of his audience, and it would be his recompense *sui plausu gaudere theatri*. But this place is not the proper scene for exhibiting such elegances."

Whereat Sheridan replies—"With regard to the partic-

ular species of personality which has just been introduced,
I need not comment on it. The House will have appreciated
its taste, its point, its propriety. But let me assure the person who has had recourse to it, that whenever he may think
proper to repeat such allusions, I will meet them with perfect good humor. Nay more, encouraged by the encomiums
bestowed on my talents, should I ever again engage in the
occupations to which he alludes, I may, by an act of presumption, attempt to improve on one of Ben Jonson's best
characters, the Angry Boy [slang for vapourer] in *The
Alchemist*."

2.

If there is one cause Sheridan has at heart, it is Ireland,
and he lends his eloquence in support of that unhappy
country. Ireland has her independent parliament, but English tariffs still cramp her commerce. Distress culminates
in riots, and Pitt sets himself to create fair trade for Ireland.
This is not one of his unmixed causes but an expedient to
meet an exigency. Doubtless his intentions are good, but
the manner of their execution lays itself open to double
dealing. His eleven original propositions before they are
laid on the table of the House of Commons have no fewer
than sixteen others foisted on them while the measure proceeds. The fourth proposition fetters Irish independence;
others try to use Pitt's benefits as a lever for exacting naval
and military support in times of peace. Ireland, in Sheridan's
burning words, is asked "to contend for the distraction of
fastening her own shackles. Newly escaped from harsh
trammels and severe discipline," she is now "treated like
a high mettled horse, hard to catch; and the Irish Secretary is to return to the field soothing and coaxing him with
a sieve of provender in one hand, but with a bridle in the
other, ready to slip over his head while he is snuffing at
the food."

Pitt's bounty to Ireland is not disinterested benevolence.

His inexperience betrays him while his opportunism ends in displeasing both remonstrant Ireland and the England that cherishes her birthright of trade monopoly. Not long afterwards Lord Mansfield exclaims, "Pitt is not a great minister; he is a great young minister."

On May 12, 1785, he opens the debate before a crowded House in a memorable discussion which lasts till past eight in the morning. Fox denounces the King's confidant, Jenkinson, as the prompter behind the scenes, nor does Jenkinson reply to the charge. On May 19 the discussion is renewed and the acrimony heightened. Burke lets loose his full fury. "I envy not," he says, "the statue its pedestal, nor the pedestal its statue." Fox exclaims—"My only pedestal is the British Constitution," and so on, all personality and recrimination. On May 30 Sheridan recalls the House to the real issues. He makes a telling onslaught on those clauses which in effect compel naval and military succor. Nothing is left to generosity; it is a mean bargain. All has been delusion, trick, and fallacy. "A new scheme of commercial arrangement is proposed to the Irish as a boon, and the surrender of their constitution is tacked on to it as a mercantile regulation." It is "neither more or less than a direct fraud, cheat, and robbery, stripping Ireland of all the commercial advantages she has obtained, as well as of the Constitution which secures them to her, and giving nothing in return but a right to render herself odious to this country by an attempt at rivalship which cannot be profitable to herself, though it may be mischievous to Great Britain."

The speech strikes home and circulates broadcast. It is published in Dublin in pamphlet form. From Mrs. Sheridan (then at Crewe Hill): "They tell me Sheridan has made the best speech on the Irish business . . . that ever was heard—I hear nothing but his praises which (between you and I) I have great pleasure in, tho' he is my husband." When Pitt's proposals suddenly collapse next August in the Irish Parliament, an eyewitness of the scene raises his paean to Sheridan—"I wish you joy a thousand times. We have the effects of a complete victory." Sheridan is regarded as the Bill's destroyer in the House of Commons.

Pitt, observes a contemporary, is a very discreet man and is right nine times out of ten where Fox is wrong. But that once where Fox is right is worth all the other times put together. The Irish Bill is one in point. Throughout the debate Pitt speaks with a hesitating air and a faltering voice. His thoughts are as uncertain, for with Pitt eloquence promotes thought. Sheridan once says of him, "His is a brain that never works but when his tongue is set going, like some machines that are set in motion by a pendulum."

Sheridan speaks often during 1785. He speaks on the servant maid tax (*"not* an Irish proposition"); he speaks several times on general taxation; he also speaks on a motion by Pitt for an inquiry into some of the public office accounts. In this matter he takes a characteristic course. Fox thunders against the inquisition as unconstitutional; Burke brands it as "a direct violation of Magna Charta." Sheridan, recoiling from extremes, contents himself with calling it unnecessary. In a debate on the partial repeal of excise duties on cotton stuffs he has occasion to allude to *The Rolliad,* a political satire issued by the Opposition.

The Rolliad makes its first appearance early in 1785 and runs to twenty-two editions. It is a mélange of pasquinades in prose and verse, pointed, humorous, polished, dealing with every Foxite grievance and every Pittite foible. Its satire emanates from the Foxites who meet over their flowing bowls in the parlor of Becket the bookseller and its source is the "smoking and spitting party" formed by Rolle in the House of Commons to annoy and interrupt by coughing, hawking, and other unseemly noises the speeches of Mr. Burke. The confederates in *The Rolliad* are numerous: Richard Fitzpatrick and George Ellis, Dr. Lawrence, fat and heavy outside ("he takes possession of the room") but within sparkling and irrepressible, Lawrence the polyglot, for he writes in Latin, Greek, French, and Italian—lean

UNCORKING OLD SHERRY:

Isaac Reid with his green room flavor and nasal twang, Bate-Dudley, the writing and fighting parson, Tickell ambitious to shine, and John Townshend repeating his last *jeu d'esprit*. And then there is Joseph Richardson who shadows Sheridan and whose gaucheries are beyond calculation.

To Sheridan, whom he resembles in countenance, Richardson becomes indispensable, smoothing conjugal troubles, assisting him in every department, and rarely absent from the table in Bruton Street. He loves nothing so much as disputation. "Tell Richardson where you dined yesterday, and he would immediately inquire, 'Had you a good day? *Was there much argument?*'"

Sheridan often takes Richardson down with him on visits to his place at Bognor. On one particular occasion Richardson sets his mind on going down to Bognor with Sheridan because it happens that Lord Thurlow with whom he is on terms of intimacy is there. "So," says Richardson, "nothing can be more delightful, what with my favoriate diversion of sailing—my enjoyment of walking on the sands—the pleasure of arguing with Lord Thurlow, and taking my snuff by the seaside, I shall be in my glory."

"Well," says Sheridan to Michael Kelly, "down he went full of anticipated joys. The first day, in stepping into the boat to go sailing, he tumbled down and sprained his ankle and was obliged to be carried into his lodgings, which had no view of the sea. The following morning he sent for a barber to shave him, but there being no professional shaver nearer than Chichester, he was forced to put up with a fisherman who volunteered to officiate and cut him severely just under his nose, which entirely prevented his taking snuff; and the same day at breakfast, eating prawns too hastily, he swallowed the head of one, horns and all, which stuck in his throat and produced such pain and inflammation that his medical advisers would not allow him to speak for three days. So thus," says Sheridan, "ended in four and twenty hours his walking—his sailing—his snuff-taking—and his arguments."

CHAPTER 5

SANCTUARIES AND RESORTS

THE OPPOSITION LEADERS against Pitt certainly are the spoiled darlings of great houses. Three palaces lie open to them. Devonshire House, the rallying point of wit and beauty; Burlington House with its Italian galleries; and Carlton House, the Prince's plaything. Carlton House has been the abode of Frederick, the Prince's grandfather. When he is given the place as a residence, he finds it in a dilapidated condition and calls in Holland the architect to do it over. Holland adds Ionic screens, Corinthian porticoes and a row of pillars which serves no particular purpose—

> dear little columns all in a row,
> what do you there?—Indeed we don't know.

It has a fine entrance hall and a grand staircase with gilded railings leading to well lighted state apartments. But externally there is little to recommend the building. It is one of the meanest edifices that disfigure London. Canova calls it an ugly barn.

On March 10, 1784, the House, refurnished and redecorated, is opened with a ball, and this is followed a month later by a breakfast to six hundred people. It is the unofficial headquarters of the Whig party.

Devonshire House also is Whig, but those who bow to the charm of its mistress are strangely varied in temperament, politics, and disposition. Some, despite their genius, are wearisome in society. Burke's presence is more coveted than enjoyed. Doctor Johnson does not appear to best advantage in the Piccadilly salons. But he is by no means insensible to the tangible advantages of being admitted into so select a circle. When Mrs. Thrale praises Garrick's song in *Florizel and Perdita,* dwelling with peculiar pleasure upon the line—"I'd smile with the simple and feed with the poor," Dr. Johnson replies, "Nay, my dear lady, this will never do. Poor David! Smile with the simple!—What folly is that? And who would feed with the poor that can help it? No, no, let me smile with the wise and feed with the rich."

Then there is the Strawberry Hill Coterie formed of men who have passed the first flush of youth. Most of them are striving to live up to their reputations. It is as easy to gain a reputation for wit as for wickedness, but the first is far more difficult to sustain. Horace Walpole, who is ever ready to sacrifice friendship to an epigram, is the leader of this small companionship. His allegiance to the Duchess is not wholehearted and the "Empress of fashion" is always at the mercy of his destructive criticism. George Selwyn also is welcome although it is never definitely settled whether he is to be classed among the wits or humorists. He too has a bitter tongue.

Then there are Charles Fox and the men about town who follow Charles Fox—Colonel Fitzpatrick, soldier, politician, poet, James Hare—the "Hare of many friends"—whose bow at the opera is a more valued distinction than an invitation from the Prince of Wales, the Earl of Carlisle, the most finished macaroni of his time, and Charles Grey, handsome and distinguished, a rising statesman and the Duchess's darling. (Her affection is returned. He has a daughter by her). And of course there is Sheridan. At Devonshire House he meets the Prince and strikes up a fatal friendship. George the unsaintly lacks a heart; Sheridan's fancy supplies the void.

Another gathering place for the Whigs is Brooks's Club. Dinner is served at half past four, and the bill is brought in at seven. Supper begins at eleven and ends at half an hour after midnight. There is no gaming in the eating room except the tossing up for reckonings. Brooks himself is a most accommodating manager. Tickell describes him—

> Liberal Brooks whose speculative skill
> Is hasty credit and a distant bill;
> Who, nursed in clubs, disdains a vulgar trade,
> Exults to trust and blushes to be paid.

In consequence of the above mentioned diffidence he dies a poor man.

Party feeling runs so high at Brooks's that when George III becomes insane, it is the custom for card players to cry—"I play the lunatic" instead of "I play the King." The Club later acquires a very staid reputation so that it is said that "dining at Brooks's is like dining in a Duke's house with the Duke lying dead upstairs."

At Brooks's one day the Prince is expatiating on the far fetched idea of Dr. Darwin's that the reason the bosom of a beautiful woman is the object of such exquisite delight for a man to look upon arises from the first pleasurable sensations of warmth, sustenance, and repose which he derives therefrom in his infancy. Sheridan replies, "Truly hath it been said that there is only one step from the sublime to the ridiculous. Consider those children who are brought up by hand. I believe noone heard of any such when they arrived at manhood evincing any very rapturous or amatory emotions at the sight of a wooden spoon."

The conversation turns upon the projected tax upon iron. One member says that as there is so much opposition to it, it would be better to raise the proposed sum upon coals. "Hold! my dear fellow," says Sheridan, "that would be out of the frying pan into the fire with a vengeance."

2.

In 1784 the Prince rents Brighton Pavilion. He changes the pleasant seaside resort into a semi-oriental palace. Something of the building is Grecian and something Gothic, but the central dome is Turkish; the pinnacles are Moorish, if anything; one part seems to be Egyptian, another Chinese, and another to be reminiscent of Hindustan. It is a nondescript monster. It appears like a mad house or a house run mad, as it has neither beginning, middle, nor end. The alterations of the Pavilion never cease. There is a China gallery, a music room with gorgeous frescoes and green and golden dragons, a yellow drawing room with oriental colonnades, a saloon or rotunda, and above all a banqueting room with a domed ceiling representing an Eastern sky.

On the other hand there are balconies and verandahs so as to admit the air and exclude the heat and a view of the sea obtained from almost every window. (But in the hall the Prince places a patent stove designed to impart an even heat throughout the building. As a result, though the temperature of the upper rooms is pleasantly warm, those on the ground floor are as hot as an oven, and Sheridan and other guests sit sweltering and sweating around the dinner table.)

The Prince builds his mistress's house close to the Pavilion on the Steyne and is often to be seen upon her balcony, especially of an early morning. (How he gets there is a mystery to many.) He will sit there talking to her by the hour; sometimes he will honor by a bow or a smile some one of his acquaintances passing on the Steyne below.

His own rooms are on the ground floor and he has sliding screens put up round his bed in which are mirrors so arranged that they reflect the promenade on the Steyne. Here on the shining surface of the mirrors he can see as he lies at ease on his pillows little figures hurrying towards him, figures that continually walk and yet never reach him, but walk on into nothing, unconscious all the while of this recumbent Gulliver watching the human menagerie.

The Prince rides on the downs, attends the races, walks on the Steyne unattended, drinks tea with the rest of the company at the Public Rooms. Sometimes there will be the clown Grimaldi to see or some new play. Often in the haze of a summer afternoon there arises from the Pavilion the wooden crack of bat against ball, for one of the Prince's favorite amusements at Brighton is playing cricket. He is not much good at the game, but he enjoys it immensely. He is thought to look particularly well in his white beaver hat, flannel coat edged with blue ribbon, white jean trousers, and highly polished shoes. After hitting about in an inexpert manner, the Prince and his fellow cricketers pleasantly conclude the day by dining in a marquee put up on the lawn.

Occasionally the Prince engages a bathing machine, and "Smoaker," his dipper, keeps a strict watch on him. Once when the Prince ventures further that Smoaker considers prudent, he shouts, "Mr. Prince, Mr. Prince, come back." Finding himself disobeyed, he dashes in after him, and drags him by the ear into shore. "I arn't ago'en to let the King hang me," he grumbles, "for letten the Prince of Wales drown hisself, not I, to please nobody, I can tell 'e."

In old age it is Smoaker who when asked by two exquisites from London where they can obtain asses' milk for their health, advises them, in reply, to suck each other.

Besides Burke, Fox, Sheridan, there come frequently to the Pavilion such convivial spirits as George Hanger, the Duke of Norfolk, Captain Morris, and the Barrymores.

Duke "Jockey" Norfolk is a great drinker and an enormous eater, and a man so dirty and slovenly that his servants are used to take advantage of the times when he is drunk to wash him. So notorious is this fact that a friend from whom the Duke demands a cure for rheumatism, makes the inconsequent reply, "Pray, my Lord, did you ever try a clean shirt?"

The Duke prefers to dine in cheap taverns and consume his chop and porter in the company of professional men who treat him with patronizing familiarity, little knowing that this grossly fat, uncleanly old man in a threadbare suit is the first peer of the realm. "I am not, at best, much of a beau, perhaps too regardless of my costume," he remarks to a friend, which sometimes subjects him to little inconveniences. Walking into a cockpit where they are fighting a match, and desirous of doing as the others do, he offers to bet upon one of the birds. But not being so well attired as the company, no one heeds him. Presently, however, a smart young fellow (a gentleman) with a generous spirit which the Duke cannot but admire calls out, "Come, my honest butcher, I will take your bet."

Plain boiled fish and grilled steaks are the Duke's favorite dishes—and still more to his taste—wine—streams and cascades of wine. The Duke possesses a remarkable capacity for liquor. He will drink everyone else under the table and then move on to finish the evening elsewhere. Until suddenly he becomes speechless in his chair, he never betrays any sign of intoxication. Then he signals a servant who rings the bell three times. Four footmen immediately answer it, bearing a kind of stretcher. In absolute silence and with long practised dexterity, they lift him on to it and with gentle and swinging motion remove his enormous bulk from the room.

In the number of his illegitimate children the Duke rivals Charles II—in their variety he far excels him. By the time he is an elderly man, the number of women he supports has swelled to an army. The money is distributed to them in the form of checks, all of them payable on the same day and time, at the same bank. And brown eyes and Jewish noses alternate with blue eyes, Gypsy skins, and woolly black hair as the mothers with their infants or stalwart children bustle in to be paid. Meanwhile the Duke sits with a friend in the back parlor where he can observe each pensioner through a glass partition without being himself visible. "What a dowdy!—What an old hag!" is his running commentary. Or. "I' faith, she looks as young as twenty years ago!"

Whenever the Duke comes to Brighton, his appearance is the signal for an orgy. On one of these occasions he quarrels (he is always quarrelsome in his cups) with the Royal brothers over some imaginary slight and orders his carriage to drive him back to Arundel. The Prince is determined he shall not go, but it is useless to argue with him in his present condition. When the coach comes round, the Prince escorts the Duke to the door and privately orders the coachman to drive for half an hour round the Pavilion grounds. The Duke is so drunk that he does not know whither he is going; he falls asleep in the coach and when it stops he thinks he is at the end of his journey. He is carried back into the Pavilion and put to bed.

Charles Morris, the bard of the group, is wont to sing songs of his own composition which are sometimes tender, sometimes convivial, always clever. He is born of a good family, moves in the best society, and is persona grata at Carlton House. He trips mirthfully along down the hill of life without languor or gout or any of the dues exacted by Time for the mournful privilege of living. His face is always resplendent with cheerfulness. "Die when you will, Charles" says Curran to him, "you will die in your youth."

The third member, George Hanger, is a good auld Irish gentleman, and many are the stories told of his wild youth. He joins a band of gypsies, falls in love with one of the girls, and marries her according to the rites of her tribe. Proud of his conquest he introduces the bride to his brother officers and is much disgusted when the beautiful dark-eyed creature elopes with a tinker. On the death of his brother he becomes the fourth Lord Coleraine, a title which, however, he never assumes. When an acquaintance once addresses him, "I hope I have the honor to see your Lordship in perfect health," his lordship angrily replies, "What do you mean, you scoundrel, by calling a man a name he is ashamed of? Whether Lord Coleraine be up there" (pointing to the skies) "or down there" pointing in the opposite direction), "I know not, or care not; but I am, as I always was, plain George Hanger.

Hanger makes his first appearance at Court on the occasion of a ball in celebration of the Queen's birthday. Having fought in America in the Landgrave of Hesse-Cassel's Jager corps, he wears the uniform of a Major in the Hessian service—a short blue coat with gold frogs, with a very broad belt and sword—which being in marked contrast to the full trimmed suits of velvet and satin of the others, attracts much attention, and inquiries as to his identity are made throughout the assembly. When he leads out the beautiful Miss Gunning to dance a minuet and on the first crossing of his lovely partner, puts on his hat, which is of the largest Kevenhuller kind, ornamented with two large black and white feathers, the figure which he cuts is so truly ridiculous that even the gravity of his Majesty cannot be restrained. The grave faces of his ministers relax into smiles and the Prince of Wales is actually thrown into a convulsive fit of laughter. Even his fair partner can scarcely finish the minuet, but Hanger himself joins in the laugh which is raised at his expense and thereby extricates his partner from her embarrassment.

The absurdity of his antics in the minuet and afterwards in a country dance forms the mirth provoking subject of the Court, and it is resolved to play a joke upon him. To this end the Prince indites a mocking letter which is copied by Sheridan with whose handwriting the Major is not acquainted.

On the next day Hanger is asked to dine with the Prince to which repast Sheridan is not invited. The Prince with great gravity compliments Hanger on his appearance at the ball, and Hanger, completely deceived, shows the anonymous letter he has received. When his host agrees with him that it can only be intended as an insult, "Blitz und Holle," cries the Major, "If I could discover the writer, he should give me immediate satisfaction."

"I admire your spirit," says the Prince. "How insulting to talk of your grotesque figure!"

"And then to turn your stately, erect, and perpendicular figure into ridicule!" Fox assents.

"And to talk of your gesticulations!" remarks Captain Morris.

In the end the Major is told that the handwriting is Sheridan's and a duel is arranged. At the third fire Sheridan falls. "Killed, by God," says Captain Morris. "Let us fly instantly."

At dinner that night to Hanger's great relief Sheridan appears. "How? how? how is this?" he stammers. "I thought I had killed you."

"Not quite, my good fellow," says Sheridan, "I am not good enough to go to the world above—and as to that below, I am not yet fully qualified for it. Therefore I considered it better to defer my departure from this to a future period—but I die well, Hanger, did I not?" The duel was fought without bullets.

When Hanger is in good form, he and the Prince race country girls on the Steyne for the prize of a new smock or go out shooting together at the chimney pots of their neighbors' houses.

But life at Brighton lacks lustre and is humdrum without the amiable Barrymores. The eldest brother, remember, is known as Hellgate, the second, clubfooted from birth, as Cripplegate, and the youngest as Newgate after the one prison he has never entered. There also exists an elder sister known as Billingsgate. The Barrymores are irresponsible children, rowdy and diabolically clever. Left without parents at an early age they remain the same naughty little boys who went out one night, armed with hammers, hatchets, and ladders, to change the signboards of the inns for miles round their home. Thus one of Lord B's pastimes after reaching manhood is to drive out at night in a very high phaeton through the narrowest streets he can find, laying about him with his whip and cracking or breaking the windows as he passes. This he calls "fanning the daylight."

Lord B. finds himself equipped with a large fortune for squandering. Everything about him is carried out regardless of cost. "Damn the expense" continues to the end his favorite expression. He enjoys nothing so much as a scrap with his fists. He retains Tom Hooper, one of the finest pugilists of the time, in his service as footman and sparring partner and they go out together in disguise at night, picking quarrels with strangers for sheer love of a row. On one occasion he turns Brighton promenade into a ring. He picks a quarrel with a young Fox, whose father manages the Brighton theatre, and is getting the worst of it, when the Prince, who is refereeing the bout in front of a mob of spectators, shouts, "Damn me, Barrymore, behave like a man."

Lord B's second brother, Henry, and a Mr. Howarth, M.P., quarrel over a game of whist at the Castle Tavern. They agree to meet on the Steyne at 5 A.M. the same morning to settle their differences with pistols. Mr. Howarth, stout and elderly, proceeds with perfect solemnity to take off his clothes and to face his adversary clad only in his drawers. He has been a surgeon, he explains, in the East India Company and has there learned by experience the importance of keeping wounds clean. Happily the affair ends in laughter and random shots.

Even the Prince's mistress is not spared by the B's. Henry is inspired to ride a horse up the staircase of her residence. He reaches the top floor, but once there nothing can induce the animal to come down. Finally a couple of blacksmiths have to be sent for.

Lady Haggerstone often comes to stay with her sister, George's mistress. A pretty woman but just a little silly by nature. Once, for example, she invites the Prince to a fête champêtre in her garden. To complete the picture she hires three Alderneys. As the Prince arrives with his friends, her ladyship darts out from a side wicket dressed as a milkmaid with the charming intention of making him a syllabub—one of his favorite dishes. She has a silver pail in one hand and an ornamental stool in the other. Lady H trips along with ribbons flying from her dainty little milking hat and the smallest little apron tied below her laced stomacher, till she comes opposite his Royal Highness to whom she makes a graceful rural curtsey. Then passing lightly over the plaited straw and tucking up her gown (to show her pretty little ankles) she places her stool and pail conveniently for use. Leaning against the flank of one of the crossest of Alderneys, she attempts to commence her rustic labors. But not having selected the right sex, the offended animal does not fancy such masquerade, for he first kicks out and then trots away, nearly upsetting the stool, the pail, and Lady Haggerstone, who then covered with confusion makes a hasty retreat back into her little dairy and is too shamefaced to reappear.

The Prince without moving a muscle praises the neatness of the farmyard in an audible voice, looks up at the sky and remarks on the fineness of the weather, and then makes his way to his carriage.

Fox the Brighton manager is another very odd character. He is a kind of Caleb Quotem in real life—can combine twenty occupations without being clever in one. He is actor, fiddler, painter, machinist, and tailor, besides check-taker and bill-sticker on occasions. He prides himself more especially on his talent as a painter. He executes all his own scenery. Sheridan is down at Brighton one summer and Fox, desirous of showing him some civility, takes him all over the theatre and exhibits its beauties. "There, Mr. Sheridan," says he, "I constructed this stage—I built and painted those boxes and painted all these scenes." "Did you" says Sheridan, surveying them rapidly. "Well, I should not have known you were a Fox by your brush."

The Prince and his intimates take to hobnobbing with a low set of friends. Lord Thurlow in his old age expresses his opinion of the curious assortment. The Prince meets him in Brighton and asks him why he has not been in to see him. "I cannot do so," Lord Thurlow replies, "until your Royal Highness keeps better company." Once when Lord Thurlow is invited to the Pavilion, Sir John Lade (whom Thrale thought of marrying to Fanny Burney) turns up unexpectedly from London and the Prince feels obliged to include him among the guests. So he leads Lord Thurlow aside and apologizes tactfully, explaining at the same time that Sir John is an old friend. "I have no objection to Sir John Lade in his proper place," growls out the old lawyer, "but that I take to be your Royal Highness's coach box and not your table." When Thurlow is laid up with gout in his house on the cliff and the Prince offers to visit him, the Chancellor delivers his most severe rebuke: "Say to his Royal Highness that I shall be honored by a visit, but he must leave his scum behind."

There is, for instance, Lady Lade who has been the mistress of "Sixteen String Jack" whom she has seen hanged at Tyburn. From him she learned her extensive vocabulary. So that the Prince says of anyone usually foulmouthed: "He swears like Lady Lade." The Prince is never attracted by her, but he admires her horsemanship.

Then there is MacMahon, the illegitimate son of a butler and a chambermaid who has permitted his wife to accept the attentions of the Duke of Clarence and in return has risen in the world. He is a short man with a red pimply face and dresses in the Prince's buff and blue uniform. . . . And there are others—amusing but disreputable.

Society at Brighton consists chiefly of opulent merchants, needy fortune hunters, broken down Cyprians, fishermen's daughters, and several fat city dowdies from the environs of Norton Folgate. The officers of the Blues are the great dashers of the place; they associate with no one but their own corps. Most of them keep their blood horses, their curricles, and their girls. At one o'clock they appear on the parade to hear the word of command given to the Subaltern Guard; afterwards they toss off their goes of brandy; dine about five and come about eight to the theatre—*Vivent L'Amour et Bacchus.*

There are two taverns in Brighton, namely the Castle and the Old Ship where the rich visitors resort, and at each of these houses a weekly assembly is held where a master of the ceremonies arranges the parties, not according to the scale of morality, but to that of aristocracy. There are card assemblies, there is a hotel or grand dormitory intended for a country Hummums, there is a theatre, there is a sort of Vauxhall called Promenade Grove, befringed with a few gawky poplars and decorated with flowers, bowers, zigzag alleys, a ditch, and a wooden box for the minstrels. The coast is like the greater part of its visitors—bold, saucy, intrusive, and dangerous. The bathing machines even for the ladies have no awning as at Weymouth, Margate, and Scarborough. Consequently they are severely inspected by the aid of telescopes, not only as the ladies ascend from the sea, but as they kick and sprawl and flounder about its muddy margin, like so many mad Naiads in flannel smocks. There is a Subscription House or Temple of Fortune on the Steyne where the minor part of our blessed nobility are accustomed to reduce their character and their estates at the same time. The signal for admission is *habeo,* for rejection, *debeo.* There are lodgings of all descriptions and fitness, from £20 per week on the Cliffs to half a crown per night in a stable—the keepers of the lodging houses, like the keepers of madhouses, having but one common point in view—to bleed the parties sufficiently. There are carriages and caravans of all shapes and dimensions, from a wagon to a fish cart, in which you may move like a king, a criminal, or a crab—that is, forwards, backwards, or laterally. There are two libraries on the Steyne replete with every flimsy species of novel. There is a parish church, where the canaille go to pray, but as this is on a hill and the gentry find their Sabbath visit to the Almighty very troublesome, the amiable and accommodating master priest consigns the care of his common parish mutton to his journeyman, the curate, and kindly raises a Chapel Royal for the lambs of fashion, where a certain sum is paid for every seat. And this, it must be admitted, is as it should be, as a well bred Deity will assuredly be more attentive to a reclining Duchess, "parrying" the assaults of the devil, behind her fan, than the vulgar piety of a plebeian on his knees. There are books open in the circulating libraries where you are requested to contribute your mite of charity to the support of the rector, as his income is somewhat less than £700 a year; the last incumbent died worth £30,000.

Morning rides, champagne, dissipation, noise and nonsense—jumble the phrases together and you have a complete account of all that passes at Brighthelmstone.

CHAPTER 6

FLORIZEL'S FOLLY:
THE SWEET LASS OF
RICHMOND HILL

A BEAUTIFUL WOMAN excites a violent
passion in the Prince. When in the spring of 1784 Mrs. Fitzherbert puts aside her widow's weeds and goes to London
for the season, a new constellation makes its appearance in
the firmament: golden hair—unpowdered—unrouged cheeks,
lustrous eyes, a sunny smile. Her profile is exquisite, and the
curves of her beautiful figure are not yet marred by being
too round. The Prince succumbs quickly.

After their meeting he takes care not to lose sight of
her again. He eagerly seeks her society and finds her not
only beautiful but gifted and sensible. He makes opportunities of meeting her, he follows her everywhere, he is
always at her side, and his attentions to her are so marked
that before long they become the most engrossing topic of
conversation.

She insists on regarding the gay and graceful badinage
between them as nothing more than the amusement of a
passing hour. She trusts to her good sense to keep his devotion within due limits, but the Prince does not recognise
any limits where his passions are concerned. He seeks to
obtain her on those terms which a man of his rank would
propose to a woman of her condition. But Mrs. Fitzherbert
is a woman of spirit and virtue, and she spurns the dis-
honoring advances of the first prince of the blood. Amazed
by a resistance so unusual, if not unprecedented, and unac-
customed to be denied or to deny himself, His Royal Highness grows more impetuous and more fervid, and opposition

and evasion only serve to make him keener. She cannot parry an attack so ardent and so prolonged. She becomes alarmed and strives to break off the acquaintance, but the Prince is not to be baffled. The more she opposes him, the more persistent his attentions become. Whatever she does only serves to increase his ardor.

To all these demonstrations she is insensible. She is not obstinate, but her terms are of the highest—marriage or nothing at all. Yet the difficulties in the way of a legal union seem insuperable. Mrs. Fitzherbert is a Roman Catholic, and by the Act of Settlement a successor who weds a Papist forfeits its Crown. And by the Royal Marriage Act (designed "to encourage Fornication and Adultery in the descendants of George the Second") the union of a Prince under the age of twenty-five without parental consent is null and void. True the Duke of Gloucester has married a lady beneath him in the social scale, but the cases are not parallel. The Duke of Gloucester was not the heir apparent, the Royal Marriage Act was not then in existence, and his wife was a member of the Church of England.

Marriage and an irregular union being equally out of the question, Mrs. Fitzherbert, after a touching interview with the Prince, refuses to see him again or answer his letters. The Prince is in despair. He testifies to the sincerity and violence of his passion by rolling on the floor, striking his forehead, tearing his hair, falling into hysterics and swearing that he will abandon the country, forego the Crown, sell his jewels, and scrape together enough money to fly with the object of his affections to America.

Rumors of her going abroad reach the Prince's ears, and he stabs himself. (Perhaps he has been blooded by his physician Keate to relieve the violence of his passion and has dabbled blood about his clothes to make himself more interesting in the eyes of his beloved.) But Maria goes.

The Prince is at his wits' end—he would follow her but does not know where she has gone. For a moment he determines to go to the Hague. He cries by the hour. At last in desperation he sets himself to discover her hiding place.

In this he is more successful. He despatches emissaries far and wide and soon discovers where she is concealed. (His messengers set up such a clatter along the French roads that three of them are arrested on suspicion that some political plot is afoot.) Having once found her, he has her shadowed wherever she goes. Then he begins a ceaseless correspondence. He writes to her pages and pages of passionate pleadings, of heart-rending appeals, of prayers for her aid, of threats, of self-destruction if she remains obdurate—of everything, in short, that can touch or move the heart of a susceptible woman. (One letter runs to thirty-seven pages.) Whether she moves from Paris to Switzerland or from Switzerland to Lorraine, she is still followed by the Prince's emissaries and by his letters.

Mrs. Fitzherbert hesitates, and hesitating is lost. She believes implicitly all he tells her, all his promises, all his vows. She can no longer doubt the sincerity of his love. He has answers for all her objections, he grants all her stipulations, he is willing to risk everything for her sake. And so, at last, worn out with his pleading and moved by his devotion, she throws down her arms and promises to return to England and become his wife. Once she surrenders she knows no half means. Beyond the one condition demanded by her conscience and her church, she leaves everything else to the honor of the man to whom she is henceforth to devote her life.

Her motives are not interested. Perhaps she persuades herself that she must make the sacrifice for his sake. Perhaps she deludes herself that she is necessary to him. Perhaps she conceives it her mission to rescue him from evil advisers and make him worthy of the position which one day he is destined to fill. But the simplest explanation seems the truest. She yields because she loves him.

Rumors of the intended marriage get about, and Fox in a long and respectful letter urges its extreme danger. It would be dangerous to the Prince, dangerous to Mrs. Fitzherbert, dangerous to the nation itself. (Fox prefers to see Mrs. Fitzherbert the royal mistress and scouts all notion of the royal bride. He is cynical in his attitude to most women except his future wife.) The Prince answers in a few lines, "Make yourself easy, my dear friend. Believe me, the world will now soon be convinced that there not only is but never was any grounds for these reports which of late have been so malevolently circulated," and he turns abruptly from the subject. This letter is written on December 11, 1785. Just four days later the Prince is married.

Mrs. Fitzherbert has a beautiful skin. At sixty it is like a child's of six years old. She has a great deal of tact in concealing the Prince's faults. She will say, "Don't send your letter to such a person—he is careless and will lose it," or when he is talking foolish things, she will tell him, "You are drunk, tonight; do hold your tongue."

At the trial of Warren Hastings, Mrs. Fitzherbert, then in full bloom of womanly beauty, attracts more attention than the Queen or the Princesses. She is the only woman to whom George is ever sincerely attached. He inquires for her in his last illness, and he dies with her portrait round his neck.

His passion satisfied, the Prince once more seeks amusement in an endless round of routs and masquerades, boxing matches, horse races, and drinking bouts. He lavishes vast sums on the alterations and decorations of Carlton House. He spends £30,000 on his stud. By the end of the year he is £160,000 in debt. He appeals to the King for aid and talks of living incognito on the continent in order to retrench. The King refuses either to help him or to allow him to travel. With every month he becomes more and more embarrassed. He is willing to be the pensioner of the dissolute Duke of Orleans on degrading terms, but Sheridan dissuades him from this step. He appeals to the ministry for a Parliamentary vote of £250,000, breaks up his establishment, shuts up part of Carlton House, and sells his horses and carriages at auction. He lives in borrowed houses, travels in borrowed chaises, squanders borrowed guineas. At length he throws himself on the mercy of the House of

Commons, and Mr. Alderman Newnham gives notice on April 20, 1787 that he proposes to bring forward a motion to rescue the Prince of Wales from his present embarrassed and distressed condition.

When the matter comes up, Rolle, rough and rustic, hears rumors of the Prince's marriage and throws a bombshell into the ranks of both sides by threatening an inquiry into the question. Sheridan rises, wishing to stave off any declaration that the Prince has wedded a Catholic: the Gordon riots may be renewed. Pitt is driven to back out. That night Sheridan repairs to Carlton House where his distracted master answers, "Pooh! Nonsense! Ridiculous!"

Meanwhile a treaty is in course between Pitt and the Prince's friends. It is hoped the King will relent. Fox receives the lover's laughing denial of his marriage, and Sheridan visits Mrs. Fitzherbert and tells her that Parliament will exact some explanation of her footing with the Prince. Sheridan reassures her: a denial in general terms will satisfy both the public and the prevaricators.

But on the evening of April 30, Fox is hurried into indiscretion and overshoots his mark. "Speaking from *the immediate authority* of the Prince of Wales," he is ready to assure his Majesty and his Majesty's ministers "of the utter falsehood of the fact in question, which never had, and common sense could see, never *could* have happened."

But Rolle goes behind all sophistry and stands his ground. Though the marriage could not have taken place legally, it still might have been solemnized without the sanction of law. Fox (perhaps with three bottles in him) once more starts to his feet and outdoes himself. He denies the calumny in question, "in toto, in point of fact as well as law." Fox exceeds his commission by this absolute denial, and George is extremely perturbed.

The next morning the Prince breaks the news to his friend quite airily, and clasping her hands exclaims, "Only conceive, Maria, what Fox did yesterday. He went down to the House and denied that you and I were man and wife. Did you ever hear of such a thing?" Maria is silent and turns pale. All England, every print shop, will parade the slander. Her name has been tarnished. She threatens to quit the Prince unless her character is vindicated, and she is indignant with Fox for besmirching her character. She has never liked Fox, and naturally her dislike now approaches to hatred. She vows she will never speak to him again, and when Sir Philip Francis endeavors to effect a reconciliation, he finds his efforts in vain. She says that by his unauthorized declaration in the House of Commons, Fox has rolled her in the kennel like a street walker.

The Prince sends for Grey, who finds him tremendously agitated and pacing in a hurried manner up and down the room. He at once explains his object in sending for Grey. It is to induce him to frame some sort of explanation for Fox's denial of the marriage—to modify in some way the terms of the denial so that Mrs. Fitzherbert may be pacified. "Charles certainly went too far last night," he says. "You, my dear Grey, shall explain it." Grey observes that Fox must unquestionably have supposed that he had authority for all he said and that if there was any mistake, it could only be rectified by his Royal Highness speaking to Fox himself and setting him right on matters. But to discuss the matter with Fox is the last thing the Prince desires. Grey knows this and like most of the Prince's friends delights at the public denial of the marriage whether it be true or untrue. He tells the Prince how prejudicial a continuance of the discussion must be to him, and positively refuses to do what he wishes. This refusal "chagrins, disappoints, and agitates" the Prince. He terminates the interview abruptly and throwing himself on the sofa mutters, "Well, if nobody else will, Sheridan must." The Prince never forgives Grey for his refusal, and there exists a coolness between them.

Possibly to forget the stress of mind from which he is suffering over this affair, at a ball given in Albermarle Street by Lady Hopetoun, the Prince arrives stupefied with drink. At first he is fairly quiet sitting "pale as ashes," but at supper a bottle and a half of champagne rouses him, and he posts himself in the doorway to the terror of everybody that goes by, flings his arms round the Duchess of Lancaster's neck and kisses her with a great smack. Then he threatens to pull Lord Galloway's wig off and knock out his false teeth and plays all the pranks of a drunken man upon the stage, till some of his companions call for his carriage and almost force him away. This is a little hard on Lady Hopetoun.

Eventually Sheridan smooths over the matter in Parliament, throwing doubt on Fox's denial, "paying a delicate compliment to the lady to whom it was supposed some late parliamentary allusions had been pointed," and complimenting the House on disdaining to press an investigation which the Prince courted. So skilfully is the tribute worded, so ambiguous is all of it but the praise, that Mrs. Fitzherbert is gratified and remains grateful.

Reflection sobers the effect. Lord Auckland's Journal notes that the panegyric seems inconsistent with its context. And caustic George Selwyn, applying a line from Othello, remarks—"Villain, be sure you call my love a whore." But Sheridan's tact is applauded, and Mrs. Fitzherbert is acclaimed and welcomed even more than she has been before.

Yet the party of Opposition has been damaged by the affair, and it takes shelter under the fine frenzy of Burke against Hastings to repair its errors and restore its credit. From such small beginnings do mighty issues arise.

CHAPTER 7

J'ACCUSE

WARREN HASTINGS stands charged with cruelty and fraud, the East India Company is known to be corrupt, and behind the whole question lowers the menace of George III with his threat of personal government. The Whigs, therefore, and Sheridan amongst them, seize the opportunity to make an example of the ex-governor, to win a victory for freedom, and to glorify the subject against the ruler.

Sir Philip Francis, supporter of the Opposition and sworn rival of Hastings, presents Indian affairs in such a light as to rouse public indignation by attributing all its evils to the latter's personal ambition and to his disregard of orders. Francis has fought a duel with Hastings and been wounded. From that time on he mistakes malevolence for virtue, nurses it as preachers tell us that we ought to nurse our good dispositions, and parades it on all occasions with Pharasaical ostentation.

He is the leading spirit in Hastings's impeachment—instigates the movement and advises and informs its managers. He is not only the prompter behind the scenes, but the author, producer, and stage manager of the whole performance. Burke, Fox, Dundas, Sheridan—all the host of brilliant orators arranged against Hastings—are actors in a stupendous drama conceived by his tortured brain. The materials for the twenty-two charges brought forward by Burke are furnished by Francis. His form of presentation is a result of conscious design—a mass of unassorted materials, bitter invective, cunning insinuations, irrelevant accusation, and diffuse argument—to buttress the shaky grounds of charge.

The personal animosity of Burke gives that underpinning earnestness and emotional power. Burke's kinsman William has gone to India to make his fortune, but returns in 1793 broken in health, penniless, and with a shortage in the accounts of the Crown. He trails a reputation of chicanery from England to India. William has two schemes for enriching himself: 1) through a complicated juggle with the Indian provincial exchanges; 2) through conjuring up a vast paper debt in India in order that he may make a profit of 25% by remitting it to England. Edmund Burke pushes William's schemes. Yet Burke accuses Hastings of peculation and jobbery. Lord Cornwallis calls William's juggling with the exchange scandalous. Does Burke start the prosecution of Hastings because William has not been used by Hastings as he thinks he should be? Of course, to a certain extent. Burke is constitutionally unable to believe that a rogue can be on his side. He looks upon his friends and relatives as God's noblemen and their adversaries as unmitigated villains. He is naïve and gullible respecting human nature. Undoubtedly an odor of financial adventureship surrounds his domestic ties. He writes to William: "Oh! my dearest, oldest, best friend—you are far off indeed! May God, of His infinite mercy, preserve you! Your enemies—your cruel and unprovoked persecutors—are on the ground suffering the punishment not of their villainy towards you, but of their other crimes, which are innumerable. I think . . . the reign of Hastings is over."

Again a sensational matter intensifies ill feeling. Sir Francis hates an intimate friend of Hastings, Sir Elijah Impey, formerly Chief Justice of the Supreme Court of Bengal, who is also impeached. One night in February, 1779, before he leaves India, Francis is caught climbing down the balcony of a delicious seventeen year old beauty, Mrs. Grand. Mrs. Grand's servants bind Francis with ropes and are astonished that instead of a burglar, they have caught a member of the Supreme Court of Bengal. The husband divorces his wife and sues Francis for damages. He collects fifty thousand rupees before the Supreme Court under Impey. The lady goes to France and marries Talleyrand. One of the serious matters in the impeachment relates to Nuncomar, who preferred charges against Hastings. Hastings disdained to reply, but the hostile Council, of which Francis was a member, resolved he was guilty. Immediately afterwards Nuncomar was accused before Impey of forging a bond. Was English law to be applied to the Indians in such cases? Impey ordered Nuncomar imprisoned and hanged.

Wide as seems the area singled out for impeachment, it forms only the border of that vast sphere of public service which Hastings has rendered. It leaves his most signal achievements untouched. He has reduced chaos to order, cleaned the Augean stable of Bengal administration, succeeded in putting down its worst abuses, and prevented British rule in India from being overwhelmed. His great task has been to teach the servants of the Company that their work is not merely to trade, to fight, much less to pillage, but to govern.

When Hastings lands in England during June of 1785, universal calm reigns throughout his dominions. The disasters of years have been retrieved by the salvation of India. He stands poor where most have battened on plunder. He is not among those who have "shaken the pagoda tree." Lord Cornwallis, who starts to govern India early in 1786, governs it on the foundations laid by the recalled ruler.

But undoubtedly Hastings has made use of the exaction and rapacity common to the East to maintain the desperate struggle for British supremacy. The Company urged him to replenish its coffers, and he has done so. Underhand bribes too have been received and queerly accounted for in the juggle of the Company's books. The East has not been governed by the standards of the West.

Three chief charges are brought against him. He has lent British troops to England's ally, the Nawab of Oude, to enable the latter to conquer a predatory tribe, named the Rohillas, who dwell on the northern boundary of the Nawab's dominions. He has imposed an enormous fine (£500,000) on a vassal prince, the Rajah of Benares, who was culpably remiss in paying his tribute (£50,000) during the war with Tippoo. Lastly he has allowed the Nawab of Oude (who promised to contribute to the expenses of that war) to obtain money that he needed by plundering the Begums, the Nawab's own mother and grandmother, who had hitherto been placed under British protection.

From the first Hastings is unwise. He allows his nominee Major Scott to overdo details, disdains to rest his case on his merits, scorns his enemies and provokes their fury. The vindicators of India desire to set up a better system, but a system unintelligible to the man who has had to decide on the destinies of millions in a moment and at a distance which forbade communications. Still more alien are they to the mercantile standards of Leadenhall Street, which have been perpetually dinned into the governor's ears as his mainstay for the sinews of war.

Of all this Sheridan is aware, but like the rest of his colleagues he casts it aside. The chance of display tempts him. He is ambitious, and here is an unrivalled opportunity for all the powers at his command—eloquence, raillery, dramatic presentation, a grasp, too, of facts which few imagine within his reach. He has not entered politics to play second, third, or fifteenth fiddle as Assistant Under-Secretary or Assistant Party Manager in opposition. He has it in him, and by God it shall come out. Still another incentive is added. Pitt completely changes front and casts a hostile vote against Hastings. He is led to the conviction that he cannot in conscience defend Hastings and associate his own government with the despotic acts which have marked the Governor's administration.

Sheridan would spare Hastings if he could. He constantly favors the middle course: all political wisdom lies in compromise. But he is swept along by Burke. Burke's

Hastings is no man, but the evil spirit that has desolated Bengal and lost for England America. His whole theory of government may be summed up in the phrase—"Fraud, injustice, oppression, peculation, engendered in India are crimes of the same blood, family, and caste with those that are born and bred in England."

On February 7, 1787, the House sits in Committee with a Mr. St. John in the chair. Over five hundred members are present when, at midnight Sheridan rises. For nearly six hours he rivets his audience by an utterance exceedingly rapid though singularly distinct, and at the close his voice sinks to a whisper. When he sits down, the whole House— members, peers, strangers—for the first time within record breaks into a tumult of applause and loudly and repeatedly clap with their hands. Sheridan's friends rush up to him and hang about his neck. Burke declares it the most astonishing effect of eloquence, argument, and wit on record. Fox says, "All that I have ever heard, all that I have ever read, when compared with it dwindles into nothing and vanishes like vapor before the sun." Pitt acknowledges that it surpasses the eloquence of ancient or modern times. It causes "the bone" to rise repeatedly in Sir Gilbert Elliot's throat, and brings tears to the eyes of unemotional Dudley Long, and after it is over, the former finds it impossible to sleep "one wink." It entirely changes the sentiments of Mr. Stanhope and staggers the convictions of Mr. Montague. It so much overwhelms Mr. Wilberforce, Mr. Martin and others that they clamor for an adjournment in order to collect their reason before voting. It is like a fine intoxication which nobody can resist.

A Mr. Logan, author of a masterly defence of Hastings, goes that day to the House of Commons prepossessed for the accused and against the accuser. At the expiration of the first hour he says to a friend, "All this is declamatory assertion without proof." When the second hour is finished, "This is a most wonderful oration." At the close of the third, "Mr. Hastings has acted most unjustifiably." The

[213]

fourth, "Mr. Hastings is a most atrocious criminal." And at last, "Of all monsters of iniquity, the most enormous is Warren Hastings."

The astonished members, afraid of themselves, dare not venture on any practical step until they have cooled down a little. For the moment all other topics are effaced. Nobody can talk of anything but Sheridan's speech about the Princess of Oude.

He splashes on color thickly—the Ganges, the Jumna, viziers, begums, eunuchs, rajahs, zenanas, and harems add enormously to the effect. He is partisan and his diatribes are overdrawn. But they strike and stir the national imagination.

(Sheridan's oratory cannot evoke the original impression—his personal fascination plays a large part in his rhetorical effects. "The brilliant eyes, the expressive looks, the arresting voice are gone. There remains the cold print.")

"I declare, Sir, from my conscience, that the system which Mr. Hastings followed in his government of India may be termed a series of unparalleled cruelty, oppression, and plunder. He acted diametrically opposite to the command of Parliament and the East India Company; and the Committee of the Commons have frequently reprobated his principles. But, says Mr. Hastings, 'Look not back to the records, weigh not the enormities of my past crimes. Listen to my own defence. I will prove that every article of peculation, rapine, and murder, ascribed to my measures, proceeds from the antipathies of my enemies. . . .' Poor, unfortunate gentleman! He happens to have his tranquil moments annoyed by the cries of injured innocence! I protest that no man but the immaculate Mr. Hastings would have dared to come to the bar of this House, and argued upon the grounds of his innocence.

"There is undoubtedly something about him either of parts or property which for a number of years has exercised a most fascinating influence. . . But to try the truth of the position, it is proper to define the quality in question.

In what then does greatness of mind consist but in great actions well directed; in executing the best purposes in the best manner; in doing most good by the purest means. False greatness of mind is indeed often mistaken for the true. It includes boldness of conception, strength of resolution, readiness of enterprise, and an utter contempt for the obvious distinctions of right and wrong. A mind of no principle, or the worst of principles, may embrace a daring and profligate measure and pursue it with alacrity and effect to a bad end. But a conduct even of this black and abandoned description implies a certain degree of foresight though misapplied, and of wisdom though perverted. I affirm without apprehension of contradiction, that the public capacity of Mr. Hastings exhibits no proof that he has any just claim to either the one or the other species of greatness. We see nothing solid or penetrating, nothing noble or magnanimous, nothing open, direct, liberal, manly or superior, in his measures or his mind. All is dark, insidious, sordid, and insincere. Wherever he has option in the choice of his objects, or his instruments, he instinctively settles on the worst. His course is one invariable deviation from rectitude. And the only trace or vestige of system discernible in the whole of a dozen years' administration is that of 'acting without any.'

"His crimes are the only great thing about him, and these are contrasted by the littleness of his motives. He is at once a tyrant, a trickster, a visionary, and a deceiver. He affects to be a conqueror and law-giver, an Alexander and a Caesar; but he is no more than a Dionysius and a Scapin. His very writings, though here he wants not for admirers, discover the same intrinsic poverty of intellect, are marked with the same mixture of littleness and pride. All his letters and minutes are dry, obscure, inflated, and uninteresting, without point, spirit, simplicity, or intelligence. He reasons in bombast, prevaricates in metaphor, and quibbles in heroics. So that in composition he hurts the mind's taste, as much as in conduct he offends every feeling of the heart."

Dundas has said that the greatest defect in the politics

of India was that they were uniformly founded on mercantile maxims. "Mr. Hastings's administration carried this sordid system to its utmost extent.

"It was in this manner that nations have been extirpated for a sum of money, whole tracts of country laid waste by fire and sword, to furnish investments; revolutions occasioned by an affadavit, an army employed in executing an arrest, towns besieged on a note of hand, a prince expelled for the balance of an account, statesmen occupied in doing the business of a tipstaff, generals made auctioneers, a truncheon contrasted with the implements of a counting house; and the British government exhibited in every part of Hindostan holding a bloody sceptre in one hand and picking pockets with the other."

As for the attack on the Begums: "Who would not have resisted acts of such enormity? The treasure of these unfortunate women was their treason . . . The country was depopulated, famine was aided, and the bloodhounds of war let loose upon the innocent natives. . . Wherever the British army was removed, the downtrodden oppression sprang up and called aloud for vengeance. The inhabitants of Oude might be compared to a flight of birds. With fluttering trepidation they crowded together in the air on discovering the felon kite, who, having darted at one bird and missed his aim, singled out a new victim and sprang on his prey with redoubled vigor of wing and keener lightning in his eye. . . I am utterly at a loss in what terms to describe the attack on the zenana. . . The confusion, the uproar, the screaming of females, the barbarity of the troops, and the trepidation of the neighborhood are unrecountable. . . Let the Commons picture to themselves any of the British Royal Family thus surrounded, assailed, and forced to surrender their property and their servants, their bosom friends, at the point of a bayonet. To us at least who live in a land where every man's house is his sanctuary, where the arm of power dares not intrude, where the Constitution has erected an insuperable barrier to every encroachment or outrage, such an instance of violence cannot but appear monstrous and atrocious beyond all example or idea."

The Governor's excuses Sheridan demolishes in order and then begins his long peroration: "It is thus that he sports with all the ties of nature and justice. . . God forbid his idea of justice should ever be adopted in this country. . . It is high time that this House should vindicate the insulted character of justice. It remains with the Committee to dispossess her of Mr. Hastings's splendid drapery, and exhibit her in her true majesty and form; not as a syren soothing the profligate in their crimes, but as the inflexible friend of the oppressed, and the steady pursuer of the oppressors, active, inquisitive, and avenging. . . Need I state that this is no party question? I am aware what factions divide the House. Even prerogative has lately found its advocates among the representatives of the people. . . The measures of every minister are supported by one class of men and opposed by another. But on great occasions have not the whole body of the Commons often laid aside all considerations of party and interest? . . . When the majesty of justice is to be supported, it is our duty, our glory, our interest, to be unanimous. Inhumanity is now before us in such a monstrous shape that we are bound to regard it as a common enemy. I trust we shall not relax in our pursuit. . . I trust the Committee will step forward regardless of the minister or the influence of the Crown, or the prepossessions which individual interest may affect. . .

"We are challenged by all the laws of God and man to relieve millions of our fellow creatures from a state of misery and oppression. It is true we do not see the swarms of human beings who call upon us for relief. We do not hear the bitter lamentations of those who are ready to perish. . . But in redressing their grievances, and reckoning with their oppressor, our relief will be magnanimous in proportion to the distance of the sufferers. Is a British Parliament to wait till its bar is surrounded with the screams of starving children, and crowds of helpless women shrieking under the pangs of hunger and wretchedness, before it vouchsafes the assistance of its power? . . . No! Let the Commons of Great Britain set an example to nations of stretching the strong arm of justice across the habitable globe in protection of injured innocence. . .

"The omnipotence of a British Parliament will be demonstrated by extending protection to the helpless and weak in every quarter of the world. And the blessings of people thus rescued from the grip of avarice armed with authority, will not be lost. . . Heaven itself will condescend to be your proxy in receiving the heartfelt gratitude of thousands. . . I thank the Committee for their indulgence in a speech that has carried me far beyond the limits of their time or my strength, and move that the Committee, on hearing evidence and considering the said charge, are of opinion that there is sufficient ground to impeach Warren Hastings, Esquire, of high crimes and misdemeanors."

CHAPTER 8

THE TRIAL

THE DOORS of Westminster Hall are flung open, and Mr. Burke at the head of the Committee makes his entry. He holds a scroll in his hand and walks alone, his brow bent with care and thought. Then begins the long procession, the clerks entering first, the lawyers according to their rank, the peers in gold and ermine, the bishops and officers all in their coronation robes, concluding with the Princes of the blood and the whole ending by the Chancellor with his train borne. They then all take their seats.

The grey old walls are hung with scarlet, the long galleries crowded with a glittering audience. Round the Queen are the fair-haired daughters of the House of Brunswick, and the lively little frizzled head of Fanny Burney, looking over her Majesty's shoulder. There too are majestic Siddons, Gibbon, Reynolds, and Parr, the lovely Duchess of Devonshire, haughy Mrs. Fitzherbert, and sweet Mrs. Sheridan.

In the midst of the blaze of red drapery, an open space has been fitted up with green benches and tables for the Commons. The managers of the impeachment appear in full dress. Even Fox the negligent wears a bag wig and sword.

A sergeant at arms arises and commands silence in the court on pain of imprisonment. Then some other officer in a loud voice calls out—"Warren Hastings, Esquire, come forth. Answer to the charges brought against you; save your bail or forfeit your recognizance." A thin and bald man in a poppy colored suit with a diamond hilted sword comes forth, preceded by the gentleman usher of the black rod and flanked at each side by his bail. He makes a long bow to the Chancellor and court facing him. He moves on slowly to his own box, and there lower still bows again, and then advancing to the bar leans his hands upon it and drops to his knees. But a voice in the same minute proclaiming he has leave to rise, he stands up almost instantaneously and a third time profoundly bows to the Court.

The crier makes in a loud and hollow voice a public proclamation: "That Warren Hastings, Esquire, late Governor-General of Bengal was now on his trial for high crimes and misdemeanors with which he was charged by the Commons of Great Britain, and that all persons whatsoever who had aught to allege against him were now to stand forth."

A great silence follows, and Chancellor Lord Thurlow now makes his speech that seems intended to convey the assurance that the high authority and adverse temper of the Commons shall not prejudice his fair trial. The speech is uttered in a calm and solemn manner. At the end Hastings again bows to the Court, and leaning over the bar, answers with much agitation—"My Lords—Impressed—deeply impressed—I come before your lordships equally confident in my own integrity and in the justice of the Court before which I am to clear it. . ."

Another general silence ensues, and then one of the lawyers opens the cause. He begins by reading from an immense roll of parchments the general charges against Warren Hastings, but he reads in so monotonous a voice that the audience cannot follow him. When he finishes, another lawyer rises and reads so exactly in the same manner that it is utterly impossible to discover whether it is the charge or the answer. Such reading as this sets everybody at his ease.

This ceremony occupies two days. On the third day Burke rises and begins a speech which lasts the next four days. The ladies in the galleries, excited by the solemnity of the occasion, are in a state of uncontrollable emotion.

Handkerchiefs are pulled out, smelling bottles handed round, and hysterical sobs and screams heard. Mrs. Sheridan is carried out in a fit. But public excitement rises to its greatest height when Sheridan's turn comes.

His speech on the Begum charge renowns him throughout Europe. It occupies him four days (June 3, 6, 10, 13), during one of which he is taken ill. Many who hear it are moved to tears, Mrs. Siddons faints, and the whole space of Westminster Hall is crowded to suffocation—thronged with the most brilliant of brilliant audiences, including the Prince of Wales and the Duke of Orleans. All the rank, wealth, genius, wit, and beauty of England are gathered together in the building. Only the Duchess of Devonshire is absent. And it is upon this occasion that Gainsborough, who just before has promised Sheridan to attend his funeral, contracts a chill which brings on his fatal illness.

The curiosity of the public to hear Sheridan is unbounded. There is a positive stampede. Tickets cost fifty guineas, yet the rage and clamor for them is so great that people are almost putting their hands into one's pocket for them. Ladies are dressed and mobbing it in the Palace yard by six, and they sit from nine till twelve before the business begins. The crush is so terrible that it is a wonder people do not lose a limb or two, or have a rib broken. Shoes, however, are the principal and most general loss. Several ladies go in barefoot. Some losing their own get stray shoes of other people and go in with one red and one yellow shoe.

A thousand pulses beat as Sheridan rises. His opening is regarded as too stiff, more like a lawyer's than a member's and too much in the manner of his father when he acts King John. But he betters as he goes on, and his speech wins universal applause. Burke is vehement in its praise, and Walpole holds the national decadence not irretrievable when "history and eloquence throw off such shoots." Mrs. Sheridan thus acquaints her sister-in-law with "the news of our dear Dick's triumph—of our triumph. It is impossible, my dear woman, to convey to you the delight, the astonishment, the adoration, he has excited in the breasts of every class of people. Even party prejudice has been overcome by a display of genius, eloquence, and goodness which no one with anything like a heart about them could have listened to without being the wiser and the better for the rest of their lives. What must my feelings be, you only can imagine. To tell you the truth, it is with some difficulty that I can 'let down my mind,' as Burke said afterwards, to talk or think of any other subject, but pleasure too exquisite becomes pain, and I am at this moment suffering from the delightful anxieties of last week. I am a poor creature and cannot support extremes."

When Sheridan's father returns to England at the close of July, he is greeted by his faithful ex-servant Thompson with the remark—"Sir, your son is the first man in England; you will find everyone of that opinion." Alicia, too, who hears the close of Sheridan's speech is "haunted" by its effect.

In a sitting of the House, held on the sixth of June, after an exciting morning spent in Westminster Hall, a certain Mr. Burgess gets up to call the attention of the members to some small matter of finance. He is transfixed immediately by the spear of Burke. "I cannot avoid offering my warmest congratulations to the honorable gentleman on his having chosen that glorious day, after the triumph of the morning, to bring forward a business of such an important nature," cries the great orator with contemptuous sarcasm. And he goes on to applaud the powerful mind of the stolid partisan who has proved himself capable of such an effort "after every other member had been struck dumb with astonishment and admiration at the wonderful eloquence of his friend Mr. Sheridan who had that day again surprised the thousands who hung with rapture on his accents by such a display of talents as was unparalleled in the annals of oratory and so did the highest honor to himself, to that House, and to the Country."

Towards the close of his long inquiry on June 10, Sheridan nearly faints, and Burke has to occupy his place. Fox, who leads him out, comes back to tell the court that his friend is so unwell that he is quite unable to proceed, and therefore he trusts the House will indulge him by adjourning to some future day. June 13 is fixed for the termination, and Sheridan, in resuming his speech, apologizes for the delay and thanks that tribunal for their indulgence.

He undertakes to prove that for all his iniquities Hastings must answer. The culprit has shifted the blame from his own shoulders to those of his tools and masters. Yet he has deliberately sanctioned their methods. "I won't say that they are mine, but they are just, honorable, humane, and politic." "This," Sheridan comments, "crowns the whole. This shows the monstrous falsity upon which his defence is founded. . . And am I now to be told, when I have brought such proof before your Lordships, that when he gives an agent authority to awe, to force, to compel, to kill—when he inflames and pronounces dreadful responsibility—when he has communications of it, and says—'I am happy to hear of it, and shall return with a delightful mind to Calcutta'—when he afterwards makes it a charge against his agent that he was not cruel enough—when finally he calls all the measures just, humane, and politic—am I then to be told that he is not responsible because I cannot prove the number of the lashes or the weight of the irons? Shall I be told that he was not the cause this noble tree was felled, because he ordered them to lay an axe to the root, but did not bid them tear the bark—because he ordered them to tear out the heart, but did not order a drop of blood to be shed? . . . I say I have brought home these crimes, and laid them full upon Warren Hastings at your bar; that he is answerable for them to law, to equity, to his country, and to his God. . .

"My Lords, I have closed the evidence. I have no further comments. When I have done with the evidence, I have done with every thing that is near my heart. It is by the majesty, by the form of that justice, that I do conjure and

implore your lordships to give your minds to this great business. That is the only exhortation I have to make. It is not
to exhort you to decide with a perfect clear conscience. . .
It would be presumption to warn you against that; I know
it cannot be the case. But what I exhort you to is, that when
you lay your hands upon your breasts, you not only cover
that pure, sublime, and clear conscience, but that you do
cover a mind convinced by a diligent application to the evidence brought before you. It is to that I quote the example
of the Commons, to exhort your Lordships to weigh and
look into facts—not so much to words, which may be denied
or quibbled away—but to look to the plain facts, to weigh
and consider the testimony in your own minds. We know
the result must be inevitable. Let the truth appear and our
cause is gained. It is to this I conjure your Lordships for
your own honor, for the honor of the nation, for the honor
of human nature now entrusted to your care; that I for the
Commons of England speaking through us claim this duty
at your hands. They exhort you to it by everything that
calls sublimely upon the heart of man, by the majesty of
justice which this bold man has libelled, by the wide frame
of your own renowned tribunal, by the sacred pledge which
you swear in the solemn hour of decision, knowing that that
decision will bring you the greatest reward that ever blessed
the heart of man—the consciousness of having done the
greatest act of mercy for the world that the earth has ever
yet received from any hand but Heaven's.

"My Lord, I have done."

And as he falters, Burke catches him in his arms.

The reception of Sheridan's speech, a contemporary hu-
morist describes with this gibe—

> The gallery folk, who, misled by the sport,
> Conceived 'twas a playhouse, instead of a court,
> And thinking the actor uncommonly good,
> They clapp'd and cry'd "Bravo!" as loud as they could,

Then Edmund gave Sherry a hearty embrace,
And cry'd, as he spluttered all over his face,
"At Supper this night thou shalt have the First Place!"

The trial comes to nothing. It lingers over years of tedious discussion. The spectacle loses the attraction of novelty. The great displays of rhetoric are over. What is left behind is not of a nature to entice men of letters from their books in the morning or to tempt ladies who leave the masquerade at two to be out of bed before eight. There remains examinations and cross examinations. There remain statements of account. There remain the reading of papers, filled with words unintelligible to English ears—lacs and crores, zemindars and aumils, sunnuds and perwannahs, jaghires and nuzzurs. There remain the bickerings between the managers of the impeachment and the counsel for the defense. There remain the endless marches and countermarches of the Peers between the House and the Hall, for as often as a point of law is to be discussed, their lordships retire to discuss it apart. And the consequence is that the judges walk and the trial stands still. Then in the following year the debates on the Regency and the situation in France completely divert public attention from Indian affairs.

Burke chafes at the delays. He becomes daily more vehement, violent, and quarrelsome. So wearied is Sheridan of his impetuous tempers that he tells Georgiana in jest how much he wishes that Warren Hastings would run away and Burke after him. Imagine the sensation during the trial when Burke hearing a tumult and certain that the victim is about to escape, throws all remnants of decency to the winds and roars out, "Put him in irons!"

Yet in the midst of legislative and judicial duties, it is impossible that the Upper House give more than a few days to an impeachment. Besides, to expect their Lordships to give up partridge shooting, in order to bring the greatest delinquent to speedy justice or to relieve accused innocence by a speedy acquittal, would be unreasonable indeed. (A

[225]

well constituted tribunal, sitting regularly six days in a week and nine hours in a day, would have brought the trial of Hastings to a close in less than three months. The Lords do not finish their work in seven years.)

Sittings of the Court

1788—35 days
1789—17 "
1790—14 "
1791— 5 "
1792—22 "
1793—22 "
1794— 3 "
1795—24 "
_____

142 days

At length in the spring of 1795 the decision is pronounced: the accused whose sin by this time has been half forgotten, whose foolish plans for himself are altogether out of mind, and whose good qualities have come round again to the recollection of the world, is solemnly acquitted.

Parliamentary redress, which Hastings longs for, is never formally accorded. But in 1813 he receives it in an indirect form. Being summoned before the House on a renewal of the East India Company charter, he reappears at that bar where he pleaded as a culprit. Applause greets him now from both sides. He is offered a seat and courteously questioned, and when he withdraws at the close of the examination, the members rise and uncover. (Those who do not sympathise pull their hats over their brows). Next day the Lords receive the old man with similar tokens of respect. The University of Oxford confers on him the degree of Doctor of Laws, and in the Sheldonian Theatre the undergraduates welcome him with prolonged and tumultuous cheering.

Sheridan and Hastings meet many years after the trial as guests of the Prince Regent in the Pavilion at Brighton and Sheridan advances to Hastings and says—"The part which I took in events long gone by must not be regarded as any test of my private opinions, because I was then a public pleader whose duty it is, under all circumstances, to make good if he can the charges which he is commissioned to bring forward." Hastings draws back a step, looks Sheridan in the face, makes a low bow, and remains silent. "Had he," Hastings subsequently says, "confessed as much twenty years ago, he might have done me some service."

The former Governor is known never to have lost a friend. His generosity is unbounded. His own private interest is lost in his regard for the public welfare. On the 22nd of August, 1818 he passes away, his last act being to lay a handkerchief over his face lest the last change distress the women who are watching at his bedside.

CHAPTER 9

THE KING'S MADNESS

THE KING breaks out into a violent delirium at dinner, flies at the Prince of Wales, clutches him by the throat, and throws him against a wall, crying, "You will know how to dare keep the King of England from speaking his mind." The Prince is overcome and begins to shed tears.

His Majesty, whose curt answers and suspicious bluntness indicate a phlegmatic temperament, is really the reverse. Shortly after his marriage it is feared that his brain is affected, and his thwarted passion for Lady Sarah Lennox is given as the cause. So early as May, 1788, disquieting symptoms revive. His feet and legs swell, and he even speaks of abdication. The hereditary gout is thought to have settled in his head. But George turns his back on his courtiers and declares that whatever is the matter with him, it is not the gout. Since back turning is his favorite posture when he is vexed, little is made of this for the moment. Some there are who rumor that his wet nurse was a lunatic and that quack medicines unhinged his balance.

He is put under the care of Willis, a clergyman doctor. He demurs at first to having a clergyman for his doctor. Willis reminds him that the Saviour healed the sick. "Yes," says his Majesty, "but I never heard that he had £700 for so doing."

During the summer he drinks the Cheltenham waters, but no improvement ensues. His daily behavior becomes more odd. He runs a race with a horse. He asks a Mr. Clements if it is he who eloped with his old flame, Lady Sarah. He sits with young Court ladies embroidering and pretends to play the fiddle. He tells West, the artist, that he will teach him how to mix colors, and illustrates his ability by mixing them with his foot. He bows to an oak, seizes one of the lower branches, and shakes it with the most apparent cordiality and regard—just as a man shakes his friend by the hand. He pulls off Sir George Baker's wig and forces him down on his knees to gaze at the stars. He shows unwonted sharpness. On one occasion he remarks that the Prince is dead, so women may after all turn honest. On another, when Colonel Manners appears, he says instantly, "That is *good Manners.*" Which causes Burke to remark that it is a strange way of reason to revisit a man in the shape of a pun. His queer demeanor is noticed by ambassadors at the levees, but his courtiers make light of it. Lord Fauconberg swears that all the world has seen him in a strait waistcoat, and Lord Salisbury that the King has as much sense as he has—which perhaps is true.

But gradually his real condition leaks out. He mumbles much about Lady Pembroke whom he has long admired, and eventually declares that she is Esther while the Queen is Vashti. He imagines he is married to her, and when he fancies himself with servants only, takes a glass of wine and water and drinks to the health of "conjugia mea dilectissima Elizabethia," meaning Lady Pembroke. His eyes are affected. To see his wife he pushes the candle into her face and nearly sets her on fire.

Dr. Warren (dubbed by the King, Sir Richard) is summoned, the ministers meet, and the Opposition sit in conclave at Burlington House. Fox, touring Italy with Mrs. Armistead, is urgently recalled, and to Sheridan the Prince turns for counsel during Fox's absence.

George's ill symptoms gallop apace. At Windsor he sits dictating Cervantes and the Bible—at the same time and with incredible speed—to pages whom he afterwards creates Baronets and Knights of the Holy Roman Empire. He talks for thirty-two hours on end—of everybody and everything. He howls and screams and clasps the palms of his hands. He suspects his sons and deprives the Duke of York of his regiment. He looks over a Court Calendar and marks the names of persons whom he means to dismiss from office. He makes a page go to sleep as an anodyne for his own insomnia and then immediately picks his pockets. He sees Pitt, who is much affected, and raves of the money that he fancies due to him from his minister. There can be no doubt now of his lunacy.

Ere long Lord Chancellor Thurlow sits closeted with Sheridan. A Regency will be demanded, Pitt will go out, and what then will become of Thurlow? Even the most loyal of Lord Chancellors has to think of himself, and he tells Sheridan he is not a party man.

Fox returns on November 24. He has journeyed in eight days post-haste from Bologna, distracted by a false rumor on the road that his beloved boy nephew, the future Lord Holland, is dead. Exhaustion and suspense tell on his figure. He is thin and very ill. For a time he fancies himself dying. He talks feverishly with his friends at his bedside the whole day long. He cannot concentrate his thoughts. But eventually he is removed to Bath where with inborn elasticity, he soon recovers.

Nothing galls him more than his lieutenant's conference with Thurlow. This parleying with the foe makes him suspicious of Sheridan's every step. But what he really, if half consciously, resents, is that under the circumstances, Sheridan now has the upper hand with the Prince.

Night and day Sheridan toils, now in council with his party, now hauled out of bed near midnight to consult with the Prince till the small hours of the morning—now harried forth to meet him at Bagshot. For days he is not asleep till five or six. He is the recognised intermediary of the Prince, the Vizier of Carlton House. Jockey Norfolk lends him Deepdene, and his post horses may often be seen on the road from London to Leatherhead or from that to St. Anne's where he consults with Fox.

The expectations of the Whigs run high. Reports of the King's critical state increase daily. A Regency seems certain, and the leaders join in a mad scramble for place and power. They squabble with the jealousy of schoolgirls. Sheridan looks on and refuses to press his claims. The Prince offers him the Chancellorship of the Exchequer in the event of his Regency, but Sheridan declines. He prefers, he says, to reach that eminence by degrees. (When the offer becomes known, a fiery partisan addresses "A Letter to Mr. Fox," exclaiming, "Mr. Sheridan at the head of finances!—why, sir, the streets of Paris would be illuminated, public rejoicings would be made, and thanksgivings offered up to Heaven by all the enemies of Great Britain.")

On November 27 the King is removed to Kew. His antics are sad and ludicrous. He dances a minuet with his apothecary in a new tie wig which he orders for the purpose. He tears two of his attendants almost to pieces and displays some aversion to the Queen. He proposes a match between one of his keepers and that fat, awful Mme. Schwellenberg, the court bully of Frances Burney. He is cowed by the domineering Willis who brandishes a straitjacket before him, and he clasps the little Princess Emily tight in his arms till they bring her mother to him. He parts with his pages and as a farewell gift gives each a pair of razors. He fancies himself a Quaker and is dressed like one from head to foot.

Meanwhile the physicians are split into two camps, Whig and Tory, the Doctor of Opposition and the Doctor of Pitt. At the same moment the King is reported dying and recovering, sane and imbecile. The tide of rumor ebbs and flows. Few give thought to the poor patient.

The Prince introduces Lord Lothian into the King's room when it is darkest in order that his lordship may hear the King's ravings at the time that they are at the worst. And at Brooks's he mimics the gestures of his stricken father.

Pitt is in no friendly mood. He pooh-poohs the necessity of appointing a Regent at all. The Opposition attempts more than one ruse to gain time, and Pitt meets them by demanding a fresh inquiry into historical precedents which consumes weeks and only results, as Sheridan says, in "a little bad Latin and worse French." It is all a trick to prolong the debate till the Tory doctors can pronounce the monarch recovered.

And now Queen Charlotte emerges on the scene. She has a difficult game to play. The King's malady seems fixed. The Regency problem is imminent. She mistrusts her favorite son and she abominates his advisers. Her other sons she almost dislikes. Pitt she fears. He may use this juncture to become paramount and for a time may turn England into a virtual republic. What she wants—if she can get it— is a joint regency where she can pull the strings. George is furious at his mother and is indiscreet in his remarks about her. Jack Payne, his secretary and confidential man, one day utters some ribaldry about the Queen in the presence of the Duchess of Gordon. "You little, insignificant, good-for-nothing, upstart, pert, chattering puppy," says her Grace, "How dare you name your royal master's royal mother in that style?"

Parliament meets, and the physicians' reports are laid before the House. Fox, rising boldly, asserts the Prince's constitutional right to the Regency. Pitt, slapping his thighs energetically with his hands, instantly sees the advantage which he has gained and exclaims to a friend who sits next to him on the treasury bench, "I'll un-Whig the gentleman for the rest of his life." Accordingly, as soon as Fox sits down, Pitt starts to his feet. The doctrine, he says, to which the House has just listened, is treason to the Constitution. The heir apparent has no more right to the executive power than any other person in the realm. In the case of the incapacity of the sovereign, it belongs to Parliament to make provision for the temporary interregnum. "Let not the House, therefore," he concludes, "rashly annihilate and annul the authority of Parliament, in which the existence of the Constitution is so intimately involved."

Sheridan feels that pressing a decision on the question of right is injurious, and he tries to discountenance Fox's course. But the result of the debate is a complete success for the ministerial party. That night at White's all is hurrah and triumph; at Brooks's all is despondency.

Pitt, ignoring the Prince's right, first brings forward

Queen Charlotte, then finally proposes a number of Regency restrictions which reduce the Prince's office to a mere cipher. Sheridan, realizing that the restrictions are the only possible compromise, persuades the Prince and his party to accept them. But a deliberate answer to Pitt's proposal is imperative, and the Prince shuts up his myrmidons in separate rooms, each engaged on his secret business. He now employs Loughborough and Burke, and afterwards, Fox and Elliot. Finally he urges Sheridan to make one missive of two—a compound of Loughborough's (all ice and snow) and of Burke's (all fire and tow).

But before Sheridan does so he saunters into Devonshire House. It is his habit to flâner there, and he loves to banter the Duchess. He sends a note to Fox making an appointment for nine of the next morning. But he stays too late and cannot get the writing done and copied by Mrs. Sheridan till two the next day. When he comes to Fox's he finds his note, saying he would be ready at nine, pinned up on the chimney. Charles speaks crossly to him. To which Sheridan replies, "I am as God made me and hate personalities."

Many more letters are composed for the Prince—a long one by Sheridan about the Queen, a shorter one by Elliot to her, a memorial by Sheridan to the King—communications to everyone. The royal controversies know no end. The Regency Bill is passed. Ireland protests in the Prince's favor and delegates come over. They are spoken of as Indian Chiefs, and at one assembly some of the ladies groan and hoot at them as they come into the room. They are feasted, however, at the great houses. At Carlton House the entertainment is grand and elegant—"the Feast of Reason and the Flow of Soul." Burke and Sheridan are among the guests. The talk is bright as the champagne they drink, and the champagne is the best in the world.

But all in vain. By February 24, 1789, the King's recovery is pronounced—much to the disgust of the Whigs. In mid-March the town is illuminated and bells are rung. Ere long the monarch returns a public thanksgiving in St. Paul's Cathedral. Sheridan receives the news with characteristic cheeriness. Sheri or Cheri, as his wife and the Duchess call him, simply raises his glass amid a throng of expectants, and gives the toast—"To His Majesty's Health."

His Majesty's recovery is the signal for festivities—galas, masquerades, balls, operas, and plays. The Queen and her daughters attend Covent Garden, showing her displeasure with Sheridan by not visiting Drury Lane. A magnificent gala is held by White's Club in the Pantheon attended by two thousand persons. Brooks's Club, anxious to remove any impression of disloyalty, holds a celebration at the Opera House in the Haymarket. Captain Robert Merry— "this furious zealot for liberty,"—writes An Occasional Ode. In congratulation of the King's recovery, he exclaims—

"Long may he rule a *willing* land,"

but adds immediately,

"But oh! for ever may that land be *free!*"

Mrs. Siddons, condescending to be Britannia, declaims this Ode with solemn and melodious dignity. At the end, to the gratified astonishment of the spectators, she sits down in the exact attitude of the figure on a penny piece. (This coup de théâtre is, of course, attributed to Sheridan.)

A great masquerade is held at Mrs. Sturt's mansion at Hammersmith—attended by three Princes. The hall and stairs are ornamented with colored lamps and the Duke of York's band plays. About one o'clock the Princes arrive all dressed as Highland chiefs. George, with his father's passion for knowing who and what everyone is, gives Betsy Sheridan such an enquiring stare that Mrs. Sheridan thinks it best to introduce her. Mrs. Sheridan sings in a trio with the Prince of Wales, and Lady Duncannon spends her time casting many tender looks across the table which are not much attended to.

Boodle's Club holds a gala at Ranelagh, also attended by the Prince and the Duke of York, who that morning has fought a duel with Lieutenant Colonel Charles Lenox. The duel originates with an incident at the mess of the Coldstream Guards where Colonel Lenox, intoxicated, toasts Pitt in the Prince's presence and continues the toast at Daubigny's where the Duke disparages his second in command on the parade ground. When the duel becomes then inevitable, the Prince, who is greatly perturbed, tells the circumstances to the Queen in the hope that the duel will be stopped. But she conceals the matter from the King, although ten days elapse between the incident on parade and the duel on Wimbledon Common.

The Duke of York is accompanied by Lord Rawdon as his second and Colonel Lenox by the Earl of Winchilsea, one of the Lords of the Bedchamber. The ground is measured at twelve paces and both parties are to fire upon a signal agreed upon. Only Colonel Lenox fires, his ball grazing the Duke's curl, but undisturbed by this narrow escape, the Duke declines to fire. He came out, he says, only at the Colonel's desire to give him satisfaction, and he has no animosity against him. Lord Winchilsea then says that he supposed the Duke will have no objection to saying that he considers his opponent a man of honor and courage. The Duke replies that he shall say nothing, and does not intend to fire, though if Colonel Lenox is not satisfied, he may fire again. On this they leave the ground. The seconds conclude that "both parties behaved with the utmost coolness and intrepidity."

Meanwhile the Prince is pacing up and down the grounds of Carlton House in great agitation. The Duke returns to him saying very coolly that he is unharmed, but cannot stay to tell any more as he must keep an appointment to play cricket. However the Prince insists upon hearing the full story, and that evening they go together to Boodle's gala.

The Prince in the fullness of joy for his brother's safety takes too many bumpers to his health. Sheridan goes up to him and tries to persuade him to stop. Finally he pushes the bottle from the Prince, saying, "You *shall* not drink any more." The Prince, fired at this, says, "Sheridan, I love you better than anyone, but *shall not* is what I can't put up with." However, with the help of one of the guests, Sheridan gets the Prince away.

When the Duke goes to Kew for the first time since the duel, he finds the King sitting in an outward room with the door open to where the Queen is. The minute the King sees the Duke he goes softly to shut the door, then running to him, embraces him affectionately and with tears congratulates him on his safety. On the Queen's entering, he draws back and becomes reserved. She takes no notice of her son other than asking with a cold and distant air whether he has been amused at "Bottle's Ball."

At the Duke of Clarence's Ball and at the King's Birthday Ball, the Queen shows Colonel Lenox great favor, though the Prince and the Duke of York refuse to dance in the minuet with him.

The upshot is that the officers of the Coldstream Guards at his own request meet to consider Colonel Lenox's conduct. Their resolution is that "he has behaved with courage, but not . . . with judgment." This is virtually a censure, and Colonel Lenox exchanges into another regiment.

Before the end of May, the King sends a letter to the Duke of Clarence, complaining of his sons' conduct during the Regency discussions. The Prince summons a conference at Carlton House for the purpose of drafting two letters to the King, one explaining and justifying their actions, and another protesting against the Queen's conduct over the duel. Burke, Sheridan, and Elliott are present. The letter of justification is entrusted to Elliott and the protest against the Queen to Burke. When another council is summoned to consider the drafts, the remonstrance against the Queen is found to "out-Burke Burke" in violence. The epistle takes two hours reading—it is exceedingly eloquent but fiery and untamed. The Duke of Portland looks more stupid than usual—not that he is at all as stupid as he looks—he has very good sense. He is really in a maze. Lord North keeps up a perpetual noise between a cough and a growl, and Fox keeps digging his fingers into the corners of his eye, a trick he has when anything perplexes him.

Fox and Lord Stormont consider the letter too bitter and it is withheld.

For a few weeks the matter is held in abeyance. Finally on some pretext the Prince, expressing his regrets at the King's displeasure, sends a letter which is written by Sheridan and its conclusion reduces to one dignified sentence the complaint about the Queen:—"I cannot omit this opportunity of lamenting those appearances of a less gracious disposition in the Queen towards my brothers and myself than we were accustomed to experience; and to assure Your Majesty that if these most unpleasant sensations should be happily removed, it would be an event not less grateful to our minds than satisfactory to Your Majesty's own benign disposition."

2.

Sheridan loses his father. The impaired state of the old man's health makes him resolve to undertake a voyage to Lisbon as Fielding did thirty-four years earlier. Elizabeth accompanies him on the journey from Dublin to Margate. But at Margate, disregarding his physician's orders, he takes a hot salt water bath and is attacked with a violent fever. When young Sheridan arrives, his father is strongly impressed by his son's attention, and before he dies, says with considerable emotion, "Oh, Dick! I give you a great deal of trouble."

CHAPTER 10

EXODUS

EVERYTHING with Burke is the handiwork either of God or the Devil. The French Revolution is the handiwork of the Devil. The new constitution of France is to him "the unprincipled, plundering, ferocious, bloody, and tyrannical democracy of a people whose government is anarchy and whose religion is atheism."

To the Americans, Whigs like himself, arguing decorously on a constitutional principle and then proceeding to fight for it, Burke can extend a very practical sympathy. But in the challenge of Paris, the vast upheaval of popular passion, the prophet of ordered freedom can see no good and no hope. In his further opinion, not only are such Englishmen who look with favor on the French Revolution, enemies to the state, but he even includes in his anathemas the advocates of parliamentary reform. Fox and Sheridan are regarded as apostles of atheism and sedition. In turn they brand Burke as the deserter who revisits their camp as a spy.

The breach between Burke and Sheridan first comes to a head in the latter's speech on February 9, 1790 on the Army Estimates and the French Revolution.

The debate should limit itself to the subject: the increase of the army. But Fox jumps to his feet and chooses to wander into France. France, he argues, can offer no present danger to Britain, and it would be base to assail her now. After a few words from Pitt, Burke throws down the gauntlet against his colleagues. He knows that Sheridan wishes that evening to make a popular speech in praise of the Revolution, and he is determined to counteract it in advance. He launches out into an abuse of France. She is "expunged out of the system of Europe"; she is in "a swoon." Her soldiers are not citizens but "base hirelings and mutineers, mercenary, sordid deserters, wholly destitute of any honorable principle." He feels genuinely concerned that "this strange thing called a Revolution in France should be compared to the Glorious Revolution in England." And he impresses the House with a suspicion that Fox has yielded to younger and less fit advisers.

The innuendo points to Sheridan whose answer provokes a final farewell from Burke. Burke's brain is now possessed by France fully as much as by Warren Hastings. His distinctions of reform from innovation, says Sheridan, seem quibbles. Nor do his flatteries march with his inner meaning. Everyone knows that he has come down prepared to anti-gallicise the situation. If he wishes to be quit of his old friends, let him say so and have done. Then Sheridan goes on to assail Burke not for his principles, which he exalts, but for his present application of them. He upholds the French Revolution as a movement quite as just as the English. He defends the National Assembly. How can it be said to have overturned the laws and revenues?—laws that were "the arbitrary mandate of capricious despotism," revenues that were nothing but "national bankruptcy." "But what is the striking lesson, the awful moral that is to be gathered from the outrages of the populace? What but a supreme abhorrence of that accursed system of despotic government which so deformed and corrupted human nature as to make its subjects capable of such acts. A government that sets at nought the property, the liberty and lives of the subjects, that deals in extortion, dungeons, and tortures, shows an example of depravity to the slaves over which it rules. And if a day of power comes to the wretched populace, it is not to be wondered at, however much it may be regretted, that they should act without those feelings of justice and humanity which the principles and practice of their governors have stripped them of?" And Sheridan ends where he began, by controverting Burke's comparison of the Revolution in France with the Glorious Revolution in England.

The tone exasperates Burke beyond measure. He publicly proclaims that henceforward he and his honorable friend—"as he has been in the habit of calling him"—are separated in politics. Even so he might have expected fairness and kindness. Sheridan's comments were not such as fitted "the moment of departed friendship." It is clear that he "sacrificed friendship for the sake of catching some momentary popularity."

While Sheridan listens to Burke's reproaches, he winces and changes color. He is moved by Burke's statement that henceforth they are political strangers. He makes every effort for a reconciliation, but Burke is implacable. He tells Sir Gilbert Elliot that while he has no animosity against Sheridan, their former friendship cannot be restored even if this episode is patched over. The wound will admit of nothing more than a temporary cure.

Fox now takes his line and the foxhounds follow his halloo. Burke is bent on a final break. On one occasion in the House, when Burke happens to be absent, Fox gives great offence to his old friend, not only by his encomiums of the French Republic and by his ridicule of hereditary rank and titles as antiquated absurdities, but he offends Burke's pride as an author by sneering at one of the beautiful passages in the *Reflections on the Revolution in France*. To this speech Burke hopes to have an opportunity of replying on the 15th of April, 1791. Fox, however, not only anticipates him by speaking first, but gives fresh umbrage to Burke by launching into an enthusiastic praise of the new constitution adopted by France. In his judgment he says it is "the most stupendous and glorious edifice of liberty that has been erected on the foundation of human integrity in any time or country." Immediately Fox sits down, Burke rises to reply, but it is by this time three o'clock in the morning, and accordingly, amidst mingled and opposite cries from both sides of the House of "Chair! Chair! Hear! Hear! Order! Order!" he is compelled to repress the expres-

[240]

sion of his sentiments, though not his indignation. It is a scene, he complains bitterly, which is only to be paralleled in the political assemblies of a neighboring country.

At length on April 21 an opportunity to reply presents itself. It is Burke's intention to bring into play all his eloquence, his learning, and his powers of invective to disparage the principles of the French Revolution and its admirers in England. The Whigs are aware of his intentions. This intention if persisted in must necessarily terminate his long connection with the Whigs as well as his private friendship with Fox. Accordingly the latter calls on him at his residence in Queen Anne Street in the hope of being able to divert him from his design. Burke receives him cordially, speaks to him of the kind manner in which the King is said to have lately mentioned his name, nay even confides to him the arguments which he intends to make use of. Burke, however, has fully convinced himself that he has a duty to perform to his country, and consequently Fox's words fall upon deaf ears. They never again meet in the same apartment. When at the end of the interview they walk together to the House of Commons, it is the last time that the arm of Fox is ever placed in that of Burke.

The final break occurs on May 6, 1791. Burke is determined to warn and convince his fellow countrymen of the danger of imitating the example of the French. The Quebec Bill (to provide a constitution for the province of Quebec) comes up in committee and some latitude for general discussion is therefore claimed. It is a question, Burke asserts, of framing a new constitution for a French colony under English rule, and is that constitution, he asks in effect, to be one in accordance with the spirit of the National Assembly? But he has not proceeded far before he is interrupted by cries of "Order!" Fox says that Burke can hardly be held to be out of order as it seems to be a day of privilege, and Burke may just as well discuss the "Gentoo government or that of China or of Turkey or the laws of Confucius." The clamor grows louder. There are hootings, catcalls, hisses. The groundlings take their cue from their leaders, and they interrupt Burke no less than eight times. Facing them with unutterable scorn, he hurls at them the cry of the maddened Lear—

The little dogs and all,
Tray, Blanche, and Sweetheart, see they bark at me!

The debate turns for a time on the question of relevance. But the contending passions of the two principal actors will not be denied their outlet. The Speakers seem to abdicate, and the eyes of all become riveted on Burke and Fox.

Burke opens quietly enough, but before he has ended, his hearers witness an explosion of feeling expressed in heightened and impassioned language. At one point he suddenly checks himself and turns to the Speaker with the words—"I am not mad, most noble Festus, but speak the words of truth and soberness." At another point, as he is dilating on the difference between the British and the French constitutions, he is angered to see Fox apparently fulfilling his previous threat of leaving the House. A band of Fox's followers rise also, but it is a false alarm. Fox returns immediately eating an orange.

Burke goes on to recall the circumstances of a friendship of twenty-five years standing, a friendship which has never been clouded by political differences. Old as he is, if he has to choose between loss of friendship and loss of his principles, he will choose, and with his last words, exclaim, "Fly from the French Constitution." Fox is now really alarmed. Leaning across to Burke he whispers, "There can be no loss of friends." Burke pauses a moment, then faces Fox relentlessly. "Yes, I regret to say there is. I know the value of my line of conduct. I have indeed made a great sacrifice. I have done my duty, though I have lost my friend. There is something in the accursed French Revolution which envenoms everything it touches."

Fox rises but is unable to proceed for some moments. He not only sheds tears, but he sobs, and the whole House is moved as it has rarely been moved. He recalls the kindness which he received when little more than a boy at

Burke's hands, and refers to the ignominious terms in which Burke has spoken of him. "I do not recollect having used any," cries Burke. "My right honorable friend," replies Fox, "does not recollect the epithets; they are out of his mind. Then they are completely and forever out of mine. I cannot cherish a recollection so painful and from this moment they are obliterated and forgotten." But it is to no effect, and the concluding speeches do nothing to change the situation. Pitt winds up in businesslike fashion by remarking on the singular situation in which the House stands on the subject under discussion, namely, the Quebec Bill, but adding that he does not think Burke can be said to have been out of order.

The members return home. One member, taking Burke home in his carriage, is led to express some approval of the line taken by Fox. "You are one of those people—set me down," cries Burke, and he is only with difficulty prevented from getting out into the rain.

The results of the rupture are critical. Burke, the mentor, the St. Paul of his party, goes out and with him other great props of the cause. It is a Whig exodus, and the scattered Foxites are left alone. The Opposition votes, which once numbered one hundred and sixty in the House of Commons, sink in the end to fewer than twenty-five.

CHAPTER 11

TRAGEDIES

"DEAR SHERI, believe me and love," writes Mrs. Sheridan to her husband who is extremely jealous, for many men are enslaved by her. "May I never see God if ever I had even a thought that could give you a moment's uneasiness. . . I will do or not do anything to make you happy, but if you have confidence in me, you will not wish to make me do anything remarkable or studiously avoid every person whose society happens to be more agreeable to me than Mr. R. Wilbraham's or such people. . . Whilst I live in the world and among people of the world, I own to you that I have not courage to act differently from them. I mean no harm. I do none. My vanity is flattered, perhaps, by the attendance and preference which some men show towards me; but that is all. They *know* I care for nothing but *you* and that I *laugh to scorn* anything that looks like sentiment or love."

But after the death of Mary Tickell, Elizabeth's standards relax perceptibly. Her letter to Mrs. Canning, wife of Stratford Canning, (Sheridan's amiable friend) underlines the change. "People have taken to drop in as they say of a morning and interrupt me in my occupation of School Mistress. The Duke of Cla.[rence] lives within a hundred yards of me and he generally pays me a visit most mornings. . . Mr. Fitzpatrick and Ld. John Townshend seldom miss calling of a morning too. Mr. Horne has been in once or twice lately—in short, as S—— says, all the gentlemen are very obliging indeed. Ch. Fox is at present on a visit to Mrs. B——. Mr. B is gone into Suffolk to shoot, so Lord Rl and Ch. thinking no doubt they shd. have as good sport here are supplying his place—they all meet here every evening and in general they are very agreeable I assure you."

(Elizabeth is still a very beautiful woman. The number of admirers who wish to console her for her husband's inattentiveness is not exaggerated. However, Sheridan for his part is unfaithful to her more than once.)

But however flighty she may be, she loves Sheri devotedly and is jealous in her turn. "Do you really long to see me? And has nothing but business detained you from me? Dear, dear Sheri, don't be angry. I cannot love you and be perfectly satisfied at such a distance from you."

She has more common sense than he. She begs him to give up his expensive way of life and to live quietly in the country with modest rooms in town. "Do think of this, my dearest Dick, and let me have a little quiet home here that I can enjoy with comfort. . . Take me out of the whirl of the world, place me in the quiet and simple scenes of life I was born for, and you will see that I shall be once more in my element, and if I saw you content I should be happy."

He does not comply, and his fragile young wife, who once so nearly fell a victim to Mathews, tried beyond her strength and her patience, gives way.

In 1791 she very nearly parts from Dick—very nearly too throws herself into the arms of the Duke of Clarence, who is frantically pursuing her. Sheridan's relations with Lady Duncannon are so notorious that Lord Duncannon threatens to bring a criminal suit against him. The Duke of Devonshire hastens over to England to set matters right and hush things up. And then when Sheridan is pleading forgiveness from Elizabeth on this account, and swearing and imprecating all sorts of curses on himself, his wife, and his child if ever he is led away by any motive to be false to her again, he throws "the whole family at Crewe into confusion and distress by playing the fool with Miss Fd. (little Emma's governness) and so awkwardly too, as to be discovered by the whole House, locked up with her in a Bed Chamber in an unfrequented part of the house."

It is a gross offense, heinous, unforgivable. Mrs. Sheridan determines upon a separation. "But I don't know how it is. I have been talked over by Mrs. B[ouverie], Ch. Fox, and S. himself has been so terribly frightened and affected by my behavior that at last I have received him once more into favour, tho' I own to you I have lost all confidence in his professions and promises."

On returning to the Capital she plunges into the gaieties of London society with ardor, seeking distraction at the gaming table. She tells Sister Christian, as she calls Mrs. Canning, that she and Sheridan are both "descending the Hill pretty fast." There is foul backstairs gossip that Sheridan has obliged her to grant the last favor to the Prince of Wales, whom she detests, in consideration of his receiving £20,000 from the Prince. And indeed her feelings for the Duke of Clarence are perilously sympathetic. "I cannot find in my Heart to be harsh and brutal to him," she sighs, and she speaks of the necessity of being "stout" and putting an end to the pursuit at once. Finally, outraged by Sheridan's repeated infidelities, she turns to Lord Edward Fitzgerald who is a perfect madman about her. In her last illness she acknowledges that the child she has borne is Lord Edward's. This shocks Sister Christian so much that she refuses to see her. But Sheridan intervenes to implore *"the friend she loved best in the world"* not to abandon her, "knowing as I do, and as I did hope you knew, that God never formed a better heart, and that she has no errors but what are the Faults of those whose conduct has created them in her against her nature."

A strange, highly strung couple, a fragile, spirited young beauty not completely grown up. Mrs. Canning on one occasion discovers Sheridan dashing his head frantically against the wall at one end of the room while Mrs. Sheridan repeats the operation at the other.

"You will think," she writes Mrs. Canning, "I am a little touch'd with the Royal Malady when I tell you that I ventured to the Brooke's Ball Tuesday in sphight of remonstrances. My physician and hairdresser met together at my toilette in the morning and prescriptions and papilotes went on very amicably at last, for I cd. not bear to have all my money and my pretty dress wasted—so I tell you Justin patch'd me up, and I bore my raking better than even I expected."

But she does not bear her raking well. In the spring of 1792 she gives birth to a daughter, christened Mary in memory of Mrs. Tickell. The mother's health fails after the child's birth, symptoms of the hereditary curse appear, and the story of the younger sister is repeated almost step for step in that of the elder. She too is ordered to Bristol Hot Wells, and Sheridan and Mrs. Canning accompany her. Dr. Bain, a young physician who has cured himself of consumption, attends her and gives the verdict that the case is not yet beyond hope. Twice a day she goes on the Downs in a sedan chair, her husband at her side. "Tomorrow," Mrs. Canning reports to her daughter, "we go into a charming house, the white bow-windowed one that overlooks the strawberry garden." Within a short time, however, Dr. Bain sees reason to change his favorable opinion. And he pronounces Mrs. Sheridan to be really a lost case and that she cannot live for six months.

On the road to Bristol, Sheridan sends a letter of melancholy self reproaches. "I am just returned from a long solitary walk on the beach. Night, silence, solitude, and the sea combined will unhinge the cheerfulness of anyone where there has been length of life enough to bring regret in reflecting on many past scenes, and to offer slender hope in anticipating the future. . . How many years have passed since on these unreasoning restless waters, which this night I have been gazing at and listening to, I bore poor E., who is now so near me fading in sickness, from all her natural attachments and affections. . . What has the interval of my life been, and what is left me but misery from memory and a horror of reflection."

His diary is one of hopes and fears and panics and despair. He is summoned to her at four in the morning; she has a violent pain in her side. Next day she is bled and blistered. "I cannot describe to you," he moans, "how horrid the solitude of the night is to me." Now she shows a gleam of returning strength and again her forces ebb away. She longs after heavenly things. "Ever since the child was born, she has turned her mind almost wholly to think and talk and read on religious subjects, and her fortitude and calmness have astonished me. She has put by every other contemplation. . . Last night she desired to be placed at the pianoforte. Like a shadow of her own picture, she played some notes with the tears dropping on her thin arms. Her mind is become heavenly, but her mortal form is fading from my sight, and I look in vain into my own mind for assent to her apparent conviction that all will not perish. I mean to send for my son and she wishes for him."

Sister Christian makes some allusion one day to her past behavior with Lord Edward which throws Sheridan into a paroxysm of grief and remorse. "Oh! not a word of that kind," he exclaims, "she is an angel if ever there was one. It is all my fault. It is I, I that was the guilty fiend."

The "angel" is reconciled to the "guilty fiend," but her confidence in him is gone and she confines the care of her infant daughter to her dear, dear Mrs. Canning. She writes some words for him to sign—"I here solemnly promise my dear Betsy never to interfere on any account with Mrs. C. in the education or in any other way of my poor child. I cannot write all I wish but he knows my Heart. Swear or I shall not die in peace—."

She receives the sacrament some weeks before the end. To Eliza Canning, her god-daughter, she leaves her watch, charm, and some jewels; to Jane Linley her pearls. To a servant she bequeaths much of her wardrobe and she specially requests that her mother may not interfere. The "*fausse montre*, containing my dear husband's picture," she leaves to "my dear and beloved friend Mrs. Canning," also a portrait of herself, to be painted by anyone but Cosway,

[248]

and a ring both to her and her daughter. She desires that "the picture of my dear Mary" be unset and "one copied of me joined to it, and the hair blended, and this, I trust, Mrs. Tickell will permit my dearest Betty to wear in remembrance of her two poor mothers." To her own mother she gives a "new black cloak which will be comfortable for her in the winter." She disposes of all her ornaments and desires that £25 shall be settled on George Edwards, Sheridan's butler, and on the woman servant. "There are other circumstances," she concludes, "which I have mentioned to Mrs. Canning which I hope will likewise be considered as my earnest wish—I am now exhausted."

The son in whom they delight arrives. The Linleys then at Bath visit her on one of her better days, and depart. But on June 27, 1792, a turn comes for the worse. She can no longer rise, and Sheridan recalls them. They are introduced one at a time at her bedside, and she gives some kind injunction to each one of them and tries to comfort them. They then part in the hope of seeing her again in the evening, but they never see her more. Sheridan and Mrs. Canning sit up all night. At about four they notice an alarming change and send for the physician. She says to him, "If you can relieve me, do it quickly; if not do not let me struggle, but give me some laudanum." He answers, "Then I will give you some laudanum." Before she takes it, she desires to see Tom and Betty Tickell. There is an affecting scene. Sheridan kneels at her bedside till he feels the last pulse and then withdraws. She dies at five in the morning. Till her last moment she is perfectly tranquil and sensible.

Her wish is to lie near her sister. The funeral takes place on the thirteenth at Wells. It proves a function. A long and representative cortege attends the hearse, the populace lines the road all the way to Bristol, and in the Cathedral at Wells the crush and tumult are so great that the powerful voice of the priest can hardly be heard, and he is almost pushed into the vault.

Tributes to Mrs. Sheridan's sweet form, voice, life, character abound. Not the least touching is the Latin epitaph composed in her honor by Dr. Harrington, the friend of her childhood. It is thus ill translated—

> Sure every beauty, every grace
>   Which other females share,
> Adorned thy mind, thy voice, thy face,
>   Thou fairest of the fair!
> Amidst the general distress,
> Oh! let a friend his grief express.
>
> But whilst, alas! each mortal mourns,
>   Rejoice, ye heavenly choir;
> To your embraces she returns,
>   And with her social lyre,
> Eliza now resumes her seat
> And makes your harmony complete.

Sheridan sits and cries like a child night after night. He descends into the vaults of Wells Cathedral and there kneels over the corpse of one whom in life he by turns adored and provoked. In an attitude of prayer he pours out his misery, and continues in the chamber till the clock is heard to strike midnight. Then he arises and bids farewell.

Yet the source of his sorrow is already contaminated by attempts to overcome it. Within two months of his wife's death, all the world knows he is in love with the radiant and beautiful Pamela, supposed to be the natural daughter of the Duc d'Orleans and that interesting refugee, Mme. de Genlis. He tries to compliment her by writing poems in French, though he hardly knows anything of the language, and he has mother and daughter at his seat at Isleworth for five or six weeks. Before they sail, he makes a declaration of love to Pamela who is charmed by "his agreeable manner and high character" and she accepts the offer of his hand with pleasure. It is settled he should marry her on their return from France in a fortnight.

So far as Sheridan is concerned that is the end of his

romance with Pamela. For in June of the following year, Lord Edward Fitzgerald sees Pamela for the first time and is instantly so struck by her likeness to the "object of his bitter regret," Mrs. Sheridan, that he falls in love with her and marries her. (Within six years he dies in prison from wounds received in the Irish rising of '98, which as hero-patriot-martyr he led.)

At Wanstead, Sheridan, who can attend to nothing, is attentive to the infant Mary. He never visits the place without taking her some toy or cap or riband and stands over her cot for hours watching her. But another tragedy remains. Eighteen months after the death of Mrs. Sheridan, a party and dance are going on merrily for Tom's benefit when Mrs. Canning suddenly flings open the door crying out, "The child, the child is dying!" Sheridan is frantic. He does everything, but the end soon comes.

Many striking condolences commemorate both these occasions. Tickell and Alicia indite letters honoring the man and pointing out silver linings within the cloud. But for a time Sheridan is disconsolate; his restraint grows less, and more and more he abandons himself to the bottle.

CHAPTER 12

"HECCA"

AT A PARTY in Devonshire House little
Miss Esther Jane Ogle, daughter of the Dean of Winchester, is seated at a table when Sheridan comes up close
to her. It seems the young lady prides herself on saying
smart things or everything that comes into her head, and
she calls out to Sheridan, "Keep away, you fright, you terrible creature,"—and this, though she is not acquainted
with him. Sheridan is piqued. He wishes to show his power
and in doing so is enmeshed by the young lady who now
thinks him very clever. She decides that there will be much
éclat in the conquest of so celebrated a man. And accordingly the date of the wedding is set. Sheridan is over forty-
three, his bride not yet turned twenty.

Tom is sent for and waits vainly for his father at Guil-
ford whilst the prospective bridegroom thunders past at
midnight on his way to London, in a coach with four horses,
lamps ablaze and heart aflame. "My father," Tom writes to
his tutor Smyth, "talked to me two hours last night, and
made out to me that it was the most sensible thing that
he could do. Was not this very clever of him? You should
have been tutor to him, you see. I am incomparably the
most rational of the two."

The marriage takes place on April 27, 1795, four days
after the acquittal of Warren Hastings and following almost
immediately on the nuptials of the Prince of Wales and
the unfortunate Caroline of Brunswick. The first gentleman
of Europe is dead drunk on his wedding night; Sheridan
on his is intoxicated by a fever of high spirits. He spends

his honeymoon at the old house at Wanstead, whence Tom's "aged mother" sends her blessing.

It is an unwise marriage. Mrs. Sheldon is capricious, and Sheridan overindulges her whims. She is desperately fashionable and extravagant. She sings well and dances well, but in things intellectual she takes scanty interest. To politics she is indifferent, and Sheridan himself once assures her, "God made the country—but the House of Commons—oh!" She hunts for celebrities and lives to bore Lord Byron. She likes to feel she has caught an illustrious man. Yet she is brave and loyal, and her devotion knows no bounds. Wasted for five years by a fatal illness, she thinks only of her "dear" Sheridan. "My whole heart and soul," she exclaims to Lord Holland, "is with Sheridan."

Sheridan himself never falls out of love with his "Hecca" as he calls her. His expressions of tenderness are as novel and varied as those of Bob Acres. She is "My sweet Hecca," "my dear, dear Hecca," "my sweet, beloved," "my darling Wench," "my life and delight," "my life, my soul," "my pretty wench," "my own dear bit of brown Holland"—and by way of climax, "Prettiest of all that my eyes ever thought pretty," "dearest of all that ever was dear to my heart." The endings of his letters contain these caresses—"Bless your bones"—"Bless your low forehead and your round plump elbows and your flowing tresses"—"Bless you, my own wench, my Hecca, that I never see without loving better, nor leave but with increased neglect"—"Bless your eyes"—"Bless your knees and elbows"—"Bless you ever and ever and all over"—"Bless thy heart, my only real pleasure on earth"—"Bless your eyelids, my beloved"—"Bless your days and nights."

The mere thought of estrangement distracts him. "At no time," he writes in 1799, "has your kindness been more necessary to me. Do not fail me, my dearest." If he does not hear from her regularly he becomes frantic. "Gracious God, not a single line. If a voice from heaven had told me that any human being should have treated me thus, I should

not have believed it. No matter." But as she owns, her difficulty in writing springs from the simple fact that she has
nothing to say. "Pray, my dear S., write, for I like of all
things to hear from you, and when you write, I feel as if
I had something to say." To which he replies, "When your
dear letter this morning began 'My dear S.' as formerly, I
felt my gloomsprite more cleared away than by any other
circumstance."

To his first wife Sheridan was "Sheri"; to his second
he is plain "Dan," "poor Dan" who is "all alone *le* melancholy as a tomb," or as "a yew tree in a churchyard." He
buys an estate at Polesden. He hopes to be fortunate as a
farmer, but he succeeds in agriculture no better than Burke.
He likes to play squire as much as Sir Walter Scott likes
to play laird. He somehow manages to settle on his bride
the sum of £15,000 tied up by the commands of the Dean
so that it cannot be touched till it has become £40,000.

The birth of a son on January 14, 1796, is a source
of great rejoicing. He is christened Charles Brinsley, at
"the fount of Opposition" laugh the newspapers, for Grey
and Fox are his godfathers. Sheridan is devoted to the
child whom he nicknames "Robin," and Hoppner paints
him pickaback with his mother. Over his education Sheridan perpetually broods. He is sent to Winchester and Cambridge. "Application, application, application," insists the
father anent his training. But as Rochefoucauld well says,
"Old age, when it can no longer set a bad example, gives
good advice." None the less he suffers hardships to provide
for the son's education and the mother's comfort. He tells
her that to ensure her happiness, he would gladly with
one hand cut off the other.

Yet the day comes when Sheridan and his wife are
estranged. His nomad habits, his drinking bouts, his flirta-
tions, and her quick temper—all these cause friction and set
up a temporary barrier. She has much to bear. A friend
once discovers her walking up and down her drawing room
in a frantic state of mind and calling her husband a villain.

After some hesitation she explains that the love letters written to her are copies of those which Sheridan sent to his first wife.

He is still insanely infatuated with Lady Bessborough. He follows her around London. Once he arrives at dinner, dines, and stays the whole evening. At length, as Lady Bessborough thinks he is preparing to pass the night as well as the evening with her, and as he begins some fine speeches she does not quite approve of, she orders her chair in order to get rid of him. This does not succeed, for as she has no place to go, Sheridan follows her about to Anne's and Lady D——'s, where she knows she will not be let in, and then home again. But luckily she gets in time enough to order every one to be denied, and runs upstairs while she hears Sheridan expostulating with the porter. Again he calls after walking up and down for an hour, and Lady Bessborough sends down word she is sorry she cannot see him but that she is not well. She is not in a mood to be flattered, abused, frightened, or complimented.

He trots after her wherever she goes, and notwithstanding epigram upon epigram, and joke upon joke, she refuses to shake hands with him, which seems to be the great object of all his trouble. He follows her in and out of the room, upstairs and downstairs, and even into the nursery. He throws himself on his knees before her. He vows vengeance against her, and once when handing her into her carriage, the moment he gets her hand in his, he crushes it with so much violence that tears come into her eyes, and she can scarcely help screaming.

He implores her (whenever Lord Bessborough turns his back) to forgive and shake hands with him. He tries every trick to stay with her. When her carriage drives to the door, he shivers and coughs, complaining of a cold, of a headache, etc., and asks if it would be inconvenient to the family to allow him to stay. They cannot refuse—he stays. He waits in her box the whole night, tries to speak once or twice, and then retires to a corner, speaks to nobody, looks very melancholy, sighs, and pretends to cry. He remains motionless with his eyes fixed on her in the most marked and distressing manner. As the ladies are going, she drops her shawl and muff; he picks them up and with a look of ludicrous humility presents them to Mr. Hill to give to her. She takes Lord Morpeth's arm and walks away, but he follows and then posts himself at the outward door by the carriages.

At a ball he follows her about like her shadow and wants to sit by her at supper (always pretending to cry), but Lord Morpeth takes hold of her, and pushing her up close to the Prince of Wales, squeezes himself in between Sheridan and her, for which she is much obliged. He writes her indecent letters—anonymously. At another ball he manages to sit opposite her, looking by turns so suppliantly and so fiercely at her that everybody round observes it and questions Lady Bessborough about it. She can only say what is so, that he is very drunk. When she gets up, he seizes her arm as she passes him, and begs her to shake hands with him. She frees herself from his grasp and passes on; he soon after follows and begins loudly reproaching her for her cruelty. Lady Bessborough is extremely distressed, hurries out of the room, and by way of completely avoiding him, crosses a very formal circle of old ladies. He has the impudence to follow her and in the face of the whole circle, to enter into a loud explanation of his conduct, begging her pardon for all the offences he ever committed against her and assuring her that he has never ceased loving, respecting, and adoring her—she is the only person he has ever really loved. The formal ladies are dismayed. Lady Bessborough thinks she will sink into the earth. Luckily he is so evidently drunk that a great deal passes for that.

Hecca asks her to come, and Lady B. sends word that she will pay a visit at night when they are all in bed. At twelve she goes and is carried up to Hecca's bedroom. They have not sat long when a violent burst at the door announces the arrival of Sheridan not perfectly sober. The most ridiculous scene ensues. He begins by asking Lady B.'s pardon, entreats her mercy and compassion, saying he is a wretch and is even at this moment more in love with her than with any woman he has ever met. On which Hecca exclaims, "Not excepting me? Why, you always tell me I am the only woman you ever were in love with." "So you are, to be sure, my dear Hecca; you know *that* of course— *you know* I love you better than anything on earth." "Except her?" "Pish, pish, child! Do not talk nonsense!" Then he begins again to Lady B., upbraiding her for her cruelty, both for quarreling with him and setting Hecca against him. Hecca every now and then coming in with, "Why, Sheridan, I thought Lady Bessborough pursued you and that you reviled all her violence like a second Joseph? So you used to tell me."—and so on till three in the morning, and Lady B. gets away with difficulty. Sheridan wants to come down with her and seizes her arm with such violence before Hecca that Lady B. is obliged to call her maid to help her, and at last she only escapes by locking Sheridan in.

Indeed Hecca is sorely tried. Another affair, and she threatens to leave him. But fortunately Sheridan has already been cured of the second great infatuation of his life: his passion for Mrs. Crewe. Amoret's charms have diminished. Her eyes and hair are dark and she is still pretty. But she is grown very fat and has a considerable quantity of visible down about her upper lip. Besides Sheridan's one time inspirer and model has developed into a bore. Gilbert Elliot finds her like ninety-nine in a hundred—a mixture of good and bad. She likes good conversation, and she likes arguments and discussions of all sorts. She is a professed wit grown out of a professed beauty. She displays as much vanity and desire of admiration in her pursuit of male conversation as real taste and genuine pleasure in it. She becomes wearing. The sort of things she insists on telling of herself and of all her acquaintances makes one stare. She is avid of political news—she wants to know of how and about it, and what is thought and what is to become of, and what shape it is to take, etc. Her ideas come so quick that Lady Douglas cannot follow them nor, she believes, can Mrs Crewe herself.

Her admiration of Burke and the vanity of being his friend has made her (since the epoch of the alarm) a professed aristocrate, but her original predilection for Fox and his politics remains. Burke declaims to her on the horrors of the French Revolution and she retails what he has said to her other Whig friends, Grey, Sheridan, etc. They, on their part, do not find it difficult to refute his arguments, as represented by her, and on many points bring her round to their own way of thinking so that after this when she happens again to see Burke he finds all his good doctrine shaken or rejected by her. This happens so often that he begins to lose all patience with her and one day remarks— "Our friend Mrs. Crewe is quite intolerable. She puts me in mind of the ship in the *Arabian Nights*. When I have built her up and launched her with secure nails to keep her tight and seaworthy, she no sooner approaches the Mountain (the Democratic party in the French Assembly) than by a magnetic power, it attracts all the nails I have driven into the ship and it falls to pieces."

One of Sheridan's escapades at a later time nearly proves fatal. He is in the habit of carrying a bag of papers with him to the Coffee House where he looks over them. One day, by mistake, he takes a bag of love letters, *gages d'amour,* locks of hair, etc., which vanity has induced him to keep. Getting drunk he leaves them behind and they fall into the hands of a fellow who demands one hundred guineas from him or from the woman concerned for their restoration. Sheridan consults his attorney and the Secretary of Drury Lane. They secure the assistance of a Bow Street runner, make a forcible entry with pistols into the man's house, and after gaining the treasure, defy him to bring any action.

[258]

2.

Towards his son Tom, Sheridan acts the part of an easy going elder brother. He takes pride in his cleverness but gives him no regular education and, with the exception of a brief spell at soldiering, no regular profession. "Tom," he complacently remarks, "you have genius enough to get a dinner every day in the week at the first tables in London, and that is something, but that is all: you will go no farther." But Tom expects to get into Parliament. "I think, father," says he, "that many men who are called great patriots in the House of Commons are great humbugs. For my own part, if I get into Parliament, I will pledge myself to no party, but write upon my forehead in legible characters, 'To be let.'" "And under that, Tom," says his father, "write Unfurnished."

He is morbidly anxious after his son's safety and health. At Wanstead he is much perturbed to find that Tom and his tutor Smyth have been skating and propose to continue the fascinating sport as long as the frost holds. Smyth reasons with him and believes he has won his point. Sheridan calls for his carriage at eleven o'clock that night saying he must be at Drury Lane, nine miles off, and Smyth is proceeding triumphantly up the stairs when a violent ringing is heard at the gate. He is wanted by the master of the House, and sure enough, what should he see, "glaring through the bars, and outshining the lamps of the carriage, what but the fine eyes of Sheridan."

"Now do not laugh at me, Smyth," he says, "but I cannot rest or think about anything but this d——d ice and this skating, and you must promise me that there shall be no more of it."

Sheridan loves his lighthearted son, but he is often moneybound and Tom is therefore pinched. He bitterly complains. "Don't I allow you £800 a year," says the father angrily. "Allow it, yes," says Tom, "but it is never paid."

And on the occasion of Tom's marriage—he gets acquainted with the girl too intimately—Sheridan threatens, "Tom, if you marry Caroline Callender, I'll cut you off with a shilling." "You haven't got it about you now, have you, sir?" the rogue replies.

Sheridan thinks the match an imprudent one. He says it is very hard, for if it weren't for this marriage, Tom was going to be the richest man in England. Tom answers that though the lady is poor, his father must admit she comes of industrious parents, for her father is allowed by everybody to be the greatest swindler in England.

Mrs. Thomas Sheridan is indeed very pretty, very sensible, amiable, and gentle—so gentle that Tom insists that her extreme quietness and tranquility are a defect in her character. Above all he accuses her of such an extreme apprehension of giving trouble that, he says, it amounts to absolute affectation. He affirms that when the cook has forgotten her duty and no dinner is prepared, Mrs. Thomas Sheridan says, "Oh, pray don't get dinner on purpose for me; I'll take a dish of tea instead." And he declares himself certain that if she were to set her clothes on fire, she would step to the bell very quietly and say to the servant with great gentleness and composure, "Pray, William, is there any water in the house?"

"No, Madam, but I can get some."

"Oh, dear, no! it does not signify. I dare say the fire will go out of itself."

Tom wishes to go down a coal mine for the satisfaction of being able to say that he has done so. "Then can't you say so without going?" Sheridan replies.

One day he tries to discuss with his father the doctrine of necessity. "Pray father," says he, "did you ever do anything in a state of perfect indifference; without motive, I mean, of some kind or other?" Sheridan who by no means relishes such subjects from Tom says, "Yes, certainly."

"Indeed?" says Tom.

"Yes, indeed."

"What! Total indifference—total, entire, thorough indifference?"

"Yes, total, entire, thorough indifference."

"Then tell me, my dear father, what it is you can do with total, entire, thorough indifference."

"Why, listen to you, Tom."

Sheridan often boasts of the antiquity of his family. He is still an O'Sheridan whose sires were the ancient princes of Ireland. When presiding at a dinner of the Theatrical Fund he descants with great eloquence upon this theme till Joe Munden, at last weary of it, says, "Mr. Sheridan, I have not the least doubt of what you say. I daresay you are descended from princes. The last time I saw your father, he was the Prince of Denmark."

Tom is present once when Sheridan protests that while he is proud of being the scion of so honorable a family as the O'Sheridans, he thinks it better out of modesty to drop the O. "But who has a greater right to the O than we have?" enquires Tom. "We owe everybody."

Tom is gay, honest, jolly, and sincere. At every gala or rout in town, he is a good singer, dancer, boxer, and drinker. And one of his friends declares enthusiastically, "You might drink with Tom in the dark."

His tutor tells Sir Walter Scott—"It is impossible to put knowledge in him, try as you might." "Just like a trunk that you are trying to overpack," adds Sir Walter. "But it won't do—the thing starts out in your face."

To the last Tom realises what Dr. Parr says of him as a boy—"Great acuteness, excellent wit and humor, but not a particle of understanding."

CHAPTER 13

DRURY LANE

THE AFFAIRS of the nation and the
theatre jostle each other in Sheridan's thoughts. All the
while the theatre tangle grows more and more complicated.
After Garrick's retirement Drury Lane goes veering before
the wind, without steady ballast, without plan, without
discipline, and without an energetic and vigilant commander. Much of the chaos behind the scenes is due to
the incapacity of the acting managers. The Roman Father
appointed to the post in 1778 was not a success—he was too
pedantic, too old fashioned, too fussy. Old Sherry's successor, King, is too good natured to do well, and his regime
is memorable only for the return of Mrs. Siddons to the
London stage. The season of 1788 opens without a stage
manager, and it is not until October of that year that John
Philip Kemble undertakes the post and a period of Shakespearean revivals, well mounted and admirably acted, begins. Sheridan manages Kemble with considerable tact. He
warns Peake, treasurer of Drury Lane: "Keep as punctual
with Kemble as you can." And again, "Ten pounds will not
break our bank. Therefore by no means, I beg most particularly, fail to pay Kemble a draught today on the order I
have given him. His wife is staying at Polesden and after
what has happen'd there, for him to be sent back without
money would be the Devil."

A kingdom of misrule exists at the theatre. They play
Much Ado About Nothing and have to make an apology
for the three principal parts. About twelve o'clock Mr. Hen-
derson sends word he is not able to play. They get a gentleman from Covent Garden who supplies the part of Bene-

dick. Soon after Mr. Parsons sends word he cannot play. Mr. Moody supplies the part of Dogberry. About four in the afternoon, Mr. Vernon sends word he cannot play. Mr. Mattock supplies his part of Balthazar. The unfortunate prompter Hopkins thinks himself very happy in getting these wide gaps so well stopped. In the middle of the first act a message is brought to him that Mr. Lamash, who is to play the part of Borachio, is not come to the house. Hopkins has nobody then who can go in for it, so he is obliged to cut two scenes in the first and second act entirely out and get Mr. Wrighton to go on for the remainder of the piece. At length they get the play over without the audience finding it out. They have a very bad house. Sheridan comes in yawning at the fifth act with no other apology than having sat up two nights running. He never sits out any play, his own excepted, and those only at rehearsal.

Absence is the main impression he produces on the actors' minds—absence of cash, absence of consideration, absence of business-like habits, absence of every single quality a manager should have, absence in the flesh to obtain cash. Luckily the bevy of fair actresses whose silk stockings and white bosoms excite Dr. Johnson's amorous propensities, have other things to think about besides one irritating man. There are triumphs to recount, intrigues to unmask, and disasters to record. Even that gifted scold Mrs. Abington ("that worst of bad women, Garrick calls her) leaves him alone.

The thermometer of theatrical success—receipts—soon begins to fall. "Last night," says one of the newspapers, "the Siddons and the Kemble at Drury Lane acted to vacancy; the hollow sound of their voices was the most dreary thing in the world." Sheridan runs deeply in arrears. Tomorrow is his favorite pay day, but like the trust day at a French inn, that tomorrow never do the actors see.

Mrs. Siddons as usual is the chief sufferer. Kemble's first official act is a blunt announcement that his sister will not go on in *King John* unless £50 are sent to her that day.

She writes to a friend—"I am, as you may observe, acting again, but how much difficulty to get my money! Sheridan is certainly the greatest phenomenon that nature has produced for centuries. Our theatre is going on to the astonishment of everybody. Very few of the actors are paid and all are vowing to withdraw themselves. Yet still we go on. Sheridan is certainly omnipotent." Two years later she speaks in still greater alarm. "I can get no money from the theatre. My precious £2000 are swallowed up in that drowning gulf, from which no plea of right or justice can save its victims."

Sheridan runs so deeply in debt with Mrs. Siddons that on one occasion she declares that until she is paid up, she positively will not appear again. Sheridan makes some jocular reply. No more notice is taken by him of this conversation, and Mrs. Siddons' name appears in the bill as usual to play Lady Macbeth. On the forenoon of the day on which the announcement is made, she writes to him simply repeating what she has before told him—that she will not appear. The play is not changed, however, nor is the slightest notice taken of Mrs. Siddons' letter, and she sits down to dinner. About six in the evening, a messenger comes, reminding her that she is announced to play Lady Macbeth that night, and expressing the astonishment of the management that she has not arrived. She returns a verbal answer—she will not appear. Another emissary appears, but his remonstrances are equally ineffectual. In a short time Sheridan himself is announced. "The audience is collecting; the curtain is about to rise." *Macbeth* and no other play is to be acted, and Mrs. Siddons must make her appearance in it. "The audience may collect, the curtain may rise, *Macbeth* may be played, but Mrs. Siddons will not perform in it."

No sufficient excuse can be made. The house expects to be gratified by Mrs. Siddons' performance. The theatre will be torn to pieces if the house is disappointed. Sheridan will take no denial. He will make such representations as will throw the whole blame upon Mrs. Siddons; she will risk her popularity, she will injure an old friend. In short he remonstrates and flatters alternately and ends by handing Mrs. Siddons into his carriage and driving her off like a lamb to the theatre.

On another occasion it is Kemble who rebels. Sheridan comes in accidentally to join the party in the green room after the performance and takes his seat at a table. As usual he cheerfully begins the conversation. The great actor now looks unutterable things and occasionally emits a humming sound like that of a bee and groans inwardly in spirit. A considerable time elapses and frequent repetitions of the sound. At length, like a pillar of state up rises Kemble, and in these words addresses the astonished proprietor—"I am an Eagle whose wings have been bound down by frosts and snows, but now I shake my pinions and cleave into the general air into which I was born." He then deliberately resumes his seat as if he has just relieved himself from unsupportable thraldom. Undaunted, Sheridan draws his chair closer and at the end of a prolonged sitting, leaves the place, not too steadily, arm in arm with the exasperated eagle who is now as mild as any mouse.

Kemble has a hard time of it. He kicks against managerial proceedings, he has to implore money for colors and a little canvas. He sends frantic appeals to Peake—"It is now two days since my necessities made me send to you for £30. My request has been treated with a disregard I am at a loss to account for. I shall certainly go and act my part tonight, but unless you send me a hundred pounds before Thursday, I will not act on Thursday; and if you make me come begging again, it will be for two hundred pounds before I set foot in the theatre." He is often heard angrily complaining to his friends—"I know him thoroughly —all his tricks and sacrifices," and he threatens to go to the "Society of the Friends of the People" and stand up there and expose him.

Peake is often kept prisoner in his own insolvent territory for hours together, not daring to unbar the door to the rush of his assailants. He is harried too by constant appeals from Sheridan himself. "Saturday Night. Shakespeare Club. [In a rambling hand]. You must positively come to me here and bring £60 in your pocket. Fear nothing. Be civil to all claimants, and trust me in three months there will not exist one unsatisfied claimant. Shut up the office and come here directly. Keep as punctual with Kemble as you can. . . Borrow and fear not. . . God bless you till I see you again, when I will make a success of all difficulties." Again. "Dr. Peake—*Without fail* and immediately give the Bearer 5 guineas to buy Hay and Corn for my coach horses— they have not had a morsel of either since last night. R. B. S. I shall call on you presently."

Tom adds to the cry of distress. "If you can possibly do so, send me ten or twenty pounds. I have not, by God, been master of a guinea scarcely since I have been in town, and wherever I turn myself I am disgrac'd—to my Father it is vain to apply. He is mad and so shall I be if I don't hear from you."

Even when the managers dine together an order is given on hapless Peake.

To Margaret Gower
To Messrs. Sheridan, Richardson, and Grubb

Haunch of Venison	0	12	0
Skate and Flounders, dressed sauce	0	7	6
Port	1	1	0
Sherry	0	4	6
Waiter	0	5	0

Mr. Peake pay this bill.

It cannot be said of Sheridan that he is ambitious to raise the tone of the stage by the production of new plays of merit. He brings out haphazard farces, musical medleys, Shakespearean plays and revivals of his own comedies. Michael Kelly, a charming fellow and an excellent singer, but one with distinctly operatic views of the drama, suggests to Sheridan the possibility of filling up the treasury by spectacular pieces such as *Cymon* which the singer has seen at Naples. At the end of the play there is a grand procession and a tournament embellished by triumphal cars drawn by horses, giants, dwarfs, leopards, lions, and tigers. The description delights the manager. *Cymon* is put on. No expense is spared. The piece is produced with due splendor and magnificence and inaugurates a long line of similar productions.

Despite this additional revenue, Drury Lane finances become more and more involved. In 1791 the old theatre is reported unsafe and incapable of repair, and in the following year it is pulled down. Sheridan's company finds expensive temporary quarters, first at the Opera House, and later at the Haymarket Theatre. The magic of his name is such that the sum of £150,000 is raised without difficulty for rebuilding Drury Lane Theatre and an enormous edifice is planned on the strength of it. But expenses exceed estimates, there are costly delays, with the result that the new theatre begins life with a deficit of £70,000 which is never cleared off. (One matter, however, is ordered more wisely. The window of the Treasury is constructed to open in Little Russell Street so that on black Saturdays, when there is no money, the cashier can make himself scarce and leave his besiegers to do their worst on the other side of the entrance.)

The opening of New Drury Lane Theatre takes place on April 21, 1794, *Macbeth* (with Kemble and Mrs. Siddons in the title roles) and *The Virgin Unmasked* being the pieces chosen for the occasion. But neither the acting of Kemble nor that of Mrs. Siddons produces as profound an impression as the epilogue spoken by Mrs. Pope and containing the following lines—

> The very ravages of fire we scout,
> For we have wherewithal to put it out,
> In ample reservoirs, our firm reliance,
> Whose streams set conflagrations at defiance.
> Panic alone avoid, let none begin it—
> Should the flame spread, sit still, there's nothing in it—
> We'll undertake to drown you all in half a minute,
> Behold, obedient to the Prompter's bell,
> Our tide shall flow, and *real* waters swell.

UNCORKING OLD SHERRY:

No *river*, of meand'ring *pasteboard* made;
No gentle tinkling of a *tin cascade;*
No *brook* of *broad-cloth* shall be set in motion;
No ships be wreck'd upon a *wooden ocean;*
But the pure element its course shall hold,
Rush on the scene, and o'er the stage be rolled.*

(* Scene rises and discovers a cascade of water rushing
down from the tanks on the roof into a huge basin prepared
for its reception, dashing, splashing, tumbling over artificial
rocks, clearly showing that in such an awful event as that
of a fire, they can not only extinguish the flames upon the
instant, but actually drown the theatre. Applause.)

How like you our aquatics?—Need we fear
Some Critic, with a hydrophobia here,
Whose timid caution—caution's self might tire,
And doubts, if water can extinguish fire?
If such there be, still let him rest secure,
For we have made 'assurance doubly sure,'
Consume the scenes, your safety still is certain;
Presto!—for proof, let down the iron curtain.*

(* Iron curtain let down. Struck with heavy hammers to
prove that it is something more than stage iron. The clang
reverberates through the house mingling with the uproar of
a delighted audience.)

One night the scenery of Drury Lane catches fire, and
Suett rushes upstairs to Sheridan to tell him that the fire
is extinguished and that he is going to tell the house. "You
fool," says the manager, "don't mention the word 'fire'; run
down and tell them that we have water enough to drown
them all, and make a face."

. . . beaux and ye plum'd belles, all perch'd in front,
You're safe, at all events, depend upon't;
So never rise like flutter'd birds together,
The hottest fire shan't singe a single feather.

In 1792 the rival Pantheon Theatre burns, and Sheridan, watching the fire, exclaims aloud—"Is it possible to extinguish the flames?" A benevolent Irishman, thinking to allay Sheridan's supposed anxiety lest the rival house survive, remarks—"For the love of Heaven, Mr. Sheridan, don't make yourself uneasy, Sir. By the Powers it will soon be down; sure enough, they won't have another drop of water in five minutes."

2.

Two years after the opening of New Drury Lane Theatre Sheridan falls dupe to William Ireland, a lad of nineteen who palms off a new Shakespearean manuscript on the dramatist. The play is entitled *Rowena and Vortigern* and it produces a sensation in literary circles. Parr, and Pye, the poet laureate, and sixteen others sign a paper solemnly testifying to their belief in the manuscript. Boswell, after asking for and nearly draining a tumbler of warm brandy and water, rises from his chair, saying—"Well, I shall now die contented, since I have lived to witness the present day." Kneeling down, he adds—"I now kiss the invaluable relics of our Bard, and thanks to God that I have lived to see them."

Mr. Harris, the manager of Covent Garden Theatre, competes with Sheridan for the privilege of representing the tragedy. But Sheridan offers better terms and induces Ireland to consent to its first performance on the stage of Drury Lane Theatre. Three hundred pounds are to be paid down, and half the profits are to be given for sixty nights. Before signing the agreement, Sheridan calls upon Ireland to examine the manuscript. After reading several lines, he comes upon one which he tells Ireland is not strictly poetic. Turning to Ireland's father, a Spitalfields weaver who has converted himself into a connoisseur of books and pictures, Sheridan remarks—"This is rather strange, for though you are acquainted with my opinion as to Shakespeare, yet be

[269]

it as it may, he certainly always wrote poetry." Reading a few pages he lays down the manuscript and says in substance that some of the ideas are bold, yet crude and undigested, and must have proceeded from Shakespeare when a young man."

The world's verdict is the same—it praises many parts of the tragedy but says it is uneven. Tried experts like Porson and Malone, however, deny its authenticity. Kemble sides with them. He is prevented by Ireland's complaints from fixing the previous night, April Fool's day, for the representation. Nevertheless he adds to the program a farce, *My Grandmother*, and Covent Garden announces a play significantly entitled, *The Lie of the Day*.

At the opening Drury Lane is besieged by a crowd of playgoers eager to gain admission. The rush, roar, and confusion are astounding. The House is crammed to the roof. Every seat in the boxes is taken beforehand. Those who find the entrance to the pit blocked, pay for a box and drop down from a box seat into a vacant place below. The air is charged with the murmurs of contending factions. In the center box is the Ireland party; in the pit is the opposition led by a man named Captain Sturt whose criticisms are evidently those of the fifth bottle.

The performance begins. The young fabricator is behind the scenes, nervous and agitated. All goes well for a few acts, and Mrs. Jordan congratulates him on the success of the tragedy which he is supposed to have rescued from oblivion. But Ireland's opponents are reserving their powers. The absurdities of some of the actors then come to their aid. When Mr. Phillimore, playing the Saxon General Horsus, receives his deathly wound, either from prior intention or chance, he so places his unfortunate carcass that on the falling of the drop curtain, he is literally divided between the audience and his brethren of the sock and buskin—his legs being towards the spectators and his head, etc. inside the curtain. This, however, is not the only calamity, for as the wooden roller at the bottom of the curtain is rather ponderous and rests on his chest, he declines like Whiskerandos to "stay dying here all night" and starts to extricate himself, his groans reaching the audience and convulsing it with merriment.

But Kemble contributes most to the play's general damnation. All through he preserves a stolid bearing, not making the least exertion and delivering his lines in funereal fashion. As he speaks various Shakespearean passages, the audience with unusual intelligence calls out "Henry IV," "Othello," or whatever play the lines are stolen from. But at last this goes beyond endurance and Kemble gives the signal for the coup de grâce. When he intones the following description of death in the fifth act—

> And when the solemn mockery is o'er,
> With icy hand thou *tak'st him by the feet,*
> And *upwards so,* till thou dost reach the heart,
> And wrap him in the cloak of lasting night,

the most discordant howl "that ever assailed the organs of hearing" echoes from the pit. When Kemble can be heard again, instead of going on, he slowly and lugubriously repeats the line—"And when the solemn mockery is o'er," which provokes a fresh howl and the piece closes in confusion.

Ireland sleeps soundly during the night after the forgery is detected. Indeed he finds it easier to figure as a forger than as a Shakespeare. His bitterest disappointment is the monetary result. When he calls at Drury Lane on Monday morning, he is told that there are £206 in the treasury after the payment of all expenses. But this sum is divided between Sheridan and Ireland's father; Ireland obtains from his father £30.

Two successes of the New Drury Lane are *The Castle Spectre* and *Blue Beard.* The first by "Monk" Lewis has a prodigious run, owing partly to the sublime effect of sinking the ghost in a flame of fire and to the beautiful Gothic scenery. Sheridan does not pay the author his due and Lewis writes a bitter epigram—

UNCORKING OLD SHERRY:

There might indeed be blacker hearts
But none could be more rotten

Sheridan looks about for new sources of sensation. "Kotzebue and German sausages" being the order of the day, he produces *The Stranger,* a play adapted from the German of Kotzebue and touched up by himself. Its literary merit is nil, but it is exceedingly popular, helping to relieve a treasury exhausted by the *Vortigern* fiasco. Cheered by the success of this new departure, Sheridan adapts Kotzebue's *Spaniards in Peru,* a spectacular and patriotic melodrama, which is brought out on May 24, 1799, under the title of *Pizarro.* The piece runs thirty nights, crowds surge in torrents to see it, money pours in unceasingly, it is the talk of the day. In the same year it is printed at Philadelphia and long lingers on the stage. Someone belittles it as a paraphrase. "I am but a translator," Sheridan exclaims, "but then *what* a translator!"

The story of the masterpiece is a triumph of procrastination. When the date of the first performance is advertised and every box in the theatre is booked, Sheridan has not even started on the last two acts, nor has he given the words of a single song to Kelly. The last rehearsal is held on the day of the performance and its fourth act ended before three of the performers receive certain additional speeches for the fifth act which is being written out in the prompter's room by the author and carried down to them piecemeal. The actors are in an agony of fright, but all three are quick of study and have good memories.

Sheridan considers his own reputation involved in the success of the play. On one occasion he is found leaning half out of his box in passionate anxiety lest the fustian and rhodomontade of Kotzebue's melodrama be not well and truly scanned. He repeats every syllable after each performer, counting poetically the measure upon his fingers, and sounding it with his voice like a music master. He is in the utmost ill humor, shocked, stamping with anger at everything Mrs. Jordan says. With everything Kemble utters he is invariably delighted, clapping his hands with pleasure like a child. With some passages by Mrs. Siddons he is charmed; with others he is shocked, frequently stating to Richardson—"*This* is the way the passage *should* be spoken," and then repeating it in his own way.

Sheridan's anguish and rapture dismay his friends. *Pizarro* is grotesque. Its characters and incidents are ludicrous. Rolla is such a prodigy of disinterested love, friendship, devotion, and heroism as the world has never witnessed, and his opposite, Pizarro, is a monster of the other kind. The real disposition and motives of the adventuress Elvira are wholly inexplicable. She is alternately black and white—at one moment the friend of morality, at the next the slave of vice. She is at all events a most outrageous, wordy virago—one of those sensitive, amiable ladies with strong passions and weak intellects, much addicted to sentimental attachments in their youth and dram drinking in their old age.

The success of the play is largely political. The English nation is threatened with invasion, and the direct and palpable appeals are applauded with patriotic frenzy. In cheering Rolla's address to the Peruvians, the auditors feel that they are defying the might and power of France.

When Pitt is asked his opinion of *Pizarro,* he replies—"If you mean what Sheridan has written, there is nothing new in it, for I heard it long ago at Hastings' trial." It is the simple truth. Sheridan bedecks Kotzebue's skeleton with the glittering jewels of his denunciation of Warren Hastings: the rhetoric in Westminster Hall and the rhetoric in Drury Lane are of a piece.

Charles Fox says that Congreve's *Mourning Bride* is execrable, but *Pizarro* is the worst thing possible.

> Here shall you see how neatly we have spread
> Our English gilt on German gingerbread. . . .

Sheridan has another run of good luck. On May 15, 1800, their Majesties go to Drury Lane Theatre. The King no sooner enters his box and advances to acknowledge the wel-

[273]

come with which he is usually received than a pistol is discharged at him by a man who springs upon a bench in the
pit. Happily a person nearby sees the movement in time
to catch the assassin's arm just as the trigger is pulled.
Thus it happens that of the two balls with which the pistol
is charged, one strikes the wainscot a foot and a half above
the King's head and the other passes through the curtain
some inches high. The King, who sees the flash and hears
the report, turns to Lord Chesterfield, the Master of the
Horse, and says—"There is a pistol fired; there may be
another. Stop the Queen." Lord Chesterfield advises his
Majesty to retire to the back of the box, but the King replies—"Not an inch, not an inch." He stands firm and looks
round the house with composure. He tells an attendant that
he observed the fiddlers expected another shot, as they
covered their heads with their Cremonas. When the Queen
advances in alarm, he waves his hand to keep her behind—
"There was a squib." "A squib?" says her Majesty, "I heard
the word pistol and the report." "Squib or pistol," answers
the King, "the danger is now over, and you may come forward and make your courtesy."

For a few seconds there is an awful silence until the
audience is assured that the King is unhurt. Then cries burst
forth "Seize the traitor, tear him to pieces." In the midst
of the uproar the stage manager comes forward and announces that the man who has fired the shot is in custody.
The curtain is then drawn up, but the performance is not
suffered to continue until the royal anthem is sung. It being
demanded no less than three times during the performance,
Sheridan dashes off the following additional stanza—

> From ev'ry latent foe
> And the Assassin's Blow,
>   God save the King.
> O'er him Thine Arm extend,
> For Britain's sake defend,
> Our Father, Prince, and Friend,
>   God save the King.

The impromptu is delivered by Kelly and is received with rapturous applause. The King is visibly softened. When he gets home, he says to the Queen, "As it is all safe, I am not sorry it has happened, for I cannot regret anything that has caused so much affection to be displayed."

Sheridan wins the gratitude of the monarch by his behavior to the Royal Princesses, for he prevents them from going into their box by saying that a pickpocket has been taken in the pit which has caused a riot; his presence is required and he begs their Royal Highnesses to wait in the room. George III is touched by these proofs of sensibility and loyalty, saying they will endear Sheridan to him for the rest of his life. And the manager, his wife and eldest son are all bidden to court.

A little later the King and Queen are present at Drury Lane, the play by royal command being *The School for Scandal*. When Sheridan in attendance lights their Majesties to their carriage, the King says to him: "I am much pleased with your comedy of *The School for Scandal*, but I am still more so with your play of *The Rivals*—that is my favorite, and I will never give it up."

The monarch is ill in March, 1801, but he recovers, and he is very particular in his inquiries as to any allusions to his illness that were made in Parliament. Dr. Willis tells him exactly what passed. "One member alone moved an inquiry into the state of your Majesty's health and Sheridan in the handsomest manner got up and spoke against it and in the highest terms of your Majesty." On which the King says, "It is very odd, but ever since that attack of Hadfield's in the playhouse, Sheridan has shown a personal attention to me."

3.

Meanwhile the tide of embarrassment, which not even *Pizarro* can stem, beats with violence upon the theatre. In 1802 Sheridan is confronted by the establishment of private theatricals. A group of fashionable dilettanti assume the name of Pic-Nic Society from the manner in which they contribute to the general entertainment. There are to be farces and burlettas, feasts and ridottos, each member drawing from a silk bag a ticket which is to decide the portion of entertainment which he is expected to provide. The notion gets abroad that the Pic-Nic Society implies in some way or other an attack upon public morals and a pamphlet war begins. Professional theatricals are angry and jealous because it is thought that the support of the aristocracy will evaporate in private parties. Eventually, however, the Society sinks under the load of obloquy and ridicule heaped upon it, and Drury Lane is relieved of competition.

The respite is short. In the same year a bill is filed in the Court of Chancery by Grubb and Hammersley, the Drury Lane bankers, who deny the right of the performers to first claim upon the receipts. A greater crowd appears in Court to hear Sheridan argue in person than comes when Mrs. Siddons appears as Lady Macbeth. Sheridan speaks for two hours. The Lord Chancellor Eldon decides in his favor, but after passing a high eulogium on Sheridan quotes Dr. Johnson's last lines in the *Life of Savage*. ". . . negligence and irregularity, long continued, will make knowledge useless, wit ridiculous, and genius contemptible."

"I had thought at the time," says Kelly, "that the quotation might have been spared, and that it was perhaps harsh to speak the truth at all times."

From time to time Sheridan makes half-hearted attempts to get straight. He cuts his salary; he calls in the assistance of his talented son Tom. Tom works hard, keeps appointments with punctuality, but the accession of the second Sheridan does but little to compensate for the loss of Kemble, who after throwing up the stage management in 1796 and taking it up again in 1800, finally secedes altogether from Drury Lane in 1802, having failed to come to terms with Sheridan for the purchase of a quarter share in the theatre. Deprived of the great actor, the management has recourse to plays like Frederick Reynolds' *The Caravan*, (with real water, a real dog, a real splash, and a rescue)

[276]

and to the precocious talents of the infant phenomenon, Master Betty.

During the run of *The Caravan* an actor says to Sheridan—"There is no guarding against illness, but really—

"Really what?"

"I am so unwell that I cannot act any longer than to-night."

"You! my good fellow," is the rejoinder, "You terrified me; I thought you were going to say that the dog was taken ill."

And once Sheridan rushes into the green room calling out, "Where is my *preserver?*" Author Reynolds modestly presents himself but the manager says, "Pooh! I meant the *dog.*"

December 1, 1804. Covent Garden. A crowd is parading Bow Street and the Piazza early in the morning; by one there is a line of people at the doors of the theatre; before evening the line stretches in long impenetrable columns beyond Bow Street into Drury Lane. As the hour for opening draws near, the air is filled with shrieks. There is a crushing and fainting. The numbers become so great that a guard of soldiers is summoned to clear the entrance and approaches. Then the crowd is admitted, and the house is filled in a few moments. Yet still the crush continues. The pit, a surging sea, is filled by gentlemen who, as at *Vortigern,* pay box price, then rush in and leap over the balconies. Every lobby and passage is jammed with people content to pay any sum if they can only peep at the stage through a hole or a crevice. More than twenty people are overcome by the heat and pressure and have to be dragged up into the boxes as into a boat to be thence transported into the lobbies. Gentlemen wedged into suffocating corners are kept from swooning only by their wives who constantly fan them. Several more raise their hands as if in the act of supplication for mercy and pity. (Drury Lane with a very weak bill takes over £300 from the overflow of its neighbor.)

At last some order is restored, and Charles Kemble

comes out to speak a prologue, but he is not listened to.
He withdraws and the play begins. The first act of the
piece, which is the ranting, raging *Barbarossa* is got through
with the same confusion, the prodigy not having to appear
in it. Then comes the expected moment. At length, dressed
as a slave in white linen pantaloons, a short, close russet
jacket, trimmed with sable, and a turban hat or cap, at
the command of the tyrant, on comes the desire of all eyes—
Master William Henry West Betty. . . .

The night is one of rapturous triumph. All Betty's exertions are greeted with huzzas. The Prince of Wales, who sits
in Lady Mulgrave's box, leads the applause. Mrs. Inchbald,
who frankly hates prodigies, goes behind the scenes at the
end of the third act and finds the stage crowded with critics
airing their views. Most of them are openly declaring that
Garrick has returned to the stage, and only one or two have
the courage to whisper in her ear that "the Bottle Conjuror
is come again." But as everything in favor of the boy is said
in a loud voice and all adverse comments are uttered in a
low tone, it is not surprising that sober criticism should be
drowned beneath the flood of fulsome praise evoked by
Betty's performance.

In short a sort of delirium sets in. Betty's name is on
everybody's lips. He is feasted, feted, and petted by the
highest in the land, who wait outside the stage door to take
him to their houses in their carriages and chairs. Politicians
consult together so as to give their dinner parties on days he
does not act. Fox comes up to town on purpose to see him.
Pitt pronounces him a prodigy and adjourns the House to
witness his performance of *Hamlet*. He changes the life of
London—people dine at four and go to the play and think
and talk of nothing but the play. Even Grassini complains
that he has spoiled the opera. Sheridan takes Betty to
Carlton House where he enchants George with his manners.
Cambridge University makes the Infant Roscius the subject
of a prize poem. The two great artists, Opie and James
Northcote, are commissioned to paint his portrait, and he
appears as the central figure in several popular prints. In

one he and John Kemble are sitting on the same horse, Master Betty, who occupies the front place, remarking to his manager—"I don't mean to affront you, but when two persons ride on a horse one must be behind."

The excitement and notoriety soon bring on an illness and London society immediately overflows with sympathy for its idol. Bulletins announcing the state of his health are issued daily until he gets well. Ladies of title drive him in their carriages through the Park, stroke his auburn locks, beg from his parents snippets of them for their lockets. Philosophers go as mad as the quality and critics. Subsequently Drury Lane and Covent Garden share him between them.

He is the support of both the patent theatres. At Drury Lane, for twenty eight nights' performance, he brings in the prodigious sum of £17,201 out of which he is paid at the rate of £100 a night for nearly the whole time. At Covent Garden he attracts even more. (Kemble is engaged at £37, 16s a week.)

Unfortunately the chief result of his public appearance is to evoke a perfect mania for witnessing the performances of precocious children and stage struck striplings. Sheridan alone keeps cool on the subject of the Infant Roscius. A proposal is made to bring out Ned Kean as a rival to Master Betty. "No," says Sheridan," one bubble at a time is enough. If you have two, they will knock against each other and burst."

Though Betty is remarkably clever—he studies Hamlet in less than four days—his voice is heavy and monotonous, his delivery too rapid for distinctness, and above all he has no originality of conception. Houghton, the Belfast prompter, teaches him all—marks every inflection of the voice, every movement of the arms, and even of the legs. He owes everything to his instructor, and he is not ungrateful. One of the first uses he makes of his good fortune is to settle an annuity upon him.

Betty's inveterate habit of dropping his *h*'s adds but little to the charm of his delivery and enables Reynolds, when

[279]

asked whether the Infant Roscius does not surpass every living actor, to reply—"No, for I do not believe he can pronounce the very word by which he lives—Humbug!" But afterwards Betty is never ashamed to admit that the audiences of his youth were mistaken in him, and he is indeed, as his most cruel critic remorsefully acknowledges, no ordinary person after all.

CHAPTER 14

CORIOLANUS AND THE
ARCHBISHOP OF CANTERBURY

IN KEMBLE'S ACTING there is neither variableness nor the shadow of turning. He plays Hamlet like a man in armor, with a determined inveteracy of purpose, in one undeviating straight line. He is cold, stately, stiff.

It is so-called Roman parts that are best suited to Kemble's gifts. He is tall, very dark, with large, nobly cut features, and beautiful deep eyes. He looks magnificent in a Roman toga and has all the dignity and force suited to the costume. In *Coriolanus* the mob falls back from him as though they have run against a wild bull.

He is terribly pedantic. He turns his head so slowly that people imagine he has a stiff neck. His eccentric pronunciation of certain words is well known. Virtue becomes *vartue*, hideous, *hijjius*, beard, *bird*, cheerful, *churful*, fierce, *furse*, earth, *airth*, mercy, *maircy*, Rome, *Room*, aches, *aitches*. These peculiarities are made the subject of endless satire. A little lexicon is supplied on the back of each playbill to help the audience to understand his peculiar orthoëpy—

Conscience—conshince		merchant—marchant	
err	—air	odious	—ojus
farewell	—farwell	pierce	—purse
fearful	—furful	rode	—rod
insidious	—insijjus	sovereign—suvran	
innocence	—innocince	stir	—stare
infirmity	—infaremity	thy	—the
leap	—lep	virgin	—vargin
melodious	—melojus	ye	—jee

[281]

Aitches or aches—shall I speak both or neither?
If aches, I violate my Shakespearean measure,
If aitches, I shall give King Johnny pleasure,
I've hit upon it, Jove, I'll utter neither.

The Garrick school is all rapidity and motion; the Kemble school is so full of *paw* and *pause* that at first the performers, thinking the new competitors have either lost their cues or forgotten their parts, frequently used to prompt them.

Kemble comes up to Sheridan one evening, and they drink deeply. Kemble complains of the want of novelty at Drury Lane and that as manager he feels uneasy at the lack of it. "My dear Kemble," says Sheridan, "don't talk of grievances now." But Kemble keeps on saying, "Indeed, we must seek for novelty or the theatre will sink—novelty and novelty alone can prop it." "Then," replies Sheridan with a smile, "If you want novelty, act Hamlet and have music played between your pauses."

Even in his most convivial moments Kemble is solemn and funereal. The Parisians wonder at his talent for silence. His familiar table talk often flows into blank verse, and so indeed does his sister's—"You brought me water, boy; I asked for beer," he tragically exclaims to a footboy during a dinner. In society he is perpetually holding forth upon his one absorbing topic—himself. (Charles Kemble tells Crabb Robinson that he thinks Kemble is a better actor than his sister Sarah Siddons, an opinion shared by Kemble himself and probably by no one else.) At a Royal Academy dinner, he is discussing certain new readings with Scott, who sits next to him, when the great silver chandelier above their heads is seen slowly descending. Everybody springs to his feet, except John Philip, who remains immovable, and he afterwards rebukes Scott for interrupting his explanations. When he is living at Lausanne, he feels rather jealous of Mt. Blanc. He dislikes to hear people always asking, "How does Mt. Blanc look this morning?"

Avarice is his failing—a family failing. While he is starring in Liverpool, he promises to go over to York to play one night for his old manager, Tate Wilkinson, for thirty guineas. But when he finds the town all in excitement at the announcement, and that there is likely to be a crowded house, he refuses to appear under half the receipts.

But he is the very reverse of servile. His conduct and bearing are in keeping with his imposing outward appearance. Towards the public as to individuals, they are commanding, calmly superior, a trifle haughty. And he more than once proves capable of taming the rowdy elements in the theatre.

Once during a performance of Shakespeare's *Coriolanus*, for example, while he and his sister are on the stage, someone throws an apple at Mrs. Siddons' head. John Kemble steps forward, in the midst of the general noise and confusion, and says, "Ladies and gentlemen: I have been many years acquainted with the benevolence and liberality of a London audience, but we cannot proceed this evening with the performance unless we are protected, especially when ladies are thus exposed to insult."

A voice is now heard from the gallery shouting—"We can't hear you." Kemble then proceeds with great heat—"I will raise my voice and the galleries *shall* hear me. This protection is what the audience owe it to themselves to grant, what the performers, for the credit of their profession, have a *right* to demand, and what I will venture so far to assert, that on the part of the proprietors, I have offered one hundred guineas to any man who will disclose the ruffian who has been guilty of this act."

Loud murmurs and noise among the audience. Kemble goes on calmly, "I throw myself, ladies and gentlemen, upon the high sense of breeding that distinguishes a London audience and I hope I shall never be wanting in my duty to the public, but nothing shall induce me to suffer insult."

With these words he leaves the stage amidst loud applause from the audience, and the play proceeds without further interruption.

2.

Mrs. Siddons face is of a noble but somewhat severe and cold beauty. Her features are large, her eyebrows black and strongly marked, her mouth finely formed, and her eyes large and grave. Her nose is a little long—"there's no end to your nose, madame," Gainsborough exclaims when he is sketching her portrait. She is tall, dignified, statuesque. In short she is not petite, lively, elegant, and has not the boldly developed bust, the laughing cherry lips, and the sweet coquettish eyes which the fashion of the period demands. The prevailing style of dress with its hooped skirt, its paniers, its high pointed heels, is unbecoming to her. She is formed by nature for the draperies of tragedy.

Indeed tragedy is Mrs. Siddons' forte. It is the Mediterranean of her mind. To see her is an event in everyone's life. She makes women sob and shriek, and men weep, whenever she performs. Christopher North speaks of "the divine, inspiring awe" which she evokes, and Hazlitt speaks of her with a like enthusiasm as "not less than a Goddess or than a prophetess inspired by the Gods. Power was seated on her brow, passion emanated from her breast as from a shrine." More intelligible than these raptures is Tate Wilkinson's declaration, "If you ask me, 'What is a Queen?' I should say Mrs. Siddons." Kemble's ideal is a marble from the chisel of Phidias, hers from that of Praxiteles.

She is rich in the one great virtue which is wanting in so many of her professional sisters—and in no other. She is a grande artiste, but a very disagreeable woman. Her prudery is excessive; her boy's dress in Rosalind is a nondescript costume which has no resemblance to that of man or woman. She is by nature unfitted for the part. Her Rosalind wants neither playfulness nor feminine softness, but it is totally without archness—not because she does not properly conceive it—but how can such a countenance be *arch?* No woman is ever less of a Bohemian, and neither the temperament nor the habits of the Irish appeal to her. In

Dublin's theatre she is offended by the genial pleasantries flung to her from the pit when a man calls out, "Sally, me jewel, how are ye?" Or an impromptu dance is indulged in.

Her private character is excellent, and she retains to the last the esteem of her friends and of the aristocratic world. Of Horace Walpole she makes a convert. Washington Irving finds in her every disposition to be gracious, but, he says, she reminds him of Scott's knights who

> Carved the meat with their gloves of steel,
> And drank the wine through their helmets barred.

On the side of the passions she is throughout unassailable. She has admirers innumerable, but she never converts them into lovers. Sheridan says of her—"One can as well make love to the Archbishop of Canterbury."

In her conversation she is solemn, sententious, dull, and dry. She speaks very slowly as if she were declaiming a set speech. At times she is apt, like her brother John, to talk in rhythmic prose. When she purchases a piece of calico, "Will it wash?" she inquires of the shopman in so thrilling a voice that he starts back frightened by her vehemence. She paralyzes her dinner partner with an opening gambit like this—"I am very ignorant, but I thirst for information; pray, what fish is that?" At one of her receptions she is observed standing next to the Duke of Wellington, silent and with a haughty look upon her face, waiting for him to speak first.

Someone relates a melancholy story of a clerk in office who died suddenly in his bureau. Upon which Mrs. Siddons (not knowing the sense of the French word) says, "Poor gentleman, I marvel how he got there."

She is determined to make money for her children. She is sharp in business matters, quarrels with her Dublin managers, and incurs in a wider circle a reputation for stinginess. The limit of her ambition is £10,000; she has long since realized that sum twice over.

Sheridan takes liberties with her. One night as she steps

into her carriage to return home from the theatre, he suddenly jumps in after her. "Mr. Sheridan," she says, "I trust that you will behave with all propriety; if you do not, I shall immediately let down the glass, and desire the servant to show you out." Sheridan does behave with all propriety, but as soon as they reach her house in Marlborough Street and the footman opens the carriage door—"only think!" Mrs. Siddons adds, "the provoking wretch bolted out in the greatest haste and slunk away, as if anxious to escape unseen."

3.

A tall, superbly commanding figure strides forth from the flies. From half the audience bursts a storm of applause; from the other half, a still louder storm of hisses and catcalls. "Off with it! None of your Scotch for us!" they shout, and the cry is taken up in all parts of the house. This is not disrespect for the leading British tragedian playing Macbeth, but merely a protest against the real Scotch bonnet with the eagle's feather instead of the "shuttlecock" headdress of ostrich plumes usually worn.

A change of scene takes place, and majestic Siddons stands before us reading the fateful letter. She is greeted by round after round of applause—seven in all—carefully counted out as the just meed of her fame. A spirit of idolatry comes suddenly over the restless audience. They listen breathless to her words, not from an eagerness to follow the play, but with a sportsmanlike desire to catch the first "point" for applause. They have not long to wait. "To catch the nearest way," she utters with what spiritual cold, what depth of suggested crime! A wild cry from the "heavens" followed by a salvo of applause. The first "point" has been made, and the score is set down. The game is really on. At every familiar stroke of genius, the audience claps, stamps, and shouts its delight. When the other actors hold the stage, the excitement and interest abate. They talk or rather shout through their parts like people at some unpleasant and necessary task. They have few "points" to make, so what does it matter? The play wears on, the audience now listless or talkative, now intently and feverishly bound up in the sublime action of the protagonists. Wild is the applause that breaks in after almost every line of the sleepwalking scene. But this marks the limit of the public's patience. The play drags on to an end amid the rustling of silks and the murmur of gay voices.

CHAPTER 15

CONVERSATION AND
CHARACTERISTICS

A ROOM PANELLED in deal. Glitter of candles and sparkle of diamonds. Scarlet and blue waistcoats and powdered headdresses. Expectant and laughing voices. A door opens and a nervous red face with shining eyes appears.

"Sherry!" they cry, "Here's old Sherry," and they open their mouths to guffaw.

"Pass the bottle," he hoarsely replies. . . .

Sheridan can work like a racehorse and idle like a lizard. At an early age he writes on Chesterfield's *Letters*—"Hurry, *he* says, from play to study and never be doing nothing. *I* say, frequently be unemployed, sit and think." When Fox at the end of a session rejoices at the near prospect of lying under the trees at St. Anne with a book, "Quite so," replies Sheridan, "but why with a book?"

He is the grand master of delays. His days are generally weeks. "Punctuality," he has Joseph Surface say, "is a species of constancy, a very unfashionable quality." Halhed lectures him on his neglect of correspondence; his first wife teases him about it. He tells his father-in-law only three years after his marriage that he is the slowest letter writer in the world. "Procrastination," he assures Whitbread, "is always the consequence of an indolent man's resolving to write a long detailed letter."

He is no respecter of persons. Others than mere duns and bores are kept on tenterhooks in the castle of indolence till he emerges smart and smiling for his midday levée.

Peers and beauties take their turn with the rest and often walk "fifty miles on his d——d carpet." The Prince more than once has to see his carriage despatched for Sheridan, return to Carlton House. He will be the lackey of none. "We are all treated alike," sighs one of his martyrs, when he sees a coroneted letter lying unopened in the heap on Sheridan's table.

Certainly none can reproach him with what Mme. de Staël terms "that haste to arrive where nobody awaits you." Everyday he begins the world over again. He is addicted to "sleeping days." He constantly keeps his room till midday and usually breakfasts in bed.

His great speech on Warren Hastings is left behind at Deepdene, to Jockey Norfolk's intense amusement. Once he actually forgets that his banking account has been credited and is astonished to find that a payment to him over the counter is not a loan.

His bag of letters is all jumbled together, his table covered with papers. The mass of unopened plays in his library is called by Kemble "a funeral pile." He presses the Duke of Bedford to "consolidate" the rent of Drury Lane. Not hearing for a year, he writes in bitter complaint of the delay. The solicitor answers that his request has been granted a twelvemonth since, and sure enough, on a search being made, the welcome missive is reclaimed. He arranges with Woodfall to print some most damaging calumnies about himself in *The Public Advertiser* in order to give point to a complete refutation in the next issue. Woodfall duly publishes the slander; Sheridan never supplies the projected contradiction.

Poor Mr. Smyth has a terrible time of it with his disorderly patron. His letters are neglected, his appointments broken, his salary left unpaid. Once he is left at Bognor with an old servant, without money or occupation, waiting for a summons to London which never comes. Unable at last to live any longer on credit, after letters innumerable of entreaty, protestation, and wrath, he goes up to London determined to endure no more. But he is met by Sheridan with such cordial pleasure and surprise that he has not come sooner, and satisfaction that he has come at last, since Tom is getting into all sorts of mischief, that the angry tutor is entirely vanquished. "I wrote you a letter lately," says Smyth. "It was an angry one. You will be so good as to think no more of it."

"Oh, certainly not, my dear Smyth," Sheridan says. "I shall never think of what you have said in it, be assured." And putting his hand in his pocket, "Here it is," he says, offering the letter to Smyth. Smyth is glad enough to get hold of it, but looking at it as he is about to throw it into the fire, he sees that it has never been opened.

He breaks many appointments with Harris, the manager of Covent Garden. Harris, wearied out, begs his friend Mr. Palmer to see Sheridan and tell him that unless he keeps the next appointment, all acquaintanceship between them must end. Sheridan expresses great sorrow for what has been in fact inevitable and fixes one o'clock next day to call upon Harris at the theatre. At about three he actually makes his appearance in Hart Street where he meets Mr. Tregent, the celebrated French watchmaker, and tells him that he is on his way to call upon Harris.

"I have just left him in a violent passion," says Tregent, "having waited for you ever since one o'clock."

"What have you been doing at the theatre?" says Sheridan.

"Why," replies Tregent, "Harris is going to make Bate-Dudley a present of a gold watch, and I have taken him half a dozen in order that he may choose one for that purpose."

"Indeed," says Sheridan.

They wish each other good day and part. Sheridan proceeds to Harris's room.

"Well, sir," says Harris. "I have waited at least two hours for you again. I had almost given you up and if—"

"Stop, my dear Harris," says Sheridan, "I assure you these things occur more from my misfortunes than from my faults. I declare I thought it was but one o'clock, for it so happens that I have no watch, and to tell you the truth, am too poor to buy one, but when the day comes that I can, you will see I shall be as punctual as any other man."

"Well, then," says the unsuspecting Harris, "if that be all, you shall not long want a watch, for here (opening his drawer) are half a dozen of Tregent's best—choose any one you like, and do me the favor of accepting it."

2.

> Good at a fight, but better at a play,
> Godlike in giving, but the devil to pay.

Sheridan is the ideal borrower—"the true taxer who calleth the world up to be taxed. His exactions have such a cheerful voluntary air. What a careless even deportment! What rosy gills, what a beautiful reliance on Providence doth he manifest, taking no more thought than lilies! What contempt for money—accounting it (yours and mine especially) no better than dross. . ."

He passes long intervals in weathering the storm of the great unpaid, a fact which once leads him to observe of an actor's absence of mind, that it never extends to a Saturday. Even Garrick, reputed to be the most punctual of paymasters, is beset by actors clamoring for arrears. But where Garrick errs through caution, the reckless Sheridan errs through delay. Garrick is kind and hospitable, but he can be both jealous and stingy. His niggardliness makes him turn back on his way to a charity benefit because he has met "the ghost of a shilling."

Sheridan always finds the way out. Miss Farren on the eve of her marriage with Lord Dudley gets him to remonstrate with the manager. But Sheridan appeases the diminutive peer—"This is too bad. You have taken from us the brightest jewel in the world, and now you quarrel about a little dust that she leaves behind her."

His triumphs are due to a dangerous gift—the power of fascination. When he chooses, nobody can stand against him. Like Figaro in *The Barber of Seville,* "ce diable d'homme a toujours ses poches pleines d'arguments irresistibles." He is a veritable Deus ex Machina. Duns quit the Proteus (when they can catch him) with old scores unsettled on his desk and fresh commissions on his books. And he is deliciously cool. Shaw, the band conductor, once demands the return of £500. Sheridan retaliates by requesting for an important errand and meets his friend's anger with "My dear fellow, hear reason. The sum you ask *me* for is a very considerable one, whereas I only ask *you* to lend me twenty-five pounds." At another time as much as £5000 are granted without a murmur and his grave offer of security rejected as an insult.

He knows how to play on the foibles of others. Kelly and Sheridan are crossing the road along the churchyard of St. Paul's, Covent Garden, when up rides Holloway, the lawyer, furious at being denied admittance. Sheridan immediately begins to admire the horse, for a judgment in horseflesh is Holloway's weakness. When the flattered attorney asks if Mrs. Sheridan would not like such a mount, Sheridan replies that he may stretch a point if Holloway shows him the animal's paces. Off trots Holloway as proud as a peacock, and away ambles Sheridan as pleased as punch.

His appeals of "moneybound" from roadside inns are answered as if by magic. He turns stony Shylocks into adherents, wins over whole regiments of mortgages, and indeed may be said to recruit his bodyguard from rebels. "They tell me," says Sir Benjamin Backbite of Charles Surface, "that when he entertains his friends, he can sit down to dinner with a dozen of his own securities, have a score of tradesmen waiting in the antechamber, and an officer behind every guest's chair." He stages the bailiffs as he stages his plays. In 1792 he induces them to hand the ices at a fête given at Isleworth to Pamela and Madame de Genlis. A few years later when he banquets some statesmen, he gets the publisher Becket to stop the momentary gap in his bookshelves by lending a library. The footmen are Becket's assistants and the furniture comes from Drury Lane. Once, like Honeywood in Goldsmith's comedy, he introduces the man in possession as his guest. On another occasion an inconvenient bailiff is encouraged to drink himself into a coma and then handed over to the watch.

When he last sees Hertford Street in the crash of 1800, and Postans, the Sheriff's officer, offers him any article for which he has a sentiment or a necessity, "No, I thank you, my good fellow," he says. "Since it's come to this, all shall go. I'll make no reserve. All my affections are blunted, and I'll take a general leave of everything." He accordingly puts on his hat and is at the door when a sudden thought strikes him. Turning to Postans, he exclaims, "Yes, I have recollected one thing which I do wish to retain, and if it is no breach of honor, I will avail myself of your kindness." Postans bows assent, and he and Sheridan reascend the stairs. Sheridan goes to the library, and taking an old battered folio, says—"This is all I wish to carry with me." Putting it under his arm, he again prepares to leave the house. Postans, thinking he was going to ask for valuables, inquires the reason for this preference. "It belonged," says Sheridan, "to my father and has been the study of my life." The bailiff's curiosity is aroused and on turning to look at the title page, he finds that Sheridan has taken away a first edition of Shakespeare.

His doors are barred and damned up by gaping creditors. He is known to be so heavily in debt that the butcher actually walks off with a leg of mutton already in the pot because the cook is sometime fetching the money for it. Once a creditor finds him in unexpected possession of money. He is told that it is to meet a debt of honor. The creditor thereupon burns his bond before Sheridan's face and declares that he now considers his debt as one of honor. Sheridan pays him at once.

If a number of duns call in the morning and refuse to leave, he has them shown into various rooms, then asking, "Are the doors shut?" passes out. Once in a prodigious hurry, he leaps down the stairs. But Fozard, the keeper of a livery stable, who is on to his tricks, bars his way insisting on payment. Sheridan swears he is cleared out. Fozard leads him back to his study, goes through his letters with him, and sure enough £350 are discovered in installments in the unopened mailbags. "Lucky, lucky dog," says Sheridan, handing over the whole amount which exceeds the sum due. "Lucky dog, Fozard, you've hit it this time." And off he goes.

Out on the street. He is seriously late by now. He must take a hackney coach. But how to pay for it? Well, time will show. He hails a passing vehicle and is driven from place to place for three hours. There, by Jove, is Richardson. "I'll give you a lift, my dear fellow, jump in." And now for a good argument. Richardson soon grows warm. Sheridan affects to grow warmer and looks offended. "I cannot think of staying in the same coach with a person that will use such language." The check string is pulled and out jumps the artful dodger. Richardson still heated shouts through the window after him, then settles back in triumph in his seat, unaware that he will have to pay the heavy fare of the coach.

Smyth appeals to Sheridan's old servant to determine if anything can be done to remedy his patron's embarrassment. Edwards tells him that he found Sheridan's window, which rattles, wedged up with bank notes which the muddled reveller, returning late at night, had stuffed into the gaping sash out of his pocket.

Angelo is walking one day with Tom King in Pall Mall when they meet the celebrated clown Grimaldi approaching them with a face of the most ludicrous astonishment and delight. He exclaims—"Oh, vat a *clevare* fellow dat Sheridan is! Shall I tell you?—Oui—yes, *I vill. Bien donc.* I could no never see him at de theatre so je vais chez lui—to his house in Hertford Street, muffled in great-coat, and I say—'Domestique—you hear?' 'Yes,' 'Vell den, tell your master dat M——, de Mayor of Stafford, be below.' Domestique fly—and on de instant, I be shown into de drawing room. In von more minute, Sheridan leave his dinner party, enter de room hastily, stop suddenly, stare and say, 'How dare you, Grimaldi, play me such a trick?' Then putting himself in a passion he go on—'Go, sare! Get out of my house.' 'Begar,' say I, placing my back against de door, 'not till you pay me forty pounds,' and then I point to de pen, ink, and paper on von small tables in de corner, and say, 'Dere!—write me a check and de mayor shall go *vitement*—entendez vous? If not, morbleu, I vill—'

"'Oh!' interrupts dis clevare man. 'If I must, Grimaldi, I must,' and as if he were très pressé—very hurry—he write de draft and pushing it into my hand, he squeeze it, and I do push it into my pocket. Vell, den, I do make haste to de banker's and giving it to de clerks, I say, 'Four tens, if you please, sare.' 'Four tens!' he say with much surprise, 'de draft be only for four pounds!' Oh! vat a clevare fellow dat Sheridan is." Sheridan, enjoying the joke, pays Grimaldi the balance

He has more than one tiff about money matters with Kelly, manager of the Italian opera. This from Peake to Kelly—"I am desired by Mr. Sheridan to express his extreme astonishment at the letter you have thought fit to write. Your talking of 'lending *him* the £100 he *wants*' he considers an insult and not proceeding from ignorance, real or pretended, of the Proposition he made you, which was that you should actually abate £100 from your salary this year and certify it to the Trustees in consequence of your having taken a sum of money last year from the Theatre for doing so little."

Once Sheridan is £3000 in arrears with the performers of the Italian opera. Payment is put off from day to day, and they bear the repeated postponements with Christian fortitude. But at last even their docility revolts. They meet and resolve not to perform any longer until they are paid. As manager, Michael Kelly receives their written declaration on a Saturday morning that not one of them will appear at night. On getting this Kelly goes to Messrs. Morlands' banking house in Pall Mall to request some advances in order to satisfy the performers for the moment, but, alas, his appeal is in vain and the bankers are inexorable—they, like the singers, are worn out, and they assure Kelly with a solemn oath that they will not advance another shilling either to Sheridan or the concern, for they are already too deep in arrears themselves.

This is a poser, and with a sad heart Kelly goes to Hertford Street to Sheridan who has not yet risen. He sends him word of the urgency of his business but is kept waiting rather more than two hours in the greatest anxiety before Sheridan comes out of his bedroom. Kelly tells him that unless he can raise £3000, the theatre must be shut up and disgraced.

"Three thousand pounds, Kelly—there is no such sum in nature," says Sheridan with coolness. "Are you an admirer of Shakespeare?"

"To be sure, I am," says Kelly, "but what has Shakespeare to do with £3000 or the Italian singers?"

"There is one passage in Shakespeare," says Sheridan, "which I have always admired particularly, and it is that where Falstaff says, 'Master Robert Shallow, I owe you a thousand pounds.' 'Yes, Sir John,' says Shallow, 'which I beg you will let me take home with me.' 'That may not so easy be, Master Shallow,' replies Falstaff; and so say I unto thee, Master Michael Kelly, to get £3000 may not so easy be."

"Then, sir," says Kelly, "there is no alternative but closing the Opera House." And not quite pleased with this carelessness, he is leaving the room when Sheridan bids him stop, ring the bell, and order a hackney coach. He then sits down and reads the newspaper perfectly at his ease while Kelly is in an agony of anxiety. When the coach comes, he desires Kelly to get into it and order the coachman to drive to Morlands' and to Morlands' they go. There he gets out, and Kelly remains in the carriage in a state of nervous suspense. But in less than a quarter of an hour to Kelly's joy and surprise, out comes Sheridan with £3000 in bank notes in his hand. "Such was Sheridan—he could soften the heart of an attorney—there has been nothing like him since the days of Orpheus."

The playing Sheridan like the working Sheridan is informal. He is brimming over with fun. "Oh, how I long for Sheridan to roll with me on the carpet," writes his sister-in-law. He loves improvisation of every kind—from dressing an Irish stew to organising a sham fight with donkeys entrenched in ditches. "He is amazingly amusing," says Georgiana of Devonshire of her guest at Chatsworth. "He is going to Weirstay to shoot for a silver arrow; he is such a boy."

He can rarely withstand the temptation of tilting the board of the Italian image seller over the parapet of Westminster Bridge, though he amply compensates him afterwards. He and Tickell are always disordering the great houses, splashing like porpoises in their lakes, disguising themselves after dinner as Turks and then sending for the ladies to identify their spouses—leaping over ambuscades of cutlery, planning sham duels, pretending to be dead and returning to life again with alarming alacrity, or piquing the jealousy of husbands who live happily ever afterwards.

He frisks with the youngest—makes up as a police officer to arrest Lady Sefton for unlawful gaming, persuades a sentimental old maid to put a favorite cock to death and then hides behind her bed at night and crows faintly like the cock's ghost. Kelly begs him for a light role in *The Glorious First of June,* and Sheridan obliges him by providing the scene with a cottage at which Kelly is ordered to gaze earnestly for a moment or two and then to deliver himself of the following line—"There stands my Louisa's cottage; she must be either in it or out of it."

A distinguished company at a fancy ball where Sheridan figures as a pilgrim is convulsed by his sudden disappearance and return in propria persona. In the House of Commons he creeps quietly up to Dent, the introducer of the dog tax, and then barks like a dog at his feet. "His levities," once writes Fox to Grey, "are disgusting," but he "comes right in the end," and "right" signifies saying "ditto" to Mr. Fox.

From Horace Walpole on the Irish Strain: "Your Milesians have hearts as unsteady as the equator; they have always an ecliptic that crosses their heads and gives them a devious motion."

Sheridan partakes of the troubadour spirit—he refuses to join the Prince of Wales in any persecution of his miserable wife, exclaiming that never will he lift up his hand against a woman, and he is singularly devoted to that Prince of whom Windham remarks during the Warren Hastings' Trial, that he would rather be drowned in the Ganges than wrecked on the coast of Wales.

When the Aliens Bill is brought in, he moves to exempt ladies from its restrictions—"to show," he says, "that the age of chivalry is not gone in this country, whatever may become of it anywhere else." He allows himself to be mixed up in a dubious affair which abruptly terminates the Prince's connection with Newmarket. Jockey Sam Chiffney is suspected of spoiling the Prince's horse Escape for his first race in order to affect the betting upon the next day's race which the horse is allowed to win. Sheridan defends George before the Jockey Club and thereby loses the confidence of Charles Fox.

It is obviously an unworthy connection. Wilkes dines with or in company with the Prince who makes a little free with him and among other things presses him to sing. Wilkes declines, but the Prince insisting, he sings *God save the King*. "How long," says the Prince, has that been a favorite song with you?" "Ever since I have had the honor of your Royal Highness's acquaintance."

Disinterestedness is the keynote of Sheridan's public life. He never lobbies for grants in the West Indies, never tries to quarter himself on the pension list or to cross the floor to sit with a triumphant majority. Always a leader of the Whigs, he nevertheless refuses to sacrifice his own principles to those of his party. And at all times he disdains to be driven. "No, Hal, were I at the Strappado, I would do nothing by compulsion" is his Falstaffian answer to a publisher's offer of a £1000 for one of the speeches at the trial of Warren Hastings.

But though he can never be bribed by money to vote against his opinion, by flattery he may be bribed to do anything upon earth. The glory of his speeches hangs about him to his death. In one of his Stafford elections, no less than forty women march in his train, headed by a beautiful Miss Furnio. Poets hymn him, and poetesses. For over thirty years the pamphlets tingle with his name. He is a spectacle to the country. His four horsed coach has only to clatter through Chichester, and the whole town is out huzzaing. His popularity intoxicates his senses and enlarges his vanity to an alarming extent. He knows himself to be in the grip of a demon, and he confides to Lord Holland—"They talk of avarice, lust, ambition as great passions. It is a mistake, they are little passions. Vanity is the great commanding passion of all. It is this that produces the most grand and heroic deeds or impels the most dreadful crimes. Save me but from this passion, and I can defy the others. They are mere urchins, but this is a giant."

He enchants the most charming women of his generation. His conversation detains Lady Cork for two months at Chatsworth from a house awaiting her at Bath. It holds Rogers and Byron spellbound. It brings up Thackeray's witty and beautiful grandmother night after night to the Westminster house of her uncle Peter Moore for the mere pleasure of hearing him. It disarms and softens his opponents. It conciliates the commonplace George Rose who once boasts that he christened a son William in honor of Pitt and is told by Sheridan that a rose by any other name would smell as sweet. For a long space it "dulcifies" Burke's righteous asperity. Even Lady Holland's dislike is not proof against the spell. "Whenever I see him," she sets down in her day book, "if but for five minutes, a sort of cheerful frankness and pleasant wittiness puts to flight all the reasonable prejudices that I entertain against him." Only twice is Sheridan mentioned as speechless, once for want of the bottle, and a second because of it.

After the performance at Drury Lane, no thought of bed enters his mind. There is always Brooks's to go to or the Beefsteak Club where Charles Fox may be met with, whom of all other men Sherry delights to amaze, "firing and blazing away for the evening like an inexhaustible battery." On one memorable occasion Fox seats himself between Sheridan and Bannister and does nothing but fill their glasses and listen to their conversation, whilst they, making his head a kind of shuttlecock, hit it on each side with such admirable repartees that he roars aloud like a bull.

No wit is more cordial than Sheridan's. It has point without sting. Fox once enters the House just after Burke has floored one of a noble Lord's nine mercenaries. "What's up?" inquires Charles of Dick, as cheers rend the air. "Nothing, only Burke knocking one of the ninepins down," Dick retorts. When the Duke of York retreats before the French, he gives the toast—"To the General and his brave followers." He quickly finishes off Sheldon, a Catholic turned Protestant who has to explain matters when Sheridan condoles with him as still excluded by an illiberal system. The encounter takes place in a country house where the guests sit up till the small hours drinking and talking. At three o'clock Sheldon draws out his watch with "This is too much, I'm off." Sheridan who so far has barely referred to his friend's conversation, then quietly observes, "Damn your apostate watch and put it into your Protestant fob."

"A joke on your lips is no laughing matter," is his warning to Lord Lauderdale's threat of repeating a good story. And on entering a silent room where the same dull friend is prosing, he infers from the silence that Lauderdale has just "committed a joke."

A friend warns him that alcohol will destroy the coat of his stomach. "Well, then, my stomach must just digest in its waistcoat." To a long suffering creditor who importunes him to name a day for payment, "Certainly," he says, "the Day of Judgment, but no, stay, that is a busy day—make it the day after." A footman drops some plates with a crash but without injury. "You silly fool," says Sheridan, "all that d——d noise for nothing."

A watchman finds him in the street fuddled and bewildered and almost insensible. "Who are you, sir?" No answer. "What's your name?" Hiccups. "What's your name?" "Wilberforce."

Someone at the theatre runs after him to ask if algebra is not a language. "To be sure, an old language, spoken by an ancient people called the Classics."

Mrs. Cholmondeley asks him for an acrostic on her name. "An acrostic on your name," says Sheridan, "would be a formidable task; it must be so long that I think it should be divided into cantos."

He attacks the arch pluralist Dundas who attempts to exculpate himself by announcing gravely that his situation is not to be envied, that every morning when he gets up and every night when he goes to rest, he has a task to perform almost too great for human powers. In the flurry of the moment Dundas has forogtten his recent marriage. Sheridan instantly retorts that he himself would be very happy to relieve him from the fatigues of the Home Department.

He rallies the writhing Secretary of State on the same subject later—"Summer, autumn, winter have passed and spring is come; and yet the right honorable secretary still groans under the same load."

A reporter who sits on Cobbett's right, having missed one passage, pesters Cobbett for several minutes to repeat the words to him, swearing that he may as well go home without his *two eyes* as without the *two pies* (referring to a speech on the two Oppositions which have been compared to two Magpies), "for," he says, "you cannot imagine, sir, how fond the public are of Sherry's little jokes."

At a supper one night after a great ball at Burlington House, Sheridan and Monk Lewis get into a dispute which

Lewis will have decided by a wager and he says—"I lay
you the profits of my play (which by-the-bye, Sheridan,
you have not paid me)."

"I do not like high wagers," replies Sheridan, "but I'll
lay you a small one—the worth of it."

The little author becomes as mute as a fish from the
rebuff. "It is not every man that can carry a *bon mot*,"
Mrs. Fitzherbert observes sapiently.

Even when he is dying Sheridan retains his fine sense
of humor. In the bare hall to which bailiffs lay siege and
where duns hide in ambush, he orders a placard to be hung
with this inscription—"I know your necessities before you
ask them and your ignorance in asking."

CHAPTER 16

ALL THE TALENTS

IN MARCH OF 1801 falls the startling blow of Pitt's abdication. His pro-Catholic inclinations are one motive; the state of his health another. He wishes to palliate his Act of Union with Ireland by a full Catholic Emancipation.

He announces his intention of introducing a bill in Parliament. It is the only difference of opinion, says George III, which he has ever had with Pitt. George writes Speaker Addington urging him to use his utmost endeavors to divert his friend from his purpose. Addington sees Pitt but in vain. The Prime Minister is determined to bring in the bill or resign. George, greatly distressed, passes several sleepless nights. He unbosoms himself to one of his equerries, General Garth. "Where," he asks forcibly, "is that power on earth to absolve me from the due observance of every sentence of that oath, particularly the one requiring me to maintain the Protestant reformed religion? Was not my family seated on the throne for that express purpose, and shall I be the first to suffer it to be undermined, perhaps overturned? No! I had rather beg my bread from door to door throughout Europe than consent to any such measure."

The upshot is that Pitt resigns. On Pitt's resignation George instantly summons Addington to take the seals. The Speaker shrinks from the task. He is one of Pitt's dearest friends; they have been children together; their fathers were close friends before them. While Addington hesitates, Pitt comes forward and urges his friend to accept the vacant post. Believing that Pitt will again return to power, he modestly speaks of himself as a "sort of locum tenens."

His industry and good intentions cannot make up for his own dullness and incapacity. With the country gentry he is popular. Self-satisfied and honorable, a strong Churchman, narrow in mind and sympathies, he is trusted by them. They understand him, for he is one of themselves. He is frank and jovial, and in his old age calls himself the last of "the port wine faction." His very mediocrity suits them better than the loftiness of Pitt. He considers that no one is fit to be a public man who cares a farthing whether he shall die in his bed or on a scaffold.

For the abilities of Addington, Fox entertains the most sovereign contempt. He once observes in a large party—"My Lord Salisbury would make a better minister, only he is wanted for court dancing master."

Addington's cabinet is weak—or dull or vacuous or at least consists of amiable pedantic triflers. Sheridan compares the elements to the dregs at the bottom of a good bottle of Tokay. But arrayed against this combination, the strength of the strong is frittered away by being splintered into ten or fifteen factions.

One day Sheridan calls to discuss matters with Fox and is amazed and amused to discover his friend closeted with Lord Grenville—Fox who stands for peace at any price, Grenville, Pitt's bellicose Foreign Secretary; Fox, warm and wilful, Grenville (with the soul of a shopkeeper) cold and calculating.

Another element pervades the stage. The Prince reappears as a political factor and at this moment wavers between Pitt and Fox. Once more Sheridan plays his old part of Grand Vizier of Carlton House whither he is now frequently summoned for secret confabulations that last from midnight till four in the morning without supper or "a drop of wine." At the opening of 1803, when the King's state is parlous and it is thought again that the Prince may be Regent, Fox who despises the Prince, nonetheless waits on and listens to him. Pitt keeps aloof, but his emissaries are active. As for the Grenvilles, their haste to treat is almost indecent. But though Sheridan is high in favor, he by no means bends his knee to all the Prince's whims. He even dares his displeasure by opposing his wish for active military service. Yet his influence is still commanding. George is always requiring, dining, flattering, exploiting the inexhaustible Sheridan. And over and over again he begs and begs in vain to mark his sense of gratitude. Sheridan does take some gifts for his son—£1500 for young Alcibiades in a divorce suit, and, with a pang, £8000 to forward that son's political career. In 1804 Tom is made aide de camp to Lord Moira in Edinburgh and later appointed Muster-Master General of Ireland. Finally Sheridan accepts the office of Receiver General to the Duchy of Cornwall (worth about £1400 per annum). But when Tom marries he tries to persuade the Prince to transfer the appointment to his son. The Prince refuses on the sole ground that Sheridan's reputation is such that "it makes it not only justifiable but most honorable to him, the Prince, to make such a selection for the office."

Sheridan steadies the Prince to Foxite leanings. But though he is never weary of praising Fox, he dissents from the oracle. He refuses to endorse his policy of peace at any price and upholds the war preparations of Addington. The times are critical. It is feared that the French will invade England. Sheridan cannot approve of terms with Napoleon and refuses to hail him as an emancipator of the people. With all his might he presses on his countrymen the menace of the universal invader. "Do we not see," he exclaims, "that they have planted the tree of liberty in the garden of monarchy, where it still continues to produce the same rare and luxurious fruit? . . . It is not glory they seek for, they are already gorged with it; it is not territory they grasp at, they are already encumbered with the extent they have acquired. What is then their object? They come for what they really want—they come for ships, for commerce, for credit, and for capital. Yes, they come for the sinews and bones, for the marrow and for the very heart's blood of Great Britain." He is "the meanest and basest of mankind" who prefers some party principle to the complete protection of England. As for himself, he will never sacrifice the Commonwealth to faction. Napoleon has wholly transformed his view of the French Revolution.

"Look at the map of Europe, and we see nothing but France. It is in our power to measure her territory, to reckon her population, but it is scarcely within the grasp of any man's mind to measure the ambition of Bonaparte. Russia, if not in his power, is at least in his influence—Prussia is at his beck—Italy is his vassal—Holland is in his grasp—Spain at his nod—Turkey in his toils—Portugal at his foot. When I see this, can I hesitate in giving a vote that shall put us upon our guard against the machinations and workings of such ambition? . . ."

And then turning to Fox—"I perfectly agree with my right honorable friend that war ought to be avoided, though he does not agree with me as to the means best calculated to produce that effect. From any opinion he may express I never differ but with the greatest reluctance. For him my affection, my esteem, and my attachment are unbounded, and they will end only with my life. But I think an important lesson is to be learned from the arrogance of Bonaparte. He says he is an instrument in the hands of Providence—an envoy of God . . . to restore happiness to Switzerland, and to elevate Italy to splendor. . . . Sir, I think he is an instrument in the hands of Providence to make the English love their Constitution the better, to cling to it with more fondness, to hang round it with truer tenderness . . . I believe too that he is an instrument to make us more liberal in our political differences, and to render us determined with one hand and heart to oppose any aggression that may be made upon us. If that aggression be made, my friend will, I am sure, agree that we ought to meet it with a spirit worthy of these islands; that we ought to meet it with a conviction of the truth of this assertion, that the country which has achieved such greatness has no retreat in littleness; that if we could be content to abandon everything, we should find no safety in poverty, no security in abject submission; finally, sir, that we ought to meet it with a fixed determination to perish in the same grave with the honor and independence of the country."

The debate between Sheridan and Fox produces an amusing caricature by Gillray under the title of "Physical Aid or Britannia recovered from a trance: also the patriotic courage of Sherry Andrew and a peep through the fog." Fox with his hat pulled over his eyes cannot see the French boats which are to carry the French army to England. But the chief figure is Harlequin Sheridan who flourishes a cudgel inscribed: "Dramatic Loyalty" and blusters out this menace: "Let 'em all come, damme!—where are the French bugaboos? Single-handed, I'd beat forty of 'em! ! damme. . . ."

Fox does not mince matters in his wrath at Sheridan. He sneers at him, calls his vanity disgusting and incurable. He meets him at the house of mutual friends, and at such times, Sheridan, he says, looks "sheepish." The schoolboy knows he is a truant, but Fox plays the political pedagogue with a vengeance. At times he replies to Sheridan as if he were speaking to a swindler. This is extremely galling to Sheridan and he retaliates by abuse. Towards the close of 1803 he is often to be heard damning Charles in the midst of his enemies, and when drunk even in the presence of his friends. This goes so far once that Sir Robert Adair challenges him to a duel which Sheridan accepts. But a peace is patched up between them. The root of the trouble lies in Fox's jealousy of Sheridan's sway in Carlton House. He deprecates greatly the influence of a man whom he now mistrusts.

Besides Fox is the idol of an incense burning circle. Whatever he does is applauded to the echo by the select band of Townshends, Grenvilles, and Cavendishes. Their critical faculties are not proof against his irresistible charm. Sheridan loves to act alone. He cannot defer the whole time to Fox's judgment, which has proved invariably wrong. In a word, he is a bad Foxite and all good Foxites are bound to regard him as a traitor and renegade.

Sheridan considers himself second in command of the

Whig gentry, but Fox thinks him disqualified both by his lack of social position and by his lack of moral stamina. Possibly Fox is right. Sheridan has less stamina than a politician ought to have, but it would be difficult to prove that he has less stamina than Fox.

On May 12, 1804, Pitt comes in and Addington goes out. But Pitt's broken health and the fatalities that close the following year sound his knell. Even the rejoicings of Trafalgar are shadowed by thoughts of Nelson's death and soon bad news is received from Austerlitz where Napoleon wins a great battle. All Europe now lies in the hollow of his hand. Pitt is at Bath when a messenger seeks him out. With a sense of foreboding, he tears open the dispatch. "Bad news, indeed," he mutters and he at once makes ready to return to London. At Putney Heath Villa Lady Hester Stanhope is shocked by his wasted appearance and hollow voice. He has the "Austerlitz look" on his countenance. She leads him into his room, and as they pass a map of Europe that hangs from a wall of the corridor, he turns to her and says—"Roll up that map. It will not be wanted these ten years." A few weeks later his weakness becomes serious and he suddenly dies on January 23, 1806, at the age of forty-seven, with these words on his lips—"Oh my country— how I leave my country." Pitt is not an easy person to love, but he is a very great Englishman.

Pitt's death and Lord Hawkesbury's failure to form a government at length brings Fox and "All the Talents" into power under the leadership of Lord Grenville. This extraordinary cabinet contains far too many jarring elements to be lasting, and it soon becomes universally unpopular. The number of caricatures against the broad-bottomed ministry is very great. One anonymous print represents the King making a bowl of punch from a number of bottles, each bearing the face of one or other of the members of the coalition. He says—"Though the ingredients taken separately, may not be pleasing to every palate, yet when mixed together, they may go down with a tolerable relish." On April 21, 1806, Gillray founds a caricature on Fox's declaration that his place is not a bed of roses. Fox and his wife are pictured asleep in bed when Napoleon is attacking the minister in the midst of his slumber. The ghost of Pitt rouses him—"Awake, arise! or be forever fallen!"

The ministry of All the Talents sees Sheridan thrust aside. He is offered the Treasurership of the Navy and indignantly accepts. He writes to Fox and remonstrates, quoting his promise of cabinet rank. Fox does not deny the promise or offer to keep his word. Such a desertion breaks down their friendship.

Still his small office (nearly a sinecure with a salary of £4000 a year and apartments) tempts Sheridan to extravagance. Forty windows, five male servants, two four-wheeled carriages, five superior and ten "husbandry" and "Doss" horses, armorial bearings, and hair powder for three make up an amount of taxation which in this year of grace 1806 exceeds his house rent by nearly three pounds. Nor is his lavishness restricted to the needs of his establishment. Not only does he refurnish his official dwelling, but he gratifies his pride by restoring a large and unnecessary sum to the renters of Drury Lane while he gives a magnificent reception to the Prince and his party in honor of his grandchild's christening. All the delicacies of the season are provided. Kelly with two Italians sings a glee, and there is also a cantata on French horns and Scotch pipers.

His appointment inspires even the directors of the Bank of England with levity. When he is sworn in, the Earl of Essex writes—"I heard of Sheridan's appearing before the bank directors to open his Navy Office Account. The joke is that they all ran out of the room carrying away their books and papers."

> Oh, Sherry! Red Sherry!
> You'd make us all merry
> With your drolls, your stage tricks, and curvets;
> But don't, on Old Davy,

UNCORKING OLD SHERRY:

> Draw drafts for the Navy;
> Nor pay 'em as you pay your debts,
>   Red Sherry,
> Nor pay 'em as you pay your debts."

At the Westminster Election Sheridan stands against Admiral Hood and the nabob James Paull. He promises to give his opponents a *check*. "Oh, damn your checks, Sherry," exclaims a person in the crowd, "they're worth nothing." The vote is closely contested, and there is a great deal of elbowing, fighting, and coarse abuse. Paull, who is the son of a tailor, comes in for his share. Envious of the brilliant uniform and decorations of Hood, he observes with some spleen that if he chose he might have appeared before the electors with such a coat himself. "Yes, and you might have made it too," retorts Sheridan. And the latter once declares that he is only restrained from chastising Mr. Paull by considering that he should raise him in the estimation of society by kicking him out of it.

Viscount Petersham appears in the procession with "a gang of scene-shifters from Drury Lane" who are described by Paull as "one hundred and fifty hired armed bandits and assassins, marching in battle array from the committee room of one of the candidates."

Sheridan himself is roughly handled. He is stigmatized as "the harlequin son of a mountebank father," "a hireling Jester" whose career has been marked with every species of profligacy and extravagance.

> "Can such a MAN be fit representative for the Independent Electors of Westminster? No! ! No! ! ! Let it not be said that the dictates of an imperious minister shall determine your actions. . . Gentlemen, will you be represented by a dependent and a slave of the Grenvilles? Forbid it Justice! Forbid it Virtue! Forbid it Freedom! ! !
>   A Calm Observer."

On one occasion he is struck at and wounded. He cannot bear this unpopularity and means to give up. He is in low spirits and after taking only three bottles of port finds himself obliged to have recourse to brandy. He absolutely refuses to go to bed, declaring that his cursed ambition to represent Westminster will allow him no rest. Soon, however, he falls into a restless kind of doze, exclaiming at intervals, "Oh, my Treasury-ship! Oh, my popularity! Oh, Percy! Percy! had I but served the people with half the zeal I served myself, they had not now forsaken me." Then faintly muttering, "Cobbett, thou reasonest well!" he awakes.

He mounts the hustings. Catcalls, shouts, hisses. A large placard is waved at him—

> No Pantomimical or Farcical Shews to *trick*
> Us out of our
> Liberties
> No Mountebank Member.
> Honest Men Pay Their Debts. ROGUES
> do NOT.

"Gentlemen, you are d——d fools not to hear me," he begins. "I have always desired to hear your orators, and therefore I don't think it handsome that you refuse to hear me in my turn. When I was coming to the hustings today, I was told by my friends it was at the risk of my life, from the turbulence of the mob. But, instead of staying back, I came here on that very account. I was told that, for my safety, I must come by this door or that; but I preferred to come round Covent Garden, and through the midst of you. I am here a candidate for the cause of you all. My opponent Paull tells you what he *will* do. I tell you what I *have* done. I put facts in opposition to his pledges. I urge the whole progress of my political life against his promises, and I challenge the whole body of the lower classes of the people of England to point out a single instance in which I have not acted as their friend. I shall conclude by saying that I thank my friends and scorn my enemies." (Applause and holding up of cards and banners)—

UNCORKING OLD SHERRY:

Mr. PAULL
Three Queries
Is not Mr. Paull the agent of the Nabob of Oude?
Is he not in correspondence with Bonaparte?
Does he know that
500,000
Frenchmen are to land in this country before the meeting
of the New Parliament?

Such appeals to the patriotism of the electors are well advised: Sheridan wins by the close margin of 277.

So affairs march till Fox, soothed by his wife and at peace with the world, makes an edifying end, in the same year too which sees the death of Georgiana, the beautiful Duchess. The coldness of Fox cuts poor Dan to the heart. He begs to see the dying man and is allowed to enter the sick chamber. But Lord Holland and Lord Thanet remain in the room throughout the short and constrained interview, obviously at the request of Charles, who speaks a few cold words. Sheridan must find what comfort he can in being charged with the arrangements for the funeral at which he is one of the chief mourners. At the Crown and Anchor he gives vent to his emotions in a speech which is full of passionate regret at the death of his mentor—"With such a man to have battled in the cause of genuine liberty— with such a man to have struggled against the inroad of oppression and corruption . . . is the congratulation that attends the retrospect of my public life. His friendship was the pride and honor of my days."

The dissolution at the close of 1806 brings back thinned ranks for the ministerialists, and the King only awaits an opportunity to end the distasteful combination. The old measure for enabling Catholic promotions is revived. A bill is drafted and sent to the King, who returns it unread, a circumstance which induces Grenville to believe that he has no objection to its passage. They suppose George to be apathetic and insensible. They are deceived. He tells

Grenville that upon this subject his opinions will never change, that he never can agree to any concessions to the Catholics. "Were I to consent to a Catholic Emancipation," George says to the Duke of Portland, "I should betray my trust and forfeit my crown." Grenville waits on the King and tells him that the Cabinet cannot yield. "Is your resolution final?" asks George. "Yes," replies Grenville. "Then," says the King, "I must look about me." The cabinet's action is imprudent, and in March, 1807, the ministry of All the Talents is wrecked. "I have known," observes Sheridan, "many men knock their heads against a wall, but I never before heard of a man collecting bricks and building a wall for the express purpose of knocking out his own brains against it."

(No, no, Master Sherry, though pleasant thy wit,
For once it has failed the true matter to hit;
For men who thus wantonly build up a wall,
Have convinced the whole world they have no brains at all.)

Sheridan takes a statesmanlike view of the whole transaction. "I think they began at the wrong end. They should have commenced the measure of redress to Ireland at the cottage instead of at the park and the mansion. To have gone first to the higher orders of the Catholics, to have sought to make them judges, peers, and commoners, I do not know that such a proceeding, had it taken place, would not rather have served to aggravate discontent, as it might have been construed into a design to divide the interests of the Catholics. Sure I am that without a view to serve or to conciliate the Catholic population, I mean the poor, the peasantry, its effect would be nothing. It would be like dressing or decorating the topmasts of a ship when there were ten feet of water in the hold, or putting a laced hat on a man who had not a shoe to his foot. *The place to set out to in Ireland for the relief of the people is the cottage. . .* If you want the attachment of the Irish, begin by giving them some reason to love you. You ask Ireland for bravery

[313]

and take away the motives for it; for loyalty, and deprive them of the benefits of the Constitution. By the hapless Bill proposed but defeated, at least a Catholic officer might have been enabled to make a career, and need no longer rise to his own degradation. Charles the First asked Selden what was the best way to put down rebellion; to which Selden answered, 'Remove the cause.' Remove the cause of disaffection in Ireland, and disaffection will end."

On March 27, 1807, the Duke of Portland shelters a ministry in tatters, and on the Duke's death Spencer Perceval, the Chancellor of the Exchequer, replaces him at the helm. Perceval is a gallant fighter. "He is not," says a member of the House, "a ship of the line but he carries many guns, is tight built, and is out in all weathers."

The result of the dissolution is disastrous to Sheridan. There is a great desire among the Whigs to be rid of him altogether. He has alienated his friends at Stafford who have supported him for a quarter of a century, and Lord Holland bitterly resents his attempt to assume the mantle of Charles Fox. Partly through Grenvillite selfishness he is worsted at Westminster by Sir Francis Burdett in league with the tailor-demagogue Paull. He takes refuge in Ilchester, a borough found for him by the Prince of Wales. But his political misfortunes do not end here. He is mercilessly quizzed in the *Anti-Jacobin* and the *All the Talents Garland*—

> Alas! I cannot write or speak
> The tears run hissing down my cheek,
> My burning bosom vomits sighs
> Like fumes which from Vesuvius rise.
> Boiled by the flames of face and nose,
> My brain a melted lava grows;
> And like two meteors in the skies,
> When Northern lights disastrous rise,
> Glare in their fiery sphere mine eyes. . . .
>
> Have I not cause to deprecate

> Measures which brought me to this state,
> Which left me loafless, fishless—worse,
> Left scarce a guinea in my purse,
> Left all my duns, a clamorous throng,
> Hopeless—who lived on hope so long;
> And left that little humbug Paull
> To sneer and glory at my fall?
> What shall I do? my cash is gone,
> And credit I—alas!—have none;
> My wits may furnish me again
> With Burgundy and rich Champagne,
> But driven out of Place and Court,
> Ah! where shall *Sherry* look for *Port?*

Frederick Foster to Augustus Foster, July 30, 1806, before the death of Fox—"I am sorry to tell you that Fox is still very ill and I fear that his recovery is very doubtful. It is dropsy, and I am afraid not alone, but he has great strength of constitution and his lungs appear to be sound, so that we can't help entertaining hopes of his recovery. I must think that it would be a most amazing loss, and it's really frightful to see almost all the talent, genius, and worth of the country dying before one's eyes—Nelson, Pitt, Cornwallis, and our beloved, amiable Duchess. Heavens! what a change since this time last year; you will scarcely know the country at your return."

Lady Elizabeth Foster to Augustus Foster, October 18, 1807—"The Prince has given up politicks, is good friends with the King, and lives but for Lady Hertford. C'est vrai, je t'assure; à 50 ans près, elle a captivé le Prince. Il ne vit, ne respire que pour elle et par elle; la ci-devant amie est inquiète et triste. Je la plains, car c'est une bonne personne qui n'a jamais abusé de son pouvoir; as to the Duchess of Brunswick, you hear no more of her than if she was in Holstein."

CHAPTER 17

PLOTS OF THE REGENCY

SHERIDAN'S BRILLIANT and disordered
life goes on. A night spent in the House speaking on the
Repeal of the Additional Forces Bill and paying a magnificent tribute to the departed Pitt is succeeded by an evening opening at Lord Cowper's and continuing at Melbourne House. Thence at two o'clock "that terrible Sheridan" seduces his friend Creevey into Brooks's and it will
be four in the morning when he affectionately accompanies
his companion home and upstairs into Mrs. Creevey's bedroom, there merrily but indistinctly to repeat the jokes he
has made.

He spends an autumn at Brighton in riotous entertainment. He frolics like a boy, not like a man of fifty-five. On
one occasion when there is a phantasmagoria at the Pavilion
and all are shut in perfect darkness, he seats himself upon
the lap of Madame Gerobtzoff, a haughty Russian dame,
who makes a row enough for the whole town to hear. The
Prince of course is delighted with all this, but at last Sheridan makes himself so ill with drinking that he gets in a
perfect fever. Creevey feels his pulse and finds it going
tremendously and gives him some hot white wine of which
he drinks a bottle and his pulse subsides almost instantly.
In the evening he goes home and desires Creevey to tell
the Prince that he is far from well and is gone to bed.

When supper is served at the Pavilion about twelve
o'clock, the Prince comes up to Creevey and says—"What
the devil have you done with Sheridan today, Creevey? I
know he has been dining with you and I have not seen
him the whole day." Creevey says he is not well and has

gone to bed. Upon which the Prince laughs heartily, as if he thinks it all fudge, and then taking a bottle of claret and a glass, he puts them both in Creevey's hands and says—"Now Creevey, go to his bedside and tell him I'll drink a glass of wine with him, and if he refuses I admit he must be damned bad indeed."

Creevey excuses himself, but the Prince insists, so go he must. When he enters Sheridan's room, Sheridan is in bed and his fine eyes being instantly fixed upon him, "Come," he says, "I see this is some joke of the Prince and I am not in a state for it."

Creevey excuses himself as best he can and returns without pressing the wine on Sheridan, and the Prince is satisfied he must be ill. About two o'clock, supper having been long over and everybody being engaged in dancing, Sheridan appears powdered as white as snow and smartly dressed from top to toe. He goes into the kitchen for supper, jests with the servants, drinks a bottle of claret in a minute, returns to the ballroom, and dances away till four in the morning.

On another occasion he attends an immense assembly at Lady Caroline's, is one of the select few who sup downstairs with Lady Melbourne and the Prince and who do not separate until six in the morning. Next day he is completely and hopelessly drunk.

He needs what he rarely gets—"pure air, quiet, and innocence." He tastes these for a few days at Richmond Hill, but they figure far too little in his life. He enjoys managing his estate at Polesden, he is also fond of yachting and spends some of his leisure in this way, but for the most part he leads a completely urban existence—late nights, crowded assemblies, hectic amusements.

His faithful friend Richardson, who shares his carousals, dies. An urgent appointment with the Duke of Bedford delays him as he is starting out for the funeral, and the party arrives a quarter of an hour late to find that the ceremony has already been performed because the undertaker is pressed for time. The chief mourner is in despair. For now it will be said in town that he cannot shake off his d——d negligence even to pay respect to the remains of his dearest friend. The clergyman, touched by his grief and entreaties, consents to read the service over again which fills Richardson's unpunctual friend with a "sort of mournful exultation." On returning to London, however, he is so much overwhelmed by sorrow that he strikes his head against the door of the nearest house on entering Conduit Street. He meets Lord Thanet's condolences in a flippant way a fortnight later—"Yes, very provoking indeed, and all owing to that curst brandy and water which he would drink."

But in reality he is hard hit. "By my life and soul," he writes his wife, "if you will talk of leaving me now you will destroy me. I am wholly unwell and neither sleep nor eat." Esther, like Elizabeth in the past, is demanding a separation, but she is shortly reconciled to him.

He takes up with Tom Stepney, Groom of the Bedchamber and Secretary to the Duke of York. One day when both are drunk, Sheridan desires to introduce Stepney to some stranger, which he does by the following speech—"I always love to make my friend Stepney known when I can show him in the most advantageous light, and now, as already he can scarcely articulate, if he will drink but one other glass, he will be quite unable to speak and I will then present him to you."

Stepney, who does not quite relish this joke, takes an opportunity afterwards of saying to Sheridan that he has a question to put to him which he hopes as a friend he will answer candidly. The other says he certainly will. "Then," says Stepney, "the fact is that all the world say that your faculties are quite going and that you are almost sunk into a mere driveller. I have contradicted this report as much as I have been able, but I find it daily gains ground more and more. Now, Sheridan, tell me honestly, is that really the case?"

On the evening of February 24, 1809, while Sheridan is sitting in his accustomed place in the House and about to speak on a motion relative to the war in Spain, a red and lurid blaze streams through the windows. It is soon known that Drury Lane is on fire. An adjournment is proposed in Sheridan's honor, but he beseeches the House to waive this mark of sympathy and not to postpone the interests of empire to his private disasters. Calmly he leaves his place and goes to survey the scene.

Some time later two actors find him seated in one of the coffee houses in Covent Garden swallowing port by the tumblerful. One of the actors makes an astonished and indignant outcry at the sight of him, when Sheridan looking up replies—"Surely a man may be allowed to take a glass of wine by his own fireside." Hearing from them that they are going to observe the scene of devastation, he expresses his desire of going with them. They quit the tavern and mingle with the crowd standing for some time at the end of the Piazza in Russell Street. Sheridan looks at the blazing ruin with the utmost composure. At length the gentlemen express surprise that he can witness the destruction of his property with so much fortitude. "There are but three things that should try a man's temper," answers Sheridan, "the loss of what was the dearest object of his affections—that I have suffered; bodily pain, which, however philosophers may affect to despise it, is a serious evil—that I have suffered; but the worst of all is self reproach—that, thank God, I never suffered!"

Among the possessions that perish are an organ that belonged to Handel and a clock that was formerly Garrick's. Among them also are two treasures which Sheridan values beyond all price—a bust of the Prince of Wales by Nollekens and the harpsichord belonging to Elizabeth Linley.

At Sheridan's request Samuel Whitbread, headstrong brewer and philanthropist, undertakes to form a committee to rebuild, recast, and refinance Drury Lane. Whitbread appoints a powerful committee which Byron eventually joins. Some of the money is soon found, a scheme is set on foot, and plans for a fireproof structure are prepared. The first stone is laid in October, 1811, and the

never can see him as *deeply wounded,* as I have seen him lately, without feeling the full extent of my regard for him. . . On the subject of debate yesterday my whole heart and soul is *with* Sheridan."

2.

At the close of 1810 the death of Princess Amelia (his favorite daughter) finds the poor old King irretrievably disordered. He begins by talking of the Lutheran religion, of its superiority to the Church of England, and ends with growing so vehement that he really rants forth its praises without mentioning the real motive of his preference—the left-handed marriages allowed. Sometimes he conceives himself shut up in Noah's ark as an antediluvian; sometimes he fancies himself possessed of a supernatural power and when angry with any of his keepers, stamps his foot and says he will send them down into hell. The Queen enters his apartment during one of his lucid intervals and finds him singing a hymn and accompanying himself on the harpsichord. When he has concluded, he kneels down and prays aloud for his consort, for his family, for the nation, and lastly for himself, that it might please God to avert his heavy calamity, or if not, give him resignation under it. Then his emotions overpower him and he burst into tears. He is never again sane.

He finds much comfort in religion and on one occasion declares, "Although I am deprived of my sight, and am shut out from the society of my beloved family, yet I can approach my Blessed Lord," and thereupon administers to himself the Sacrament. Indeed he is unhappy only when he cannot have his favorite dinner of cold mutton and salad, plover's eggs, stewed peas, and cherry tart, and fearful (he who in his senses has never known fear) when it is proposed to shave his beard. "If it must be," he says, "I will have the battle axes called in."

He loves to wander through the corridors, a venerable

figure with a long silvery beard, attired in a silk morning gown and ermine night cap, holding imaginary conversations with ministers long since dead.

So pleasantly does he while away the time that sometimes his dinner is ready before he expects it. "Can it be so late?" he asks. "Quand on s'amuse, le temps vole." He is fully convinced that the Princess Amelia is alive and happy at Hanover, enjoying perennial youth and beauty, and he believes that Lady Pembroke is his wife. Her absence angers him. "Is it not a strange thing, Adolphus," he says to the Duke of Cambridge, "that they still refuse to let me go to Lady Pembroke, although everyone knows I am married to her; but what is worse, that infamous scoundrel Halford was at the marriage, and has now the effrontery to deny it to my face."

He considers himself no longer an inhabitant of this world and often, when he has played one of his favorite tunes, observes that he was very fond of it when he was in the world. He speaks of the Queen and all his family and hopes they are doing well now, for he loved them very much when he was with them. The belief that he is dead is one of his regular delusions. "I must have a new suit of clothes," he says one day, "and I will have them black in memory of George the Third, for he was a good man."

The worn Regency problem is at once revived, and Sheridan is forced into a labyrinth of intrigues with the shady, the disreputable and the corrupt. The emergency arises at a time when it is hardly possible for him to come through it with credit. He is broken in health and in a desperate case financially; he is generally drunk. Worse than all this, he is hopelessly bound by his allegiance to the Prince of Wales of whom Grenville dispassionately declares "that a more contemptible, cowardly, unfeeling, selfish dog does not exist." And it is for this man Sheridan entertains feelings of utmost devotion—"by whom to be esteemed is the glory and consolation of my private and public life. . . There never did exist to Monarch, Prince, or man, a firmer or purer attachment than I feel, and to my death shall feel, to you, my Gracious Prince and Master. . ."

Sheridan does not intend as Fox and Grenville did to use the Prince as a stick to beat the government and by holding the stick to have the real power. He is no leader. His aim is much more to stay at the Prince's elbow—unofficially if need be—with suggestion and intimacy. He prefers pulling the wires to strutting on the stage. It pleases his vanity. He has no ambition to be the central figure, but he cannot bear the thought of not being in the picture at all. The stand he has chosen has no alternative. He must cling to the Prince or disappear and Sheridan cannot face disappearance. His vanity conquers his pride. Added to this is his dislike of Grenville, who throughout treats him with arrogant contempt, and all these varied and mixed motives lead him to play a perplexing part during the Regency crisis.

The question of Regency restrictions is debated in Parliament, and the Tories under Prime Minister Perceval draft their proposals. These are presented to the Prince, who requests Grey and Grenville to draw up an answer to them. The way seems clear. Perceval will go, and they will come in and arrange the chessboard as they please. But the noble Lords compose a document which proves most distasteful to George, as it accepts the principle of limiting his prerogative with the barest murmur of protest, thus sacrificing his consistency. Sheridan is consulted and drafts a reply more in keeping with the Prince's wishes. Grey and Grenville are infuriated and go so far as to address a remonstrance to the Prince, expressing "their deep concern in finding that their humble endeavors in His Royal Highness's service had been submitted to the judgment of another person, by whose advice His Royal Highness had been guided in his final decision, on a matter on which they alone had, however, unworthily, been honoured with His Royal Highness's commands." And they go on to show the inconvenience which may arise from the interference of unauthorized advisers in transactions for which they should be practically and constitutionally responsible.

Such a declaration is bold and injudicious. The passion for pen and ink is too strong upon Lord Grenville. It outweighs every other consideration. The Prince shows the letter to Sheridan who, sore at the whole transaction, bitterly ridicules the charge of undue influence and declares that he has acted throughout on the Prince's commands and with an aim to reconcile the conflicting views of all parties in his short answer. Besides he maintains that till Grey and Grenville are actually ministers they are not technically in a responsible situation. The upshot of the wrangle is that George, incensed at the dictatorial tone of the Whig leaders and fearing from Grenville a renewal of the Catholic question, retains Perceval in power. Sheridan is supposed to have been largely responsible for the defeat of the Whigs. Lord Grenville never sees him and Lord Grey is hardly civil to him when he does.

On May 11, 1812, Prime Minister Perceval is assassinated. The cabinet is bewildered by his death; a fresh attempt is made to strengthen it but fails. No agreement being found possible, the House steps in and addresses the Regent, begging him to form a strong and efficient administration. He sends for Wellesley and offers him the premiership, but Wellesley soon finds that Liverpool and his Tories will not serve under him at all while Grey and Grenville will only serve on conditions which he cannot grant. The Catholic question, the Peninsula War block his way. Above all the Regent will have none of his bullies, the Grenvillite Whigs—that is positive. His state is hysterical. He cries long and loud; he nearly goes into convulsions and doubts are entertained of his sanity. Lord Moira is next begged to form a government but declines. The Regent calls Grey and Grenville a couple of scoundrels. But he is soon afterwards treating with these haughty Whigs to whom he commits the task of forming an administration. Grey and Grenville insist upon the resignation of the Household if they are to take office. This the Prince categorically refuses, supported by Lord Moira and Sheridan. Negotiations are broken off, and Wellesley is vainly attempting to form a cabinet when Lord Yarmouth, the Vice Chamberlain, tells Sheridan that the Household will resign once Grey and Grenville are installed. This is not quite the same thing as being dismissed by the Prince beforehand and may not satisfy the noble Lords, but it is information which certainly would interest them and which Sheridan should pass on. This he omits to do. He even makes a bet of £500 in Tierney's presence after Yarmouth's communication that the Household will not resign. The Regent finally takes the bit into his mouth and kicks over the traces. Liverpool and the Tories enter on their kingdom, and the Whigs are out till the days of the Reform Bill.

Hardly has Liverpool been installed than the truth of Sheridan's transaction comes to light. Sheridan is reviled on all sides for suppressing the information. It is even rumored that Yarmouth asked him to convey the decision of the Household to Ponsonby, the informal head of the Opposition. Sheridan strenuously denies the charge. If not actually treacherous to the Whigs, he has certainly not been loyal. The blackest thing against him is the bet.

Painful exculpations follow in the House of Commons. He hardly comes to the real point in his efforts to put himself in the right. On June 17, 1812, he speaks eloquently of the Prince and clears himself of the charge of servility and "that rubbish of secret influence." He then sidesteps towards the Catholics of Ireland, approaches the question of the Household, hesitates, and passes his hand over his forehead. The House calls on him to sit down. He does so, drinks a glass of water, and attempts to proceed, but he is overcome with faintness and obliged to give it up. On June 19 he is in better health and takes an almost too jaunty tone about the bet, but he sums up his attitude clearly—"My right honorable friend (Tierney) said to me, I hear the Household are going to resign. I replied I did not believe it. And why did I not believe it? . . . I knew that resignation was contingent upon a circumstance which, at the moment of the bet, was more remote from taking place than ever." Then off he goes again on the subject of Catholic Emancipation; finally he stresses his political disinterestedness.

"His whole speech," reports Mr. Grey Bennett in his diary, "was most doting and showed hardly any remains of what he was. He forgot all facts, and made such an exhibition that it would have been cruel to have pressed him hard, which neither Tierney nor Ponsonby did. Tierney told me he thinks him quite gone, that once during his speech his jaw became locked, so that he could not utter. I never witnessed a sight more distressing."

He speaks six times after June 19, and his final speech in Parliament on July 21 on the Overture for Peace from France is a faint echo of his old conquering glory—"The immortality of nations is not consigned to mortal custody. But to fight bravely and to perish gloriously is so. Take our country. Its conditions, with all its faults, is the best that ever existed. Take our Constitution, wanting certainly many reforms, yet practically affording the best security that human wisdom has ever given to man. Yet with all this to contend for, we may not be able ultimately to command success. Even Great Britain for her rights and honors might spend her treasure, shed more and more of her best and bravest blood, and yet at last might fall. Yet after the general subjugation and ruin of Europe, should there ever exist an historian to record the awful events that produced the universal calamity, let that historian, after describing the greatness and glory of Britain, have to say, 'She fell, and with her fell all the best securities for the charities of human life, for the power and honor, the fame, the glory, and the liberties of the whole civilized world.' "

CHAPTER 18

LAST SCENE OF ALL

THE END OF SHERIDAN'S political life is inglorious. Once more he stands for Stafford at the general election of 1812 and is defeated. He reproaches Whitbread bitterly for this, maintaining that the latter's refusal to advance him the necessary £2000 lost him the election. But the real reason is his incapacity to rouse himself to action. All is in vain—he does not leave London till it is almost impossible to reach Stafford in time to make an effective canvass. When he reaches it, he loiters inactive at the inn, the mob all the while calling clamorously for him. The consequence is that he loses the election. But such is the fascination of his manners that before he leaves the town, the electors seem to be in despair for not having voted for him.

One hope remains for Sheridan when Stafford rejects him. The favor of the Regent is not yet lost. The Prince offers to bring him into Parliament as a member for Wooton Bassett and raises £3000 for this purpose. This offer is refused as Sheridan fears to lose his political independence. But he tries to borrow the money from the Regent in order to purchase the Borough himself. The sum is actually deposited with a solicitor, a Mr. Cocker. But when Sheridan after much vacillation finally resolves not to enter Parliament, he fails to inform Cocker of the purpose and disposal of the money and the latter chooses to apply it to his own debts. George, however, later tells Croker that Sheridan swindled him out of the fund—that he accepted the offer and used the £3000 illegitimately to pay a debt to the

solicitor in whose hands the sum was deposited. He then
made an elaborate pretence of starting off for Wootton
Bassett, but in reality remained in London, having been
bribed by Whitbread with £2000 to keep out of Parliament altogether. The Prince says that the mutual recriminations of Sheridan and Cocker are like those of Peachum
and Locket in *The Beggar's Opera.*

Possibly the matter is misrepresented to the Prince, but
whatever the real cause, the rupture between him and
Sheridan is undeniable and complete. The two men never
meet or speak again, and the imputation aggravates the
burden which Sheridan has now to bear.

Tom leaves him. He has inherited his mother's constitutional weakness and quits England in 1813 as Colonial
Treasurer to the Cape, where it is hoped he may recover,
but whence he never returns. "It would half break your
heart to see how he is changed," writes Sheridan at parting.
"I spend all the time with him I can as he seems to wish it,
but he so reminds me of his mother, and his feeble gasping
way of speaking affects and deprives me of all hope." And
later, when bad news comes from the Cape—"I have en-
deavored to escape from despairing about Tom as long as
my sanguine heart could hold a hope. But now, and you
must think so too, all hope is over. If you were well I would
go to him though the scene would crack what nerves I
have left."

Reduced to the pittance of his post, fretting over his
wife's illness and his own, Sheridan more and more secludes
himself. But his glory does not depart with his fortunes.
Byron and Rogers still see much of him and admire the
brilliance of his conversation. He more than holds his own
with the new generation of wits. "I have seen him," the
poet records, "cut up Whitbread, quiz Madame Staël, annihilate Colman, and do little else with some others of good
fame and sensibility. The Staël who outtalks Whitbread
and overwhelms his spouse, is *ironed* by Sheridan."

The great wonder of the time is Madame de Staël. Every

sentence she utters is caught and repeated with various commentaries. She visits Lord and Lady Jersey, Lord and Lady Hardwicke, Lord Liverpool. She is at the Hollands' and at Rogers' literary dinners. Among her acquaintances are Canning, Grey, Erskine, Bowles, Croker, Coleridge, Byron, Wilberforce, Mackintosh and Campbell—all the celebrities of the time. She is as great a curiosity in London as Napoleon himself would be. Her appearance at a party creates a furore. People get on chairs and tables to see her. She is "an avalanche," a "spiritual Amazon," a constellation to whom all other stars sing *Te Deum*. She talks and talks, harangues, lectures, holds forth, argues everywhere. She makes long speeches to those only accustomed to hear them in the Houses of Parliament. The most voluble of all human beings, she can put her volubility into four languages—German, English, Italian, French. (When she does not talk she writes.) She quotes Latin. She interrupts Whitbread, she declaims to Lord Liverpool, she preaches English politics to the first of the Whig politicians the day after her arrival and (if we are not very much mistaken) preaches politics no less to the Tory politicians the day after. She likes all the English poets without reading them. Her tongue is in perpetual motion. But despite all this, as Byron has said, she is *ironed* by Sheridan.

Though she has those contours powerfully rounded which express a poetic organisation, she is the most singular looking foreign monster the Londoners have ever beheld. She wears a yellow turban on black hair, carries a laurel twig in her hand, and has flashing eyes in a brilliant coarse face. Her short neck and shoulders rise so much behind that they amount to a hump. With this ugliness, she has all the airs of a beauty. She flummers Sheridan upon the excellence of his heart and moral principles and he in return upon her loveliness and grace.

The Staël is a brilliant interlude. Matters march from bad to worse. Sheridan's person, no longer protected by the

House of Commons, is liable to arrest for debt. He sells his library, his pictures, his plate. Reynolds's prized portrait of St. Cecilia vanishes from his possession. His home is dismantled. Mrs. Sheridan sends harassed appeals to Peake, the faithful treasurer of old and new Drury Lane. Now it is for ten pounds—four pounds out of five for washing the house linen have been owing a year; now it is for a creditor who will not wait; at last it is for a few pounds—"even two would be acceptable." But it is all in vain. In August, 1813, Sheridan is carried off to a sponging house for a debt of £600. "Whitbread, you have no right to keep me here! For it is in truth your act. O God! with what mad confidence have I trusted *your word!* I ask *justice* from you and no *boon.*"

Three days he languishes in jail before Whitbread comes to bail him out. Directly he regains his freedom, he breaks down utterly and bursts into tears. But his melancholy vanishes after his usual allowance of two bottles for dinner.

Wine is his only visible means of support. He is a wreck of a man. His eyes, still lustrous and brilliant, become terrible indeed when he defends himself against an assailant of his character. The smile that is almost as great a passport as Mrs. Jordan's laugh is rarely now in evidence. He has fits of weeping. His geniality is vanished. He seems "dry, circumspect, sarcastic, and selfish in his talk." His wit is "always saturnine and sometimes savage; he never laughed—at least that I saw and *I* watched him!" says Byron. Nevertheless "his very dregs are better than the first sprightly runnings of others."

"Poor fellow! he gets drunk thorough and very soon." It occasionally falls to the poet's lot to pilot him home—no sinecure, for he is so typsy that Byron is obliged to put on his cocked hat for him. To be sure, it tumbles off again and Byron is himself not so sober as to be able to pick it up again.

The poet meets him at all places and parties—at Whitehall with the Melbournes, at the Marquis of Tavistock's, at Robins' the auctioneers, at Sir Humphry Savy's, at Sam Rogers'—in short in most kinds of company and always finds him convivial—and, when not drunk, delightful.

Once Byron sees him cry at Robins' after a splendid dinner full of great names and high spirits. The occasion of the tears is some observation or other on the subject of the sturdiness of the Whigs in resisting office and keeping to their principles. Sheridan, who is sitting next to Byron, turns round—"Sir, it is easy for my Lord Grenville, or Earl Grey, or the Marquis of Bath, or Lord Hertford, with thousands upon thousands a year, some of it either *presently* derived, or *inherited* in sinecures or acquisitions from the public money, to boast of their patriotism and keep aloof from temptation; but they do not know from what temptations those have kept aloof who had equal pride, at least equal talents and not unequal passions, and nevertheless knew not in the course of their lives what it was to have a shilling of their own." And in saying this he weeps.

Lord Holland remarks to a friend—"Whatever Sheridan has done or chosen to do, has been, par excellence, always the best of its kind. He has written the best comedy *(The School for Scandal)*, the best drama (in my mind, far before that St. Giles's lampoon, *The Beggar's Opera)*, the best farce *(The Critic*—it is only too good for a farce), and the best address *(Monologue on Garrick)*, and to crown all, delivered the very best oration (the famous Begum Speech) ever conceived or heard in this country." Somebody tells Sheridan this, and on hearing it he burst into tears.

In October, 1815, we find Sheridan dining at a largish party composed of Byron, Harris of Covent Garden, Douglas Kinnard, Colman and others. Like other parties of the kind, it is first silent, then talky, then argumentative, then disputative, then unintelligible, then altogether inarticulate, then drunk. Byron and Kinnard have to conduct Sheridan "down a dark corkscrew stair, which has certainly been constructed before the discovery of fermented liquors."

One day Byron sees him take up his own *Monody on Garrick*. He lights upon the dedication to the Dowager Lady Spencer. On seeing it he flies into a rage and exclaims that it must be a forgery, that he has never dedicated anything of his to such a damned, canting bitch, etc., and so goes on for half an hour, abusing his own dedication or at least the object of it.

"What a wreck is that man!" exclaims the poet. "And all from bad pilotage, for noone had ever better gales, though now and then a little too squally. Poor dear Sherry! I shall never forget the day he and Rogers and Moore and I passed together, when *he* talked and *we* listened, without one yawn from six till one in the morning."

A day of sunlight. This very year Lord Essex takes him to Drury Lane to see Edmund Kean in *Othello*. Sheridan is delighted. Between the acts Lord Essex misses him from the box and fears that he has suddenly gone home. But Sheridan has stolen away to the green room, where he is found proudly installed in all his old glory, the actors crowding round and welcoming him with "a sort of filial cordiality"—drinking bumpers of wine to his health and pressing him to return. (Even then he declares that he will be heard again, for the Duke of Norfolk will bring him into Parliament. To the last, like Congreve, he slights his theatrical triumphs.)

A few days later his illness begins. He is kept awake by eight hours' incessant coughing. His veins swell, he cannot eat or sleep, an abscess forms in his throat, and his life slowly ebbs away. He presses two guineas on the physician who demurs to take them. But "here is too much about myself,"—he will speak of Hecca. His wife and he are reunited, and he thinks more of her failing health than of his own. "Never," he writes, "let one harsh word pass between us." He follows her every footstep in search of health—to the Isle of Wight, to the tranquil garden at Windsor. Her letters to him are his "heart's food and raiment." She is indeed very ill, but she hastens home to nurse her husband.

Creditors still harass them. They have hardly a servant left. Mrs. Sheridan is about to send away the maid but cannot collect a guinea to pay the woman her wages. All the reception rooms are bare and the whole house is in a state of intolerable stench and dirt. Sheridan promises to attend the St. Patrick's dinner on March 17, 1816, but is forced to excuse himself on the score of severe illness. The Duke of Kent who presides writes affectionately to him; he suspects nothing of Sheridan's distress. But gradually it leaks out that Sheridan is in want, though not dying of it. The Regent is touched, or feels that his generosity is at stake. He proffers two hundred pounds with a promise of three hundred more—his support is respectfully declined by Mrs. Sheridan. (When the philosopher Anaxagoras lay dying for want of sustenance, his great pupil Pericles sent him a sum of money. "Take it back," said Anaxagoras, "if he wished to keep the lamp alive, he ought to have administered the oil before.") Lord Holland forwards some ice and currant water. Grey, it is said, is kind.

It is past midnight and Tom Moore is sitting with Rogers when this missive arrives—

> Saville Row
>
> I find things settled so that £150 will remove all difficulty. I am absolutely undone and broken hearted. . . . They are going to put the carpets out of the window and break into Mrs. Sheridan's room and *take me*—for God's sake let me see you."

Next morning Moore and Rogers walk together to Savile Row. A servant tells them that all is safe for the night, but that the broker's bills will be pasted over the front of the house next day. Moore brings the money, and the execution is averted. He sees Sheridan and finds him good natured and cordial, and, as ever, sanguine: he dwells on the profits from a final edition of his dramatic works—he is certain he can arrange all his affairs if only he might leave his bed.

June arrives. Sheridan is worse, and once more the bailiffs threaten. A sheriff's officer is about to arrest him in his bed and carry him off in his blankets, when his old friend Dr. Bain interferes and prevents the outrage. He tells the bailiff that such a step will be fatal, and in that case he will institute a prosecution against him for murder. However, the Sheriff's officer remains in possession. Finally an article in Sheridan's behalf is printed in the *Morning Post* by an old opponent—"I say *Life* and *Succor* against Westminster Abbey and a Funeral." The appeal evokes a widespread response and the fashionable world flocks to Savile Row. But Sheridan's real friends at this last crisis are Peter Moore and Samuel Rogers.

By mid-June his state is critical. Within a week his mind begins to wander. He can take little nourishment, and his face is convulsed. By the close of the month, however, he rallies. He sends for his son, he converses with his wife. Lady Bessborough pays him a visit and sits on a trunk in which he keeps his works. He asks what she thinks of his looks. She says his eyes are brilliant still. He then makes some frightful answer about their being fixed for eternity. He takes her hand and grips it hard, and then tells her that he gives her that token to assure her that, if possible, he will come to her after he is dead. Lady Bessborough is frightened, says that he has persecuted her all his life, and now carries his persecution into death. Why does he do so? "Because," says Sheridan, "I am resolved you shall remember me." He says some more frightful things, and she withdraws in great terror. He sends a final message to her— "that his eyes will look up at the coffin lid as brightly as ever."

On Thursday, July 4, he is raised in a reclining posture to take his last leave of Mrs. Sheridan. They are left alone together and when she appears her face is in anguish. Next day the Bishop of London prays over him and tells some ladies that Sheridan joined ardently in the prayers, but he confesses to Lord Holland and Rogers that the dying man was too far gone to do so. That night his slumber is undisturbed, and on Saturday he can even converse briefly with friends. Once more Mrs. Sheridan sits and talks with him. It is near midnight when they part.

On Sunday Peter Moore returns to Savile Row. It is about eleven. The church bells cease ringing as he passes up St. James Street to give the sad news at White's and Brooks's. He has seen Sheridan who spoke "good-bye" to all. That is his last word. As the clock of St. George strikes midday, Sheridan slumbers into death.

The funeral is fixed for the following Saturday. It is known that Westminster Abbey is to be Sheridan's resting place. It is hoped that according to his desire his remains may repose among statesmen, next to Fox. For some reason never explained, this is not permitted. Perhaps the Whig leaders prevent the profanation. It is decided that his grave shall be by Garrick's, opposite the monument of his old friend and companion, Dr. Goldsmith.

There is a funeral of unsurpassed ostentation. The "alienated" friends are expressly written to and requested to attend by Mrs. Sheridan. Among the pallbearers are the Duke of Bedford, Lauderdale, Mulgrave, Lord Holland and Lord Spencer. Among the Earls who attend are Thanet and Bessborough. The Bishop of London is a pallbearer. Then there are Canning, Sidmouth, Yarmouth, the representative of the Prince's household, and personal friends like Erskine and Lynedoch, the Dukes of York, Sussex, and Argyle. Burgess, Bouverie, and Asgill follow. Wellesley and the Duke of Wellington both write feeling letters of condolence and regret. The real friends march modestly and aloof in the procession—Peter Moore, Dr. Bain, and Samuel Rogers.

The bier is deposited at Peter Moore's house, and thence in the rain, amid crowds of weeping onlookers, the cortege wends its way to Westminster Abbey. On its arrival at Poet's Corner, the coffin is immediately lowered into the grave, and the sub-Dean officiates in the succeeding rites, but his voice is so faint as to be scarcely audible. The large slab which marks the vault is placed by Peter Moore—

Richard Brinsley Sheridan
Born 1751
Died 7th July, 1816
This marble is the tribute of an attached
Friend
Peter Moore.

Poets commemorate the brilliance, moralists deplore the lapses, patricians divide the honors of genius. "The last of the luminaries. . . The last of the giants. . . A mighty spirit is eclipsed. . . ."

CHAPTER 19

EPILOGUE: CURTAIN

LORD BYRON TO THOMAS MOORE, June 1,
1818. Palazzo Mocenigo, Canal Grande,
Venice.

"I DO NOT KNOW any good model for a
life of Sheridan but that of Savage. Recollect, however,
that the life of such a man may be made far more amusing
than if he had been a Wilberforce and this without offend-
ing the living or insulting the dead. The Whigs abused him;
however he never left them, and such blunderers deserve
neither credit nor compassion. As for his creditors—remember Sheridan never had a shilling, and was thrown with
great powers and passions into the thick of the world and
placed upon the pinnacle of success, with no other external
means to support him in his elevation. Did Fox—pay his
debts?—or did Sheridan take a subscription? Was the Duke
of Norfolk's drunkenness more excusable than his? Were
his intrigues more notorious than those of all his contemporaries?—and is his memory to be blasted, and theirs respected? Don't let yourself be led away by clamor, but
compare him with the coalitioner Fox and the pensioner
Burke as a man of principle, and with ten hundred thousand in personal views, and with none in talent, for he
beat them all *out* and *out*. Without means, without con-
nexion, without character (which might be false at first,
and made him mad afterwards from desperation), he beat
them all, in all he ever attempted. But alas! poor human
nature!

"Good night—or rather morning. It is four and the dawn

gleams over the Grand Canal, and unshadows the Rialto.
I must to bed; up all night—but as George Philpot says, 'it's
life, though, damme, it's life!'

Ever yours,

B."

APPENDIX

LIST OF ADMINISTRATIONS OF GREAT BRITAIN

Date	Party	Prime Minister
1770–1782	King's Friends	Lord North
March, 1782	Whig	Marquis of Rockingham
July, 1782–1783	King's Friends	Earl of Shelburne
April, 1783– December, 1783	Whig-Tory (Coalition)	Duke of Portland
December, 1783–1801	Whig-Tory	William Pitt
March, 1801–1804	Tory	Henry Addington
May, 1804–1806	Tory	William Pitt
February, 1806–1807	Whigs and Tories, (All the Talents)	Lord Grenville
March, 1807–1809	Tory	Duke of Portland
October, 1809–1812	Tory	Spencer Perceval
June, 1812–1827	Tory	Lord Liverpool

BIBLIOGRAPHY

THE FOLLOWING WORKS have been consulted. Walter Sichel's impressive and scholarly volumes are invaluable. I owe much to them. Eliza M. Butler's *Sheridan, A Ghost Story* has been extremely helpful, especially in dealing with Sheridan's later career.

Airlie, Mabell, Countess of, *In Whig Society*, London, 1921.

Andrews, Alexander, *The Eighteenth Century*, London, 1856.

Angelo, Henry, *Reminiscences*, 2 vols., London, 1830.

Anstey, Christopher, *The New Bath Guide*, London, 1832.

Ashton, John, *Florizel's Folly*, London, 1899.

Ault, Norman, *New Light on Pope*, London, 1949.

Baker, Henry B., *English Actors*, 2 vols. New York, 1879.

Barbeau, A., *Life and Letters at Bath in the Eighteenth Century*, London, 1904.

The Bath Anthology, edited by Chas. J. Whitby, London, 1928.

Baumann, A. A., *Burke, the Founder of Conservatism*, London, 1929

Bernard, John, *Retrospections of the Stage*, 2 vols., London, 1830.

Besant, Sir Walter, *London in the Eighteenth Century*, London, 1902.

Black, Clementina, *The Linleys of Bath*, London, 1911.

Boaden, James, *Life of Mrs. Jordan*, 2 vols., London, 1831.

Boswell, James, *Life of Samuel Johnson*, 2 vols., Oxford University Press, 1924.

Boswell, James, "Private Papers of James Boswell" from Malahide Castle, 18 vols., ed. by Geoffrey Scott and Frederick Pottle, Mount Vernon, N.Y., 1928-1934.

Broderick, George C., and Fotheringham, J. K., *The History of England*, 1801-1837, London, 1906, in *The Political History of England*, 12 vols., ed. by William Hunt and Reginald L. Poole.

Brougham, Henry, Lord, *Historical Sketches of Statesmen Who Flourished in the Time of George III*, Vol. 1, London, 1855.

Butler, Charles, *Reminiscences*, 2 vols., London, 1824.

Butler, Eliza M., *Sheridan, A Ghost Story*, New York, 1931.

Byron, Lord, *Letters and Journals*, ed. by Rowland E. Prothero, 6 vols., London, 1922.

Cobban, Alfred, *Edmund Burke*, London, 1929.

Cone, Carl B., *Burke and the Nature of Politics*, University of Kentucky, 1957.

Cove, Joseph W. (Lewis Gibbs), *Sheridan*, New York, 1949.

The Creevey Papers, ed. by Sir Herbert Maxwell, 2 vols., London, 1903.

Creston, Dormer (Dorothy Julia Baynes), *The Regent and His Daughter*, London, 1932.

Croker, John Wilson, *Correspondence and Diaries*, ed. by Louis J. Jennings, Vol. I, London, 1884.

Daghlian, Philip B., "Sheridan's Minority Waiters," *Modern Language Quarterly* (Dec. 1945), VI, 421-422.

D'Arblay, Madame (Fanny Burney), *Diary and Letters*, 3 vols., London, 1892.

Darlington, William A., *Sheridan*, New York, 1933.

Dictionary of National Biography, ed. by Sir Leslie Stephen and Sir Sidney Lee, London, 1917.

Dobson, Austin, *Eighteenth Century Vignettes*, 3rd series, New York, 1896.

Doran, John, *Annals of the English Stage*, 2 vols., New York, 1865.

Drinkwater, John, *Charles James Fox*, London, 1928.

Elias, Edith L., *In Georgian Times*, Boston, 1914.

Elliot, Sir Gilbert, First Earl of Minto, *Life and Letters*, 3 vols., London, 1874.

Family Correspondence, The Two Duchess (Georgiana, Duchess of Devonshire, and Elizabeth, Duchess of Devonshire), ed. by Vere Foster, London, 1898.

Fitzgerald, Percy, *The Lives of the Sheridans*, 2 vols., London, 1886.

——, *The Romance of the English Stage*, 2 vols., London, 1874

——, *David Garrick*, 2 vols., London 1868.

——, *The Kembles*, 2 vols., London, 1871.

Foss, Kenelm, *Here Lies Richard Brinsley Sheridan*, London, 1939.

Frampton, Mary, *Journal, 1779–1846*, ed. by Harriot G. Mundy, London, 1886.

Fraser, J. A. Lovat, *Henry Dundas, Viscount Melville*, London, 1916.

Galt, John, *Lives of the Players*, 2 vols., London, 1831.

Glenbervie, Sylvester Douglas, Lord, *Diaries*, ed. by Francis Bickley, 2 vols., London, 1928.

Gower, Lord Granville Leveson, *Private Correspondence*, ed. by Castalia, Countess Granville, 2 vols., London, 1917.

Graham, Harry, *Splendid Failures*, London, 1913.

Greenwood, Alice D., *Horace Walpole's World*, London, 1913.

Guedalla, Philip, *Fathers of the Revolution*, New York, 1926.

Hansard's Parliamentary Debates, London, 1812.

Hassall, Arthur, *The Making of the British Empire, 1714–1832* (The Oxford Manuals of English History), New York, 1903.

Hewlett, Maurice, "Sheridan as Maniac," *The Fortnightly Review*, Vol. CV, New Series, Jan.-June, 1919, London, 1919.

History of the Westminster Election, By Lovers of Truth and Justice, London, 1784.

History of the Westminster and Middlesex Elections in 1806, London, 1807.

Hobhouse, Christopher, *Fox*, Boston, 1935.

Holland, Lady Elizabeth, *Journal (1791–1811)*, ed. by the Earl of Ilchester, 2 vols., London, 1908.

Holland, Lord, Henry Richard, *Memoirs of the Whig Party*, 2 vols., London, 1852.

——, *Further Memoirs of the Whig Party, 1807–1821*, London, 1905.

Hulme, Edward M., *A History of the British People*, New York and London, 1924.

Hunt, William, *The Political History of England from the Accession of George III to the Close of Pitt's First Administration, 1760-1808*, Vol. X, London, 1905.

Ilchester, Giles S.H.F.S., Earl of, *Henry Fox, First Lord Holland*, 2 vols., London, 1920.

Jesse, John H., *Memoirs of the Life and Reign of King George III*, 5 vols., Boston, 19-?

Kelly, Michael, *Reminiscences*, 2 vols., London, 1826.

Larson, Laurence M., *History of England*, New York, 1924.

Lecky, William E. H., *History of England in the Eighteenth Century*, Vols. 5-8, London, 1887.

Lefanu, Alicia, *Memoirs of the Life and Writings of Mrs. Frances Sheridan,* London, 1824.

Lyall, Sir Alfred, *Warren Hastings,* London, 1902.

Macaulay, Thomas V., *Essays on Lord Clive and Warren Hastings,* New York, 1910.

Magnus, Sir Philip, *Burke,* London, 1939.

Malleson, Colonel G. B., *Life of Warren Hastings,* London, 1894.

Mantzius, Karl, *A History of Theatrical Art,* Vol. 6, London, 1921.

Martin, Sir Theodore, *Monographs,* New York, 1906.

Mason, Alfred Bishop, *Horace Walpole's England, New York,* 1930.

Massy, William, *A History of England During the Reign of George III,* Vols. 3 and 4, London, 1865.

Matheson, Cyril, *The Life of Henry Dundas, First Viscount Melville,* London, 1933.

Melville, Lewis (L. S. Benjamin), *Farmer George,* London, 1907.

——, *The First Gentleman of Europe,* London, 1906.

——, *More Stage Favorites of the Eighteenth Century,* London, 1929.

——, *Bath Under Beau Nash,* London, 1907.

Moore, Thomas, *Memoirs of the Life of Richard Brinsley Sheridan,* 2 vols., London, 1825.

Murray, Robert H., *Edmund Burke,* Oxford University Press, 1931.

Nettleton, George H., *English Drama of the Restoration and the Eighteenth Century,* New York, 1928.

——, "*Robinson Crusoe,* Sheridan's Drury Lane Pantomime," *The London Times Literary Supplement,* Dec. 25, 1943, Jan. 1, 1944, April 15, 1944, June 23, 1945, June 30, 1945.

Nevill, Ralph, *London Clubs,* London, 1911.

Newman, Bertram, *Edmund Burke,* London, 1927.

Nicoll, Allardyce, *A History of Eighteenth Century Drama, 1750–1800,* Cambridge, 1927.

——, *A History of the Nineteenth Century Drama, 1800–1850,* Vol. 1, Cambridge, 1930.

Oliphant, Mrs. Margaret, *Sheridan,* London, 1909.

The Parliamentary History of England, London, 1816.

Pellew, George, *Life and Correspondence of Henry Addington, Viscount Sidmouth,* 3 vols., London, 1847.

Pigott, Charles, *The Jockey Club or Sketch of the Manners of the Age,* Dublin, 1792.

Pillet, Major General (René Martin), *Views of England,* Boston, 1818.

Pückler-Muskau, Hermann Ludwig Heinrich, Fürst von, *Tour in England, Ireland, and France by a German Prince,* Philadelphia, 1833.

Rae, W. Fraser, *Sheridan, A Biography,* 2 vols., New York, 1896.

——, *Wilkes, Sheridan, and Fox,* London, 1874.

Reid, Loren D., "Sheridan's Speech on Mrs. Fitzherbert," *Quarterly Journal of Speech* (1947), XXXIII, 15-22.

Reynolds, Frederick, *Life and Times, Written by Himself,* 2 vols., London, 1826.

Rhodes, Raymond Crompton, *Harlequin Sheridan,* Oxford, 1933.

Robinson, Cyril E., *England,* New York, 1928.

Rogers, Samuel, *Table Talk,* New York, 1856.

——, *Recollections,* London, 1859.

The Rolliad, London, 1799.

Russell, Lord John, *Life and Times of Charles James Fox,* 3 vols., London, 1859.

Sadleir, Michael T. H., *The Political Career of Richard Brinsley Sheridan,* Oxford, 1912.

Sanders, Lloyd C., *Life of Richard Brinsley Sheridan,* London, 1890.

Schiller, Andrew, "*The School for Scandal,* the Restoration Unrestored," *PMLA* (September, 1956), LXXI, No. 4, Part 1, 694-704.

Sergeant, Philip W., *Liars and Fakers,* London, 1925.

Sheridan and His Times by an Octogenarian.

Sheridiana or Anecdotes of the Life of Richard Brinsley Sheridan, London, 1826.

Sheridan, Richard Brinsley, *Plays,* ed. by Iolo A. Williams, New York, 1926.

——, *Plays and Poems,* ed. by R. Crompton Rhodes, 3 vols., Oxford, 1928.

——, *Speeches,* 3 vols., London, 1842.

Sherson, Erroll, *The Lively Lady Townshend and Her Friends,* London, 1926.

Sichel, Walter, *Sheridan,* 2 vols., Boston and New York, 1909.

Sitwell, Osbert, and Barton, Margaret, *Brighton,* London, 1935.

Smollett, Tobias, *Humphrey Clinker,* New York, 1905.

Stanhope, Lady Hester, *Memoirs,* 3 vols., London, 1845.

Stokes, Hugh, *The Devonshire House Circle,* London, 1917.

Sydney, William C., *England and the English in the Eighteenth Century,* 2 vols., London, 1891.

Sydney, William C., *The Early Days of the Nineteenth Century,* 2 vols., London, 1898.

Tallentyre, S. G. (Evelyn B. Hall), *The Women of the Salons,* New York, 1926.

Taylor, George R. Stirling, *Modern English Statesmen,* London, 1920.

Timbs, John, *Clubs and Club Life in London,* London, 1872.

Trevelyan, George Otto, *Early History of Charles James Fox,* New York, 1900.

Warton, Grace and Philip (Katherine B. and John C. Thomson), *The Queens of Society,* Philadelphia, 1890.

Watkins, John, *Memoirs of the Public and Private Life of Richard Brinsley Sheridan,* 2 parts, London, 1817.

Watson, Ernest B., *Sheridan to Robertson,* Cambridge, 1926.

Wecter, Dixon, *Edmund Burke and His Kinsmen,* University of Colorado Studies, 1939.

Weitzman, Sophia, *Warren Hastings and Philip Francis,* Manchester University Press, 1929.

The Whig Club or Sketch of Modern Patriotism, London, 1794.

Whitford, Robert C., *Mme. de Staël's Literary Reputation in England,* Urbana, Illinois, 1918.

Wilkins, William H., *Mrs. Fitzherbert and George IV,* 2 vols., London, 1905.

Wilson, Beckles, *George III,* London, 1907.

Wilson, Philip W., *William Pitt the Younger,* New York, 1930.

The Windham Papers, 2 vols., London, 1913.

Withers, Philip, *History of the Royal Malady,* London, 1789.

Wraxall, Nathaniel W., *Memoirs,* ed. by Henry B. Wheatley, 5 vols., New York, 1884.

Wright, Thomas, *England Under the House of Hanover* (Illustrated from the Caricatures and Satires of the Day), London, 1848.

INDEX

[347]

Rolle, John, Baron, 206.
Rolliad, The, 187-188.
Rose, George, 299.
Rousseau, Jean-Jacques, 37, 109.
Rutland, Duchess of, 11, 31, 33, 120, 169.

Salisbury, Lady, 31, 62, 182.
Salisbury, Lord, 229, 304.
Savage, Richard, 119, 338.
Scott, John, 178-179.
Scott, Major, 167, 212.
Scott, Sir Walter, 254, 261, 285.
Sefton, Lord and Lady, 23, 26, 169, 298.
Selden, John, 314.
Selwyn, George, 21, 25, 28, 35, 67, 104, 109, 142, 149-150, 190, 208.
Shelburne, Lord, 32, 37, 150-152, 156, 158-160, 340.
Sheldon, 300.
Shelley, Percy B., 38.
Sheridan, Alicia, "Lissy," (Mrs. Jos. Le Fanu) sister of R. B. S., 53-55, 62, 71, 73-75, 77-78, 80, 83.
Sheridan, Ann Elizabeth Hume Crawfurd, "Betsy," (Mrs. Henry Le Fanu), sister of R. B. S., 53, 62, 71, 73, 80, 83, 94.
Sheridan, Charles Brinsley (son of R. B. S.), 254.
Sheridan, Charles Francis (brother of R. B. S.), 52-54, 60, 70, 71, 73, 78-81, 83, 86, 88, 99, 320.
Sheridan, Elizabeth (grandmother of R. B. S.), 42.
Sheridan, Elizabeth Ann, née Linley (first wife of R. B. S.), 12, 17, early life and career, 58-62, 69; elopement and marriage, 70-89, 91-100; 101-102, 103-107, 108, 116, 117, 120-121, 124, 125, 176, 186, 219, 221, 233, 234, 237, 244-248, 249-251, 254, 318, 319, 331.
Sheridan, Esther Jane, née Ogle (second wife of R. B. S.), 252-257, 318, 321-322, 331, 333-336.
Sheridan, Frances, née Chamber-

laine (mother of R. B. S.), 45-53, 115.
Sheridan, Mary (daughter of first Mrs. Sheridan and Lord Edward Fitzgerald), 247, 249, 251.
Sheridan, Richard Brinsley, 12, 13; drinking, 14-16; 20; gambling, 21, 26; debts, 28-29; 30-34, 36, 52; birth and early education, 53-56; 58, 60, 62, 69; elopement, duels, and marriage, 70-100; 104, 106; courted by fashion, early reviews, 108, 111-114; *The Sanctuary,* 113-114; *The Drama of Devils,* 113; *The Rivals,* 69, 115-118, 275; *St. Patrick's Day,* 117; *The Duenna,* 12, 69, 117-118; elected to Literary Club, 119; 120-121; proprietor of Drury Lane, 123-125; *A Trip to Scarborough,* 125-126; *The Foresters,* 126; *The School for Scandal,* 69, 124, 126, 127-133, 275, 332; mismanagement of theatre, 134-135; *Verses to the Memory of Garrick,* 134, 332; *The Critic,* 135-136, 332; election to Parliament, 137-138; 141, 142, 152, 158; for American Independence, 159, 160; Secretary of the Treasury, 161; attitude to Fox's India Bill, 166-167; 169-172, 176, 178, 180; eloquence, 183-185, 332; plea for Ireland, 185-187; 188; friendship with Prince of Wales at Brighton, 190-191, 193, 196-197, 199; and affair of Mrs. Fitzherbert, 205-208; role in Hastings Trial, 209-218, 221-227; and Regency, 230-237; break with Burke, 238-240; domestic troubles, 244-251; second marriage, infatuations, 252-258; and son Tom, 259-261; and Drury Lane, 262-280; *Pizarro,* 272-273; 274-275; and the Kembles, 282, 285-286; conversation, wit, characteristics, 289-302; on Napoleon, 304-306; break with Fox, 307-309, 312; Treasurer of Navy, 309-310; 311-313; on Cath-